Culture and International Relations

Culture is a popular and powerful, though often unacknowledged, idea in international relations. However, where it was once used to foster mutual understanding, in the post-Cold War era it became synonymous with ways of life that clashed.

Culture and International Relations: Narratives, natives and tourists provides an historical survey of the development of the idea of culture from the perspective of international relations (IR). It crucially demonstrates that, far from being a neglected subject in IR, culture has been important throughout the discipline's history. The author identifies two distinct concepts of culture – the humanist and the anthropological – and uses a contextual methodology to track its changing meaning across the twentieth century from cultural internationalism to the clash of cultures.

This innovative volume examines the implications of culture for IR and controversially challenges the current dominant ideology of culture in international relations, arguing that – contrary to popular belief, and some prominent international theory – it is not obvious that everyone has culture or even that culture exists. Throwing light on how we should think about people and their differences in the contemporary world, this book will be relevant to everyone working in international relations.

Julie Reeves has studied international relations at the University of Kent at Canterbury and University of Southampton. She was recently a Visiting Faculty Fellow in the Faculty of International Relations, Belarus State University, for the Civic Education Project.

Routledge advances in international relations and global politics

Culture and International Relations

Narratives, natives and tourists

Julie Reeves

Routledge
Taylor & Francis Group

LONDON AND NEW YORK

First published 2004
by Routledge
2 Park Square, Milton Park, Abingdon, Oxon, OX14 4RN

Simultaneously published in the USA and Canada
by Routledge
270 Madison Ave, New York NY 10016

Routledge is an imprint of the Taylor & Francis Group

Transferred to Digital Printing 2007

© 2004 Julie Reeves

Typeset in Baskerville by Wearset Ltd, Boldon, Tyne and Wear

British Library Cataloguing in Publication Data
A catalogue record for this book is available from the British Library

Library of Congress Cataloging in Publication Data
Reeves, Julie, 1963–
   Culture and international relations : narratives, natives, and
tourists / Julie Reeves.
     p. cm.
   Includes bibliographical references and index.
1. International relations and culture–History–20th century. I. Title.
   JZ1251.R44 2004
   306.2–dc22

                                            2004000706

ISBN10: 0-415-31857-2 (hbk)
ISBN10: 0-415-45984-2 (pbk)

ISBN13: 978-0-415-31857-0 (hbk)
ISBN13: 978-0-415-45984-6 (pbk)

Dedicated with love to David and to the
memory of Diane Reeves

Contents

Acknowledgements

Over the course of a project, one incurs many debts of gratitude. Some are directly associated with this book and some belong to the PhD research behind it; while others are long-standing but are nonetheless important for being so. I have taken full advantage of the opportunity before me to do the 'cultural' thing and to thank everyone and 'their kitchen sink.'

First and foremost, I would like to thank the Economic and Social Research Council, without whose generous support none of my postgraduate work would have been possible.

Over the years, I have had the privilege of being taught and guided by some fabulous teachers (and a few right duffers, who are best forgotten). Chief among the stars are Professors Chris Brown, Adam Kuper and Andrew Mason, all of whom deserve my immediate and obvious thanks. Chris taught me the value of being 'functional and focused' (a difficult project), Adam pointed me in the right direction and Andy made me laugh when we disagreed – thanks to all three for their encouragement, patience and support.

At the University of Kent at Canterbury, thanks go to Richard Sakwa, Chris Taylor and Andrew Williams – who messed up my mind in the best possible way.

From Wakefords Comprehensive and Sixth Form, thanks to Peter Whittaker, the late Steve Berry, Mr Franklin, Chris Rooney, Ann Stirmey and LCDTC.

Everyone at Southampton University, especially Anita Catney, Peter and Veronica Clegg, Rhoda Coates, David Francis, Dilys Hill, Darryl Howlett, David Owen, Stuart Poore, Caroline Thomas, Lisa Schuster, Jacquie Smith and Sandy Wilkins, thank you.

During the course of writing this book I received invaluable advice from William P. Keihl, Adam Kuper, Andrew Mason, Thomas R. Seitz and John Simpson – all of whom saved me from some embarrassing mistakes. Some of the aforementioned read and commented on parts of the manuscript, as did Cherry Bradshaw and Eilly Wong who both faced an unenviable task. The section on strategic culture owes much to my earlier discussions with Stuart Poore, although I am not certain he will agree with what I have written. I would also like to thank Lisa Mann and Mott Linn of Clark University, USA, for their help and the two anonymous referees at Routledge, especially with title suggestions. From my earlier research, thanks to Caroline Haste from the University of Wales Aberystwyth and Ray Gamble of the International Whaling Commission for the information they supplied.

In preparing the manuscript, I worked closely with John Reeves, who read the whole draft and deserves special attention and thanks for his hard work. His excellent 'model reader' comments helped me to focus on what I wanted to achieve.

I am very grateful for everyone's comments and excellent feedback, but, of course, I am responsible for the views expressed in this book, the excess baggage and the remaining errors.

I have met and worked with some wonderful people, who in one way or another have contributed to the way I think about the world – thanks to everyone from:

Leigh Park and Havant CND; Southern Electric, especially Peter Cardin and his jokes, Jeanne Freeman, Sue Jones, Julie Kellaway, Heather Linfield, Peter Orme, Julie Squibb, Janette Stevens; I would also like to thank Southern Electric for the insight into Stalinism – it has proven very useful; the Inland Revenue lot, especially Wendy and Julie; Havant Borough Council, especially Trisha Watts and Julia Mattison for their unbelievable kindness, the late, great, John Harvey who restored my faith in management, and the incredibly uplifting Andrea Parratt; all The Women at Zurich on the Countrywide accounts team; the CCS team at the Office for National Statistics (and everyone who suffered on 'pay'); the Civic Education Project – BUM and the students on the Issues and Perspectives course; the good people of Savory, Wyoming, and the eclectic crowd who ended up on Montejinni Station, NT, especially Susan Neal (wherever she is) – and anyone with whom I ever campaigned, danced, worked, laughed or generally did something wild with – you all know who you are.

With love and thanks to all friends past and present, especially: Michelle Aighton, Stella Anthony, John Paul Cassey, Debbie Conroy, Steve Corner, Jeff Crawford, Steve Curtis, Dave Cook, Madeleine Demetriou, Saartjie Drijver, Mark Erskine, Lisa, Ingrid and Geoff Gilbert, Lesley Hadley (and the memory of little Charlie Grant), Sarah Hamiduddin, Kathy Havering, Vida and Roy Henning, Jay Hogg, Tom, Alex and Ned King, Virginia Liu, Helen Lyons, Dave Ludlam, Peter Mandaville, Alison Moore, Barbara Muchan, Andrea and Ian Parratt, Tom and Frances Pelgrave, Charlotte Prince, Anne Reeves, Paula Roberts, Helena Romaniuk, Suzanne Snook, Peter Stanley, Kev Stanworth, Linda, Tim, Emily and Erin Woolley and Stella Timewell who took me on two of the most wonderful journeys of my life.

Special thanks to the following for their support and friendship – Pam and Hansjörg Schoss, plus Louise, Leonhard, Theodor and Mathilde; Tom Seitz and Stephanie Anderson, plus Madeleine, Chloe and 'Chirpa' cat; Monica Jacobs and Christine Weston, whose faith, support and input I could not have done without, especially during the 'dark days' of writing up; and my longest enduring friend Clare Shaw, plus Chris, Amy and Lucy. My conversations with Clare, Christine, Monica, Pam and Tom have given me great joy over the years.

Love and thanks to all the Reeves clan – Joan and Ben Parker, John Reeves, Linda Reeves, Pam and John Loftus, and their families. And last but no means least, my big brother Chris, who tried to keep discussions about my work down to thirty seconds – but was always there to hear my moans and groans.

Two people deserve special recognition – Judith King, with whom I have discussed and shared so much over the course of two decades and who has been truly inspiring – a big thank you. And above all, David William Reeves – my poor Dad who suffered every word (and tantrum) of this research … twice. I do not know how to begin to thank you – Mum would be very proud.

Introduction

In 1942, the American cultural anthropologist, Margaret Mead claimed – "[w]e *are* our culture" (Mead 1942/1943:21). She even put the word 'are' in italics seemingly to emphasize the point that culture defines us in some way. Whatever we may be, we could only be our own culture and not someone else's it appeared; which only served to underscore the uniqueness of individuals and their communities.

Yet, it might be said that Mead's claim was quite an audacious one because it is not at all obvious that 'we are our culture.' Although, most of us would recognize her idea of culture today, we did not always think this way about the word 'culture.' Prior to the suggestion that 'we are our culture,' the word 'culture' was used to refer to art, music and literature, or what the late nineteenth century educationalist and commentator Matthew Arnold described as "sweetness and light" (Arnold 1869/1994:29). Culture was, in Arnold's words, the "pursuit of our total perfection by means of getting to know, on all the matters which most concern us, the best which has been thought and said in the world ..." (Arnold 1869/1994:5). Far from making us what we are, 'culture' was the thing that would, in Arnold's view, save us from the intellectual and spiritual anarchy that industrialization had unleashed.

The difference between the idea that culture represents the 'best of everything' that had been thought, said and, for that matter, produced, and the idea that 'we are our culture,' which suggests the admittance of everything including the worst of things, is considerable. Not only is the gulf between the two ideas enormous, but in view of the contemporary dominance of the notion that we are our culture, it is easily forgotten these days that we ever thought about culture in other terms. This is especially noticeable since, from the time Mead issued her statement, the anthropological idea of 'culture' has advanced around the world at a considerable pace and has colonized popular thinking and academic discourse from Birmingham to Beijing. The fact that we now, in all probability, understand what Mead meant by the phrase, tells us that a substantial change took place – a change not only in the use of terms and in the meanings we attach to the word 'culture,' but also in the way we think about the world.

The history of the word 'culture' reveals two concepts behind the word; the humanist and the anthropological. The twentieth century witnessed the older humanist concept of culture, Arnold's notion, being replaced, in both popular and academic discourse, by the anthropological concept, i.e. Mead's expression of culture. Moreover, a specific form, or version, of the anthropological concept came to dominate the later part of the twentieth century; a version which is recognized here as the essentialist conception of culture – as though there is a specific essence of culture that makes us what we are.

When Mead wrote her statement, the anthropological idea of culture was not widely known or popularly accepted outside of Germany and the United States – many people remained to be convinced. That many people have been convinced would appear, on the surface at least, to be a considerable achievement. Margaret Mead alone cannot be held responsible for the current widespread belief that 'we are our culture.' She did not invent the concept or even the word 'culture' (this latter achievement appears to belong to the Italians in the thirteenth century as we shall see in the first chapter), but she was part of a small group of scholars who did their best to convince us that we are all natives of our culture. Arguably, or perhaps just hopefully, this achievement reached its apex in the late 1980s and 1990s when there was much talk of 'multi-cultures' and cultural 'clashes.' There are, however, serious theoretical problems with the notion that 'we are our culture,' especially when it is expressed in essentialist terms. Not least, because as the anthropologist Joel Kahn has pointed out, this concept exists, most thoroughly, in a state of "taken-for-grantedness" (Kahn 1989:17).

Today, there is plenty of culture to be found; culture is everywhere – it makes our communities and it makes us different from one another, as people, as organizations and as businesses. We must defend it when it is under threat of extinction; protect it from globalization; employ it against homogenization; celebrate it in its diversity; and find ways of living with a multiplicity of other cultures if they happen to share the same geographical space, say, the British state for example. 'Culture,' it seems, defines us and our ways of life, and what is more, everyone knows this. 'Culture' is accepted and known as the thing that distinguishes us from one another. If there are some unfortunates out there who do not know this yet, then the chances are they will soon because this particular idea of culture is a growth industry. As an example of the globalization in ideas, 'culture' has done very well for itself. Yet, it is well to remind ourselves, that although the idea that culture as a whole way of life is associated with anthropology, not all anthropologists study culture – nor do all those who do, approve of this (essentialist) understanding of the term.

'Culture' used to be, in Arnold's day and in the early part of the twentieth century, the province of art and literature, of intellectual endeavour and personal achievement, especially the 'higher' manifestations of these things. 'Culture' was an artifact to be visited at the gallery or to be witnessed at the theatre, and it was, at the same time a quality of attainment, through education and knowledge. It was closely connected to aspiration and denoted a measure of success. Moreover, it signified the progress that could (or should) be made by a society.

When, the British poet, Samuel Taylor Coleridge suggested in 1830 that civilization should be "grounded in cultivation," because the result was 'polishing' rather than the mere 'varnishing' of a people, he was making an appeal to the alternative, humanist, understanding of culture.[1] Coleridge's notion of 'cultivation' would become 'culture' and a matter of aspiration. Culture would separate the civilized from the savage, the educated from the uneducated and it would provide a benchmark for distinguishing the features of general progress among humanity. When Arnold referred to culture in terms of 'the pursuit of perfection,' it was clear that this kind of culture did not come naturally or even easily. The humanist's idea of culture, as opposed to the cultural anthropologist's conception, required conscious effort. It would be an anathema to the humanists to suggest that we could simply *be* our culture; for them, culture was something we had to work at to acquire.

The transformation from one concept of culture to the other was not obviously dramatic. We did not all wake up one morning imbued with new ideas about culture; so although the general trend is discernible, an exact date of transformation is not. However, the change from one understanding of the term 'culture' to another does signify a profound shift in our understanding of *others* and of ourselves, and this shift has made a deep impression on the social sciences. How the change occurred, from the older, humanist, concept to the younger, anthropological, concept and why this situation arose is the main concern of this book. Tracing the historiography of culture and the rise of the anthropological idea, tracking, if you like, the progress of the two ideas of culture provides the basic substance of what follows.

This book tells the story of the idea of culture from the viewpoint of one of the disciplines in social science; the discipline of international relations (henceforth IR). The story is told from within the discipline, from its founding around the time of the First World War, a time dominated by the humanist conception of culture, to the apex of the success of Mead's idea in the 1990s. In many ways, the experience of IR, of the relationship between the discipline and the idea of 'culture,' is not much different from that experienced elsewhere in the social sciences or even the humanities. IR scholars did not invent the idea of 'culture' nor could they be said to have added anything much to the concept. Whereas some anthropologists came to endow this word 'culture' with particular meaning, IR theorists and commentators have simply followed the dominant and popular trends. These trends have ensured that Mead's notion of 'culture' has become an important intellectual tool for sociologists, economists, political theorists, strategists, historians, journalists and IR scholars alike.

{ In many ways, charting the fortunes of the ideas of culture in IR acts like a barometer for reflecting changes in the rest of the social sciences and society at large. What we find is that the discipline began its life with the humanist concept and gradually moved to embrace the anthropological concept. While some IR scholars have incorporated the idea into their work from anthropology, others have relied upon their instinctive understanding of the term and have imported the idea into their work from the general social context. This book focuses on the relationship between the discipline, its scholars and the ideas of culture that have influenced their thinking about the world. It is the story, in one respect, of how Margaret Mead's idea of culture came to dominate IR and of how, in embracing one idea about culture, the discipline lost the other, much older, and arguably, more useful, humanist concept of culture.

Purpose and explanation

One might wonder why understanding the changing meaning of a term and its consequences matters? It is of interest for several reasons.

First of all, it helps to know where words come from and how they came to acquire specific meanings. In itself, this knowledge makes us more sensitive to the fact that ideas are invented to serve particular purposes. Certainly, we are more aware of the politics behind our concepts these days in social science. We are aware that our concepts carry with them social and political implications, none more so than the idea of culture. In IR, this point has considerable saliency. To say that a local practice is part of a culture, of what people are, has the more than possible consequence of placing that practice beyond our critical reach. This is especially problematic where the question of cross-cultural rights, say human, animal or environmental rights, is invoked. The argument that the genital abuse of children, or the torture of human beings or animals is none of our cultural business if it is not *our* culture, is an unpalatable one. This culture concept places a barrier between communities and, to a considerable extent, the grounds upon which a universal discourse is probable or even imaginable. Without an understanding of the culture concept, we are not in a position to challenge claims made on its behalf nor are we able to consider robust political alternatives.

Second, at the level of the text itself, mapping the changing meaning of the term 'culture' adds to our understanding of the theory or narrative being promoted by an author at a given point in time. The tendency to focus on a few key points in a text does run the risk of distorting what the author was trying to achieve, but more importantly, famous points may not be the only items of significance. We all tend to skip over the parts in texts that no longer seem relevant, or that we do not find interesting, however, these pieces did form an integral part of what the author was trying to tell us and ought, perhaps, to be reflected on from time to time. Not only should texts be re-visited in honour of the author, but it also serves as a way of checking how much the world has changed. Every text belongs to the context or age in which it was written and, in this way, may have more to reveal to us than simply what we believe is contained within its pages.

Understanding the heritage behind concepts, third, sheds light on our knowledge of the history of the IR discipline. How we achieved the position of knowledge we occupy today is not straightforwardly a case of linear development – ideas submerge and re-emerge in new guise. Some ideas, overlooked and neglected may be worth revisiting for offering us not only alternative ways of looking at the contemporary world but also for what they have to tell us about our IR history. The idea that idealism begat realism begat neo-realism and a whole load of critiques is too simplistic; at worst it creates the impression that the subsequent set of ideas are an improvement on the latter, which may not always be the case. This is noticeable with regard to the older humanist notion of culture, which occupied an important and popular place in international relations. Today there is not much talk of international cultural relations; yet, it was all the rage in the 1920s. Such is the power of an idea to impose its view on the world and write the opposition out of the textbooks.

Fourth, greater awareness of changes to our concepts challenges our contemporary assumptions about the world. Simply because we think culture is an important subject and one that speaks about the differences between communities does not mean that this was always the case, nor does it mean that the current belief is wisely held and 'true.'

This brings us onto the final and perhaps most important reason for investigating the meaning of culture in the discipline. It is by presenting the history of culture and reviewing its place in IR thinking, that the current orthodoxy which maintains 'we are our culture' can be questioned and finally rejected.

This book is an overview of the history of the two concepts of culture and their relationship to IR. There is much more that can be written on this subject, and indeed, has been written. No doubt, some will complain that this theorist or that subject has not been mentioned – this is to be expected. This is not a complete history of culture and international relations, nor does it claim to come close; what is offered is a framework for analysis and some snap-shots of time that support the general thesis. The framework of the book focuses on particular theories and specific contexts to demonstrate the point that the humanist idea of culture has been replaced by the anthropological concept. The framework is not a fixed entity as such. In the realm of ideas, there is always complexity and subtlety of approach; concepts frequently overlap, and useful ideas do not necessarily fade away, but re-emerge in new forms. This might be said of Samuel Huntington's reworking of the anthropological concept at the international level, but it might equally be true of International Society theory and its quest for a solidarist international culture. Although the framework is not rigid, it is clear that a major transformation has taken place from one end of the twentieth century to the other in the predominant meaning attached to the word 'culture.' The question, then, of how a scholar understood the term 'culture' and how they employed this to inform their narratives of international relations becomes a pertinent one, and one in which a contextual methodology proves invaluable.

A contextual method

The strangeness of *others* has always fascinated us as human beings, but the ways in which we have viewed strangeness and categorized it, have changed considerably over the centuries. We have classified ourselves in terms of whether we can be counted as the civilized, savage or barbarian. We have arranged people by categories of religion, race, class, nationality, gender, and power. Indeed, it would seem that our capacity for distinguishing between different kinds of human beings and their communities is endless.

Nowadays, it seems preferable to divide people up according to their culture. However, if we were discussing the topic of culture in 1920 or even 1620 – we would not be discussing the same thing. The meaning of words, as Quentin Skinner has pointed out, changes, and this is obviously true of the word 'culture' (Tully 1988). More importantly, the changing meaning of the word itself signifies a change in the way we identify the strangeness of *others*, what we think about that strangeness and how we have gone on to consider the place of this in the world more generally.

Although, it may be obvious to us today that 'culture' relates to specific communities of people and their different ways of life, this understanding of the word would not have been obvious to our predecessors, nor may it be obvious to our successors. The meaning of culture both in intellectual and popular discourse has varied to such an extent that commentators from both ends of the twentieth century would barely have understood each other. This is important – for if we are trying to work out what 'culture' means and has meant in the discipline then we need to avoid "writing history backwards" (Schmidt 1998:36) as Brian Schmidt has put it. Instead of first establishing a particular meaning of culture and trying to read IR texts and the history of the discipline in the light of that understanding, the aim here is to employ the general history of culture to facilitate an understanding of specific IR scholars' work.

A modest form of the contextual method aims at relocating a text or piece of work in the setting in which it was first written and constructed. It is modest because Skinner employed this methodology to analyse a single text, whereas a number of texts drawn across a ninety-year period have been analysed here. However, there are some important things to be taken from Skinner that will help the reader understand the whys and wherefores of the research behind this book.

According to Skinner, we need to become aware of two things: what a text was intended to mean by the author and how the meaning was intended to be taken by the audience (see Tully 1988:61–3). We know that different readers read differently (Clark 1993), but for the purposes of this book, it becomes essential to establish first the extent of what it was possible to read if we were the contemporary audience. This does not rule out variation within that audience, it merely determines the extent of what was most likely to occur. We might think of this methodology as the 'art of the reasonably possible.' What was it reasonably possible for authors and their readers to 'know' at the time of writing? What ideas were available to them? What discourses were informing their interests, and causing them to argue against?

We are all affected by events and ideas that we find ourselves surrounded by. Through going back to the time in which authors were operating and by relocating their work in their contemporary context it becomes possible to understand the concepts and ideas that were uppermost in their minds when they were writing.

What we need to remind ourselves of, is that the "literal meanings of key terms sometimes change over time, so that a given writer may say something with a quite different sense and reference from the one which may occur to the reader" (Tully 1988:50–1). The changing meaning of terms, even subtle adjustments, will necessarily affect our reading of a text and our understanding of it, even within a discipline as young as IR. To begin to understand what a theorist intended to impart in his/her work, it is necessary to understand the intellectual and conceptual tools they were working with, not in our terms, but in theirs.

Without exploring the relationship between the word and its attending concepts, the best that can be said of the whole idea of culture in past and present usage is that it rests upon a collection of unspoken assumptions. The assumption, for example, that early reference to the word 'culture' implies that the theorists were as interested in cultural differences as we are today. That assumption is at best, mistaken. Not only were early twentieth century theorists more interested in racial and national differences which they thought existed within the framework of 'civilization' but more importantly, early theorists would not have understood the idea of 'cultural differences' as we now do.

We can find the idea of culture being articulated in two spaces; the general social context and in a particular text. However, it is not simply the case that we uncover or reconstruct the past context and then read the text in the light of this, for we need also to maintain a sense of what Skinner calls "conceptual propriety" (Tully 1988:64). This means we have to map out the boundaries of what was possible and not possible for a writer to know at the time they wrote, and also to consider what the author was trying to achieve within the boundaries of their context. This is the heart of the contextual method.[2] As James Tully has remarked when discussing Skinner's work – the "points of a text relative to the available conventions and the author's ideological point or points in writing it" (Tully 1988:10) are not the same thing. We are all subject to this. For instance, I could write about many things concerning the subject of culture; the fact that I have chosen not to is a matter of my own ideological choosing. My idea of culture will be very different from Samuel Huntington's in spite of us both sharing, more or less, a similar context (certainly in terms of time and the conventional standards of meaning attached to the word 'culture'). Although both of us have the same conventional meanings of culture available to us, we do not employ them in the same way, nor do we see the world in the same way within the available conceptual and conventional standards.

So, available conventions in the context are one thing, which need to be identified, whereas what an author is aiming to do with or against those conventions in his/her text is something else. This is an important distinction. Knowledge of the context and close examination of a particular text for its ideas and assumptions enable us to conclude that where a text lacks any detailed statements to the contrary, a scholar must be working within the available and standard conventions of his/her age. We can be secure in this conclusion because the absence of a clear definition or detailed description of a term such as culture leads us to suppose that this is a term with which the author is almost certainly comfortable and familiar, and to such an extent that they have no need to orientate their readers.

For example, the British IR scholar, Chris Brown openly called on the 'intuitive' understanding of his readers when he told his readers in a footnote:

> 'Culture' is a highly contested term, and it would be easy to spend the rest of this article attempting a definition. For this reason it will be left here undefined, on the principle that readers will have a rough intuitive sense of what is involved in the notion . . .
>
> (Brown 2000:200 n2)

It is clear that Brown 'knowingly' shared with his audience a certain commitment to a particular understanding of the word 'culture', or a 'conventional standard.' However, Alfred Zimmern, writing in the 1920s, relied upon a very different conventional understanding of 'culture.' Unlike Brown though, Zimmern did not tell us this and the meaning has to be distilled from his work. In any case, it would have been as clear to Zimmern's audience, as it is to Brown's, what the word 'culture' meant and was intended to mean by the author at the time of writing – in spite of the fact neither author provided their readers with a definition of the term 'culture.' This lack of definition does not actually matter if the reader is reading the text at the time it was written, but it becomes a problematic issue several decades later when the meaning of the word has changed. A new audience of readers will attach a completely different meaning to the word, which will alter (if only marginally) their perception of a text.

Very few writers in IR, even today, offer an adequate definition when they refer to the term 'culture,' so it becomes crucial that we know what they mean as they rely heavily on their readers' 'intuitive' understanding. In itself, this offers considerable insight into the availability and widespread knowledge (power) of an idea. If I do not need to define my terms, it is because I assume everyone knows what I mean. Therefore, where a definition is absent we can be sure (or as sure as we can be) that this idea is familiar to the author and is assumed by the author to be equally as familiar to the audience. There is no need to explain what is already known and popularly understood; and this is what is meant by the notion of a conventional standard, where concepts are widely held and known in a familiar way.

Only when one is offering something new or unfamiliar is one compelled to spell out the terms clearly. Recovering the meaning of works from the context in which they were written and understood may tell us much more about the nature of the work than we might have previously assumed. It may reveal to us ideas that were important to the author that we have glossed over, and more importantly, it may tell us something new about ourselves – or how we have constructed our disciplinary historiography. Even if we conclude that most authors are working within, or, as is more likely, are the victims of, the prevailing conventional assumptions of culture for their time, the process of recovering the meaning in context is a useful one. It will, on the one hand, confirm that the meaning of culture has changed across the twentieth century, and, on the other hand, reveal that there has been a persistent interest in the subject of culture within the discipline – even though this may not be the issue that some authors became famous for. Moreover, we should recognize that conventional standards and prevailing assumptions can be exceptionally powerful things; this is especially so when they form part of a larger narrative about the world.

Narratives, natives and tourists

The subtitle of this book, 'narratives, natives and tourists,' requires some words of explanation. A narrative, in broad terms, is a story or tale about something – it links events or happenings in a coherent way and conveys them to the audience (see White 1987). To narrate, in the social sciences, is to give a continuous account of some aspect of the world and to provide the commentary, if you like, between action and play. As events do not speak for themselves, all scholars tell stories about the world; but a narrative is the story embedded in the story – frequently the narrative is hidden from view. The question to ask is what is the point being made behind the plot?

In this book, we will examine how scholars in IR have employed the notion of 'culture' to inform their narratives about international relations. Whether the concept of 'culture' is employed in its anthropological or humanist guise, it informs the framework for thinking and telling stories about the way the world is, or how some people think the world ought to be. The idea of culture has been and continues to be a fundamental conceptual tool enabling scholars to link events, issues and problems, at the international level: it is the concept informing the narrative that links the events in international relations.

There are several different kinds of narratives involving a notion of culture in IR, but they all derive, ultimately, from either the humanist or anthropological concepts. No two scholars will say the same things in these narratives even when they use the same concept of culture, but the possibilities and limitations of what they can say is frequently determined by the way they conceive of culture in the first place. In short, whether a scholar wishes to support a cosmopolitan (universal) or particularist (relativist) narrative of international relations will be structured by whether they are relying on the humanist or anthropological concept. Whether an author wishes to emphasize human commonality or difference will also be supported by the concept of culture they employ. What scholars are likely to say then, is to a considerable extent determined by the conventional standards they find themselves working with and the context, or "factory conditions" (Fox 1991:9) to borrow a phrase from Richard Fox, scholars find themselves working under and the conceptual choices they make. Since the 'factory conditions' have changed in IR over the course of the twentieth century, so we find scholars at varying points in time, doing different things with the concept of culture; or to be more precise, producing different narratives of world politics according to the concept of culture they subscribed to.

Who are the natives? In a general academic sense, the answer to this question depends very much on how one defines the idea of culture. The idea of 'the native' is crucial to the anthropological concept of culture, but is of less significance, especially in terms of inherent differences, in the humanist conception. In this book, however, 'the natives' are not simply the locals, born and bred – they become a shorthand term for the consequences of the anthropological outlook. They are the locals who are determined to make their idea of locality their defining feature. Who can and who cannot belong to the locale becomes a central question to 'the natives.' Searching for the 'English native' is a matter of determining who can and cannot be recognized (or is acceptable) under the definition of what it means to be 'English.' A question that is primarily political in my view, and impossible to answer with any measure of certainty, as should become apparent as this book unfolds. It is also a matter obviously complicated these days by migration, intermingling of every kind and globalization. Looking for the natives in a sea of faces in the high street or in a local cafe is unlikely to yield much. The restaurant as much as the pavement might indeed be full of 'tourists' (or non-natives) so any cursory glance will probably not reveal who the natives really are. Although we may not be able to physically distinguish between the natives and the tourists in terms of their appearance or their behaviour, the idea that we can (or should be able to) separate the local native from the passing tourist in cultural terms remains an important objective – and one not simply confined to academics.

Identifying the natives is more than a matter of description; for the locals it can be, as Walter Benn Michaels (1995) has suggested, an ambition, which clearly politicizes the idea. Where this ambition involves separating the 'authentic' and true-born local native from any foreign import, the social and political consequences can be serious. Extreme expressions of the native, by themselves or as they appear in some academic arguments that favour the native, can degenerate into something identifiable here as 'nativism.' We find Michaels quoting John Higham on nativism within the confines of the American context, where he defines nativism as an "intense opposition to an internal minority on the grounds of its foreign ... connections ..." (Michaels 1995:2). However, from an IR perspective, those 'foreign connections' have a broad basis both in theory and practice. 'Nativism' (and nativist) in the sense that I employ it here, exceptionalizes the native and glorifies them to excess. This can manifest itself within a state as animosity to *others* not deemed to qualify as pure natives, obvious examples include ethnic minorities and refugees; but it can also find expression on the world stage as suspicion of and hatred towards other generalized kinds of natives, 'Americans,' 'Muslims' etc. Nativism can give rise to an insidious form of politics. Moreover, it stands directly opposed to that free-ranging activity loosely referred to here as 'tourism.'

If the natives are the locals magnified and intensified, who are the tourists? The short answer is that the tourists are, under the terms of the natives, the people who easily do not belong. They are the people whom the native account considers as outsiders or 'passers-by.' Whether people travelling through a community do this for two weeks, two years or permanently, is not the issue. The tourists might not intend to remain within a community for any great length of time and, unlike the natives, can be easily regarded as unimportant. On the other hand, the tourists might claim a permanent space amid the natives, which is theoretically difficult. In either case, they are certainly viewed as irrelevant when compared to the force of native culture.

The place of the tourist in cultural theory is a problematic one. A cultural account is only concerned with a specific group of natives, and although the tourists may be remarked upon for the demands they make on the natives and for the disruption they cause, the underlying assumption is that the native culture can be examined and accounted for in purely their own native terms. This is to say, that in the general scheme of things, a busload of tourists do not figure significantly in the culture of the Chicano, the Mashpee Indians or the Kayapo Indians for example. Although the tremendous impact the tourists may have on a community as paying guests, visitors on business, or temporary workers might be acknowledged, as a category of people they are not counted as a serious part of the landscape or as something to be taken seriously in cultural terms. The essential features of a community and what that community is thought to share – its culture – are believed to remain isolated, if not wholly in one piece, despite the presence of tourists or cultural *others*. In short, it is a major assumption in certain forms of anthropological thinking that (borrowing an example from Michaels) a New York Jew cannot become a Mashpee Indian, and that it is the native culture (of the Mashpee) which presents the ultimate preventing barrier.[3] It is not possible to become culturally otherwise, and many a narrative involving the anthropological idea of culture proceeds as though this were a self-evident fact and minor concern. Under Mead's idea of culture, we have the culture we have, it makes us what we are and we are stuck with it. Yet, there is something very troubling with this line of thought; what might be obviously excluded from a tour group becomes uncomfortable when the tourist as *other* represents real people and real cultural *others*, such as our hypothetical New York Jew amid the Mashpee community. Turn the tourists into refugees, asylum seekers, migrant workers, immigrant settlers or second generation British Muslims and the idea that we cannot become culturally otherwise and remain forever excluded from and isolated by the native culture is not only socially unacceptable but also politically disturbing.

The theory that champions the natives' exclusivity to the detriment and banishment of the tourists in their midst needs to be challenged. For these reasons, 'the tourists' serve a dual purpose in this book. On the one hand, the tourist is a descriptive term for itinerant behaviour, including package holidaymakers and voyeurs whose interest in the native is perhaps only of momentary duration, while on the other hand, the idea of 'the tourist' is also a more generalized notion of the *other* employed to oppose 'the native.' The tourist serves as an irritant deliberately placed to upset the native and his/her theory of the world. The tourist reminds us that life is not fixed and enduring, and that what is transient can exert a powerful influence in the world. If the native represents all that is 'pure, unique, and enduring' in a culture or way of life, then the tourist stands for everything that is deemed impure and/or temporary on a mass scale. Where the native appears as a permanent feature in the local landscape, the tourist can be glimpsed flying overhead or breezing past on a bus, or setting up a corner shop. The tourists ruffle the local native's landscape with their hotels, their restaurants, their shops and various other kinds of off-shore installations, and unsettle the native's account of the world. The tourists appear in this book in order to demonstrate that what the nativist argument thinks belongs, may not, in actuality, belong anywhere. More-over, this should not bother us (although it will obviously disturb the nativists) and will not bother us, once we have released ourselves from the confines of essentialist conceptions of culture and a world dominated by fetishizing the natives. Therefore, both 'the natives' and 'the tourists' are metaphors in this book for larger categories of thought.

Key points

- There are two concepts of culture – the humanist and the anthropo-logical.
- The twentieth century witnessed the rise of the anthropological concept over the humanist concept.
- This development impacted across the social sciences – it has had special implications for the discipline of international relations (IR).
- The contextual method enables us to assess this change through the meanings and understandings which authors attached to the term culture, and to do so by recovering the meanings in their terms, not ours.
- The narrative is the story about international relations in which the idea of culture may occupy a specific place.
- The natives embody the anthropological concept.
- The tourists embody the humanist concept of culture.

1   The civilizing mission of culture

The word 'culture' appears to have begun life as the Italian term, *cultura* and we find references occurring in thirteenth and fourteenth century literature.[1] *Cultura* specifically means 'to cultivate' and, in its original sense, referred to cultivation of the soil and the tending of animals, from which sense we obtain the word 'agriculture.'[2] The French borrowed the term *cultura* from the Italians, first as *couture* and then as *culture*. 'Culture' quickly spread across Europe under the influence of the European aristocracies' fascination with all things French, making its appearance in England during the fifteenth century. The word's etymological root in the idea of 'cultivation' is crucial.

By the late eighteenth century, the idea of cultivation began to be applied to human beings in addition to the soil. The process that took the meaning of 'culture,' in Terry Eagleton's wonderful phrase, from "pig-farming to Picasso" (Eagleton 2000:1), and, if you like, from 'Picasso to the Pitjandjara,' was a long and uneven one.[3] We do not find all people employing the term in the same way, at the same time, even within the same regions. Nonetheless, certain trends can be discerned in an otherwise complex historiography, making it possible to tell a general story about the idea's progress. Yet, it is important to note, as the anthropologist Adam Kuper has pointed out, that "[c]ulture is always defined in opposition to something else" (Kuper 1999:14). In establishing its meaning in opposition to other ideas, the meaning of culture has always contained a political element, which becomes apparent as the historiography of the idea unfolds. Although the progress of the idea of culture spanned several centuries, it is a story in which the perceived inadequacies of civilization and eventually evolutionary theory emerge as crucial components. This chapter only discusses the 'pig-farming to Picasso' stage; the process that takes us from Picasso to the Pitjandjara is discussed in the third chapter.

Civilité, culture and kultur

Initially, the word 'culture' referred to the cultivation of good manners, but gradually the meaning extended to include a whole range of intellectual and social activity and improvement. However, the idea of cultivating human behaviour pre-dates uses of the word 'culture' to describe the activity. According to the social historian Norbert Elias (1939/1978), the process begins in the Middle Ages and has its roots in courtly behaviour (this is the origin of the words *courtoisie* in French and *curtesy* in English). Codes of behaviour and strictures on manners became a growth industry in the fifteenth and sixteenth centuries. Whether it was polite for one to spit under the table rather than over or on it became a matter of great importance and one in which the concept of polite behaviour is central (Elias 1939/1978:153–60). Politeness is a constructed activity and people needed to know how to behave politely in public, so much so that, as Elias indicates, books of instructions flourished during this period.

Manners and etiquette (increasingly elaborate rituals of behaviour) exert control over individuals and the self, and they call for individual and collective restraint in the presence of persons more eminent than oneself. A growing awareness and interest in the habits of table manners, personal hygiene and social relations can all be seen taking place from the fifteenth century onwards. Elias links these kinds of developments in public behaviour to the growth in feelings of 'delicacy and shame' coupled with the increasingly private nature of life in large and affluent households. He sees these developments as part of the 'civilizing process' as he calls it, but it is not until the French words *courtoisie* and *policé* (politeness) are replaced by the word *civilité* in the seventeenth century that the civilizing process becomes more visible. It is with this development that the division between individual cultivation and general social, civilizing, development becomes distinct.

Civilité from the Latin term *civilis* (to make civil) is a broad notion, indicating acceptable social behaviour not simply at court but also between social classes.[4] According to Elias, people begin, during the seventeenth century, to mould themselves, and others, more deliberately than they had previously. As this process acquires a self-conscious aspect, the idea of cultivation takes on additional appeal (in addition to pig farming, that is). And the French are among the first Europeans to employ the word 'culture' in respect of individual behavioural development. Culture has become a matter of art, literature and intellectual achievement (see Williams 1976/1988:90), as well as appreciation and knowledge of these things.

On the eve of the French Revolution a new term makes its appearance to describe growth and improvement in the larger social sense – civilization.[5] In this context, 'civilization' is initially a generic term which describes the French, their national development and all the achievements that entailed; but given the wider European tendency to follow all things French, it did not remain solely their term for long.[6]

Napoleon reportedly told his troops in 1798 as they set off for Egypt, "[s]oldiers, you are undertaking a conquest with incalculable consequences for civilization" (cited in Elias 1939/1978:49–50). The rest of Europe sat up and took note. Set against the dramatic social changes that were taking place as a result of industrialization, the term civilization seemed most appropriate for distinguishing the achievers from the underachievers.

Industrialization and "low culture"

Europeans had concerned themselves with standards of manners, education and decency. As individuals, they had aspired to better themselves and to become 'cultured,' while the term civilization encapsulated, in their view, what was common to all. "Cultivation, could be taken as the highest observable state of men in society" (Williams 1958/1993:63) distinct from civilization which was "the ordinary progress of society" (Williams 1958/1993:63). 'Civilization' was the perfect term with which to set out deliberately and consciously to conquer *others* and thereby force a better standard on them; 'culture,' on the other hand, remained a personal matter. We can see this in the characters in Jane Austen's novels, where "[e]ven the country squires – Mr Knightley, Mr d'Arcy, Edmond Bertram – were well read, appreciative of art and proud of both" (Parsons 1985:2).

It is important to grasp a sense of the 'factory conditions' of the time, and the context in which the idea of being cultured established itself, especially those things that the idea established itself in opposition to. The historical period of questioning identified as 'the enlightenment' embodied all that was rational, technical and in opposition to tradition, and had developed (during the eighteenth century) alongside civilité and the subsequent notion of civilization. Inevitably, the enlightenment was seen as indistinguishable from civilization because of its tendency to advance. The counter-enlightenment, conversely, rejected the universal and scientific basis of explanation, and attempted to return to tradition, nature and a simpler way of life. For some, the advance of civilization, especially its industrial aspect, was seen to be exerting a detrimental effect on people, society and the environment; nature was being destroyed by the factory blight.[7] The aim was to recreate or reinvent some simpler and purer time; a time before the folks became the masses. These sentiments found romantic expression in poetry, literature and art, and developed across the eighteenth century and continued during the nineteenth. Veneration of natural purity, for example, can be found informing John Ruskin and the 'arts and crafts movement' in Britain, and would eventually make its way to 'art nouveau.'

The influence of early German counter-enlightenment intellectuals, such as Johann Herder, helped to extend the meaning of culture from the cultivation of better habits to something slightly more spiritual in content.

The idea moved from one involving self development to an idea that denoted community development and group destiny. It also opposed notions predicated entirely on the scientific and rational progress of humanity. In 1867, when Matthew Arnold wrote his classic text, *Culture and Anarchy*, he drew upon German thinkers and their counter-enlightenment ideas to bolster his critical observations of the state of British civilization; Gotthold Lessing, Johann Herder and Wilhem von Humboldt, are all acknowledged and admired by Arnold (see Arnold 1869/1994:48 and 85). In *Culture and Anarchy*, Arnold clearly drew on the German idea of *Volksgeist* or "an invisible Spirit that breathes through a whole people" (Coleridge 1978:94) as Samuel Taylor Coleridge had put it. Herder's earlier connection between *Volks* (folks) and *Geist* (spirit) was an important one, because it signified that the idea of *Kultur* (German for culture) (kultur) had a spirit-like quality, or what anthropologists recognize as the humanist conception of culture.[8] It is contextually important to note, however, that although Herder associated the word *Volksgeist* with a particular community of people and his studies of folk communities, he did not conceive of this 'culture' in a fixed and unchanging way, rather it contained an intangible aspect and the element of progression.[9] For Arnold, it was the human spirit in the form of 'sweetness and light' (beauty and knowledge) that needed cultivating to a higher state. This was more than good manners; it concerned educating the mind and feeding the spirit.

Arnold began by telling his readers that:

> The whole scope of the essay is to recommend culture as the great help out of our present difficulties; culture being a pursuit of our total perfection by means of getting to know, on all the matters which most concern us, the best which has been thought and said in the world, and, through this knowledge, turning a stream of fresh and free thought upon our stock notions and habits, which we now follow staunchly but mechanically, vainly imagining that there is a virtue in following them staunchly which makes up for the mischief of following them mechanically.
>
> (Arnold 1869/1994:5)

Arnold was urging his readers to improve themselves. Not only was he criticizing the state of English society for being 'philistine and commercial' (as he saw it), but he was making a direct appeal to individual cultivation and spiritual development through the means of culture. Arnold saw culture as the tool for achieving a higher state individually and for effecting desirable social change. The source of the 'present difficulties' was civilization, and Arnold believed that culture would save society from its ugly influence. Civilization may have progressed enormously by Arnold's time, but with its 'vulgar masses' and 'dark satanic mills' it had also created unpleasant social side effects.

Arnold pleaded the case for what anthropologists would later recognize as 'high culture;' the best of everything in the arts and humanities. But for Arnold, this simply was culture; there was nothing higher or lesser to be considered as part of the word's meaning. The 'mind and spirit' versus all that is 'mechanical and material.' Industrialization may have brought technical benefits but it had undermined spiritual values and the quality of life in British society; in short, there was too much 'low culture' in Britain (although Arnold did not recognize it in these terms). A bad case of too many 'vulgar' and 'philistine' people, and not enough 'pursuit of perfection.' For Arnold, "[c]ulture is right knowing and right doing; a process and not an absolute" (Williams 1958/1993:125). Moreover, it is a process in which the idea of education plays a central and crucial role.[10] Naturally, arguments involving qualitative distinctions, i.e. 'the best of' things, are susceptible to normative critique and accusations of ethnocentrism today. Yet, at the time, it would have been obvious to Arnold and his generation that William Wordsworth and Coleridge wrote 'good' poetry, which fed the mind and soul in a manner that Victorian music hall ditties would never achieve.

belief that culture was only for the affluent

Several decades after Arnold, the British scholar F.R. Leavis worried that 'mass civilization' was "levelling-down" society (Leavis 1930:8) – culture was now in the minority.[11] The debasing of society by mass social developments is a perennial fear in some circles – for example, are computer games bad for children, is violence on television or in song lyrics having a negative influence on people? All of these normative concerns are straight out of the Arnoldian view of things. Is culture improving society and helping us to pursue perfection, or is it being hampered by the crass development of civilization?

Nearly two decades after Leavis, T.S. Eliot tackled the same question. Instead of worrying about the effect cheap paperback novels were having on English culture, Eliot opened up the idea of culture by thoughtfully including a 'boiled cabbage' in his understanding of what constituted Englishness. In a move that seemingly points the way towards popular culture and the discipline of Cultural Studies, Eliot tells us that English culture:

> ... includes all the characteristic activities and interests of a people: Derby Day, Henley Regatta, Cowes, the twelfth of August, a cup final, the dog races, the pin table, the dart board, Wensleydale cheese, boiled cabbage cut into sections, beetroot in vinegar, nineteenth-century Gothic churches and the music of Elgar.
>
> (Eliot 1948:31)

He appears to undermine Arnold's elitist view of culture by including such vulgar events as 'Derby Day' and mundane artifacts as boiled cabbage, but Eliot could not quite bring himself to adopt Arnold's egalitarian view of culture. For Eliot an aristocratic elite turns out to be the safe keepers of culture – high culture that is (see Eliot 1948:48). The English may eat Wensleydale cheese and go to the dogs, but the culture that matters, even for Eliot, is that of Elgar, not that of the bingo-players.[12] At least Arnold considered the aristocracy as uncultured and reckless as the other English classes! It would not be until the English literature critics came along in the 1950s, notably Richard Hoggart and Raymond Williams, that 'low' culture would gain a respectable place in society and the elitism of the humanist concept would be challenged.

The distinction between 'good' and 'bad' or 'high' and 'low' culture is critical to Arnold's view of the world, but whether this kind of distinction is necessary for the humanist concept itself is open to debate. Nonetheless, it has been a distinction that has generated considerable debate and interest in British academia, even spawning its own discipline of Cultural Studies.

The discipline of Cultural Studies that developed during the 1960s might be described as a working class backlash against the elitist proponents of 'high culture.' Scholars in this discipline would come to revel in the amount of 'vulgarity' that affronted Arnold, and Leavis unearthed, by arguably, 'bringing the bingo players back in,' and standing Arnoldian assumptions on their head. As John Storey has pointed out, "[a]lthough cultural studies cannot (or should not) be reduced to the study of popular culture, it is certainly the case that the study of popular culture is central to the project of cultural studies" (Storey 1996:1). This is a proposition that Arnold, Leavis and, to some extent, Eliot would have found an anathema. Remove the hierarchical thinking behind the humanist concept and everyone has culture in the Cultural Studies sense. Culture is not simply Baroque music it is also body-piercing and in this way, the discipline challenges the snobbery in the Arnoldian assumption that culture is solely certain kinds of art and literature and the 'best of everything.' At the same time, the discipline of Cultural Studies owes much to Marxist critique (particularly Antonio Gramsci's notion of hegemony); although, as Storey has pointed out, it is not necessary to be a Marxist practitioner, "[a]ll the basic assumptions of cultural studies are Marxist" (Storey 1996:3).

It is obviously easy to criticize Arnold's idea of culture for its ethnocentrism and elitism as some of his contemporaries and subsequent critics did.[13] Proclaiming, for example, that the middle classes are philistine, the aristocracy barbarous and the populace vulgar, is unlikely to win friends. Besides, at the time Arnold wrote, the humanist idea of culture had already become somewhat of an embarrassment and something to be sneered at.[14] Yet, there is a potential for universalism underwriting Arnold's thought; a potential that the critics failed to either see or conveniently ignored.

All classes, according to Arnold, and therefore all human beings (although Arnold does not say this), given the right education and environment, would recognize the value and importance of 'culture.' 'Culture' speaks with a universal voice, from and to all human beings. "It seeks to do away with classes; to make all live in an atmosphere of sweetness and light ..." (Arnold 1869/1994:48). Arnold would, as well, have poured equal scorn on the natives and the tourists if he found them to be ignorant and uneducated. The working classes may be vulgar and the aristocracy frivolous, but both could reap the benefits of culture if they put their minds to it. Indeed, the very same thesis can be located in Herder's idea of *Humanitat* or 'league of humanity.'[15] The achievements that every local community produces are capable of being recognized and admired beyond that community by all human beings. There is an element of the universal recognition of exemplary behaviour in the humanist concept. Few would dispute the lack of merit in dispatching football hooligans around the world, for example; that activity only brings shame.

Herder tells us that it was through reading Shakespeare that he felt that he not only came to understand the English to some extent, but that he also understood himself and his own community better and saw it in a new light.[16] His personal experience of reading Shakespeare shares the same relevance to culture that Arnold's thesis advocates. This comes some way to grasping the spiritual aspect of the humanist concept. This idea of culture, as conceived by Arnold and Herder then, *is* Shakespeare and the impact of reading him; there is no hint here of any difficulty involved in exchanging Shakespeare for Goethe, quite the contrary. Only by reading the best of everything, including both Shakespeare and Goethe, are the benefits of 'culture' such as art, literature and intellectual achievement derived. The benefits we gain from reading a good book, reflecting on a piece of music, or appreciating a work of art or architecture are not quantifiable or readily tangible. And the aesthetic and qualitative results derived are not confined to the individual in Arnold's view, but benefit the whole of society. If sufficient people become cultured then society would, inevitably, be transformed, or this is how Arnold saw it. The important point is that Arnold's concept of culture was not associated with innate difference as the anthropological concept understands it; the key distinction lies with the humanist stress on the quality of the educated mind. The inherent cosmopolitanism within this, the humanist conception of culture, will later play a significant role in the thinking of early IR theorists.

The idea that culture was the means for improving mind and disposition remained the primary understanding of the term for the British and French. And it remained their understanding long after their German neighbours had turned the idea into an altogether different concept.

For centuries, the aristocracies of Europe followed the French and their fashionable trends – they spoke the French language, copied their clothes, imported their furniture, borrowed their designers and were influenced by their ideas. This is as true of the German princes as it is of the English. The difficulty in Germany was that the small yet growing middle classes were alienated from the German aristocracy. Whereas Elias tells us that there was little discernible difference between the French aristocracy and the intelligentsia in France – they ate the same foods, read the same books, and could be found together in the Parisian salons – the German classes did not enjoy a similar intimacy with one another.[17] From the mid-eighteenth century onwards, and isolated from the aristocracy, the middle classes begin to develop their own coping mechanisms. The idea they draw upon is culture or kultur in German. Drawing upon their own language and taking pride in their achievements, the German middle classes begin to establish a sense of identity and self-confidence that needed no reference to things French or 'civilized' to justify its existence. Elias describes this process as a 'self legitimating' one for the German middle classes, whereby the distinctiveness of German life comes to be defined as worthy in its own right. Since the idea of kultur already embodied the idea of *Volksgeist* in German thinking, the attraction for a folk with a distinct spirit was, perhaps, somewhat obvious. This idea of kultur, however, would gradually place greater emphasis on specific *Volks* or people and be cleansed of its humanist and cosmopolitan outlook.

As the nineteenth century rolled on, so the distinction between the German ideas of 'zivilization' and kultur would become more concrete. From the German perspective, zivilization was artificial, foreign and of no benefit to the intelligentsia (it had not admitted them to court or afforded them power for example), whereas kultur was something altogether more natural and pure; something that spoke for the German people and their achievements. The main point was that, in its early life, the German concept of kultur represented a rejection of all things French. For the alienated intelligentsia, kultur was the ideal concept around which to develop a sense of self. As the German middle classes come to power, they take their concepts, including kultur, with them. Elias tells us that what had been a social antithesis between the ideas of kultur and zivilization, say as it was in Herder's day, would now become a national antithesis. Kultur represented all that was good, honest and pure for the German speaking people, whereas zivilization embodied all that was artificial, mechanical and false.

By opposing the largely Anglo-French idea of civilization, kultur appears to parallel Arnold's view of culture, but there is a crucial difference in that kultur comes down firmly on the side of the German native rather than that of the cosmopolitan aspirations of a well-educated tourist. Here, then, we can note a change in the social and national meanings, function and significance of both zivilization and kultur. The idea of kultur found in German usage during the latter part of the nineteenth century was plainly different from Herder's conception in the late eighteenth. The American anthropologists Alfred Kroeber and Clyde Kluckhohn noted that, in the 1850s, the German scholar Gustav Klemm had dropped those elements associated with "enlightenment," "tradition" and "humanity" (Kroeber and Kluckhohn 1952:46) that could be found in Herder's work. The idea of kultur had lost its cosmopolitan outlook: it was now something that only described the German speaking *Volks*; it was not something that all peoples could share and benefit from. By the time the Germans identified kultur as a community-based and, more significantly, a scientific enterprise, the term 'culture' meant something very different to most of their European neighbours.[18]

By the turn of the twentieth century, three different ideas were clearly visible. For the British and French (and Americans at this time, although their position will change on this matter as we shall see in chapter three) the idea of civilization embodied their sense of large-scale social achievement. Civilization, closely tied to industrialization, Empire and progress, represented all that was seen as good in the advancing world. Some people had expressed doubts over the benefits of civilization and for them, culture and a return to all that was natural, spiritual and pure, was an important critical tool (see Johnson 1979). In general though, no matter what one thought about the actual state of culture and civilization, the idea of culture, for the British and French, remained an individual matter. It was associated with intellectual and personal endeavour, education and improvement. Kultur, by contrast, was a national concept. It represented the spirit of the German speaking peoples and all that they had achieved, while the German term 'bildung' was employed to describe individual development.

We can see the distinction quite clearly in a remark made by the French historian Fernand Braudel in reference to a quotation from the German historian, Wilhelm Mommsen. Apparently, Mommsen said, "[i]t is humanity's duty today [1851] to see that civilization does not destroy culture . . ." (Braudel 1963/1995:5–6). Braudel acknowledged in 1963 that this "sounds bizarre to French ears because for us the word 'civilization' takes precedence, as it does in Britain . . ." (Braudel 1963/1995:6).

It has been said that the "Germans in the name of *Kultur*, opposed the encroachments of *Zivilization*," and this was especially true around the time of the First World War.[19] The Germans failed to defend kultur against zivilization in the First World War, which only served to intensify their faith in kultur. Far from questioning the concept, some drew more heavily on other ideas that had been fashionable at the turn of the century, and added to it those ideas centred on evolutionary thinking and race theory. This development would have disastrous consequences, resulting in the horror that would be the Second World War.

→ Britain / France - civilization - individual social achievement

Germany - Kultur - national concept

Race and evolutionary ideas

It is important to recognize that the concept of civilization itself under-went changes in meaning and these inevitably affected the idea of culture that took shape in its wake. Accumulated developments in industry, commerce and lifestyle that had taken place over the course of the previous two or three centuries were impacting at every level of European society and beyond during the eighteenth century. The idea that human beings could transform their environment was evident in the factory system and scientific developments. New found wealth was creating different kinds of social relationships, while consumer goods, from pottery to cutlery, were beginning to enter ordinary people's homes enabling them to change their immediate environment. These changes were not only taking people to new parts of the world as merchants, administrators and emigrants, but were also bringing people into contact with new information about the world. The big question, in the late eighteenth century, was how did everyone fit in? Whereas Spanish Catholics had previously worried about whether the American heathens had souls, the Europeans and Americans now worried about civilizing the 'savages' – a process in which religion would only be one aspect of their overall (re)education.

The concept of civilization had always been a hierarchical one, distinguishing as it did, in a tripartite system, between the civilized, barbarous and savage. During the eighteenth century, however, the idea of civilization, in spite of its inherent hierarchy, had been an inclusive concept and this manifested itself in its singularity – there was only one civilization to which all people, in theory, belonged. All people had the potential to become 'civilized' and the administrators and missionaries of Empire invested formidable effort into bringing this state of affairs about. In short, the concept of civilization easily accommodated the idea of a 'great chain of being.' The major and most meaningful differences were religious; separating the Christians from the Muslims and the Jews and other religions, as they had done for centuries. From the civilized (and Christian) perspective, all human beings derived from Adam and Eve and belonged to one great big family, although some clearly considered themselves the senior members in that family in view of their advanced state. Given the strangeness of some 'primitive' natives and the persistent inconvertibility of some religious *others*, perhaps it is not surprising that hierarchical thinking behind the idea of civilization would become pluralized and extended.

During the nineteenth century, attitudes began to harden and doubts crept into the concept, questioning to what extent everyone was linked together, if at all. Braudel tells us that around 1819 "the word 'civilization' . . . began to be used in the plural" (Braudel 1963/1995:6), but it did not become popular in the plurality until the 1860s; this development signifies a considerable change in thinking about relations in the world.

Mid-nineteenth century developments in the natural sciences would give this change in thinking a considerable boost. A paradigm shift was taking place; one in which the idea of nature and the place of all species in it would be fundamentally altered. In place of 'the great chain of being' came evolution with separate and multiple chains of being. One should not underestimate the impact that evolutionary thinking had in the social sciences, and particularly on the idea of culture. Evolutionary theory would influence the social theories of Karl Marx and Herbert Spencer, as well as thinking in sociology, anthropology, economics and politics generally.

It is popular to link evolutionary theory with Charles Darwin, but in the social sciences, much of the thinking owed more to the ideas of Jean-Baptiste de Lamarck.[20] While Darwin's theory was explicitly biological, Lamarck's theory of acquired characteristics stressed both environmental influence and biological inheritance. Adam Kuper has suggested that most late Victorian anthropologists were working with Lamarckian, rather than Darwinian, evolutionary schema. As Kuper says, "[t]here is a paradox here, for Darwin's triumph stimulated a very un-Darwinian anthropology . . . those untrained in biology were very likely to prefer a Lamarckian to a Darwinian view of evolution, if, indeed, they recognized the differences" (Kuper 1988:2). Yet, the same is true for many scholars in the social sciences, not simply those working in late nineteenth century anthropology. It is important to note that during the late nineteenth century, evolutionary thought covered a wide spectrum of ideas, many of which bore the influence of British scholars. Charles Darwin is an obvious name here, but the work of Francis Galton and Herbert Spencer arguably had a greater impact on social theory.

The collision of evolutionary theory with the concept of civilization resulted in some very unsavoury ideas when taken beyond the laboratory and placed in the social context. A most obvious outcome was the increasing interest in ideas of race that would eventually give rise to race theory; and the connection between evolutionary thinking and ideas surrounding 'race' resulted in a form of biological determinism that would be very influential at the turn of the century and dominate the first half of the twentieth century. Most obvious, here, is the idea of Social Darwinism. Although the phrase itself is not wholly accurate, these ideas would fuel the eugenics movements and racist ideology.[21] However, it is important to remind ourselves that these ideas were widely spread (in other words, they were conventional standards) in the then contemporary context.

The American anthropologist George Stocking has pointed out that, "[t]urn-of-the-century [nineteenth to twentieth] social scientists were evolutionists almost to a man, and their ideas on race cannot be considered apart from their evolutionism" (Stocking 1968/1982:112). As the idea of civilization had developed and Empires expanded, the co-existence of 'civilized white Europeans' with 'uncivilized non-white savages' became, necessarily, untenable.[22] A key question for nineteenth century thinkers was why people were different; while, the answer to this question "was increasingly to be found," as Stocking indicates, "in 'race'" (Stocking 1968/1982:35). According to Ivan Hannaford (1996), from 1890 onwards, evolutionary theory had become biologically (racially) determinist and was closely associated with the concept of civilization.[23] Hannaford suggests that the heyday for race thinking was the period from 1890 to 1914, yet arguably, the heyday for racial politics extended well beyond this point and well beyond the Second World War period.[24] The point is that race was the main category for differentiating between people and an increasingly politicized one as far as people believed they could shape society through Social Darwinism.

The changes that occur in ideas about race, which evolutionary theory enhanced no end, changed the meaning of civilization from an inclusive concept to one based on a fundamental separation of peoples based on their blood. Whereas in the eighteenth century the idea of civilization had been thought to be the destiny of the whole of humanity, by the late nineteenth century a different set of assumptions had come to prevail. These assumptions rested on ideas about the divisible nature of humanity. Given scientific support by evolutionary theory, thinking about different races became an acceptable way of looking at the social world.

It would be a serious mistake, however, to think that race theory and racist attitudes were something that belonged to the slave trade era or were confined to the Nazis.[25] Not only were attitudes towards race very different in the eighteenth century as Hannaford has pointed out, but by the late nineteenth century (and well into the twentieth), everyone thought in racial terms.[26] In turn, this profoundly affects the way people thought about civilization and what they thought the concept meant. With the power of science to lend legitimacy, the idea of race appeared a credible way of thinking about people and the differences between them. In much the same way as we talk today about the cultural differences between people, so people during that period spoke and thought in terms of differing races. So much so, that by the turn of the twentieth century, the language of race was *the* prominent discourse; and because of culture's close relationship to the civilization concept, the influence of racially determinist thinking on the civilization concept would eventually alter the meaning of 'culture' both in Germany and in the United States.

It was not simply the case that there were different races in the general sense; evolutionary theory told us people were born fundamentally different from one another. These inner differences, considered obvious and self-explanatory at the time, manifested themselves in outward physical characteristics – skin colour, facial features and stature. Observable differences were sufficient to confirm (or justify) that the white race was not only distinct from the black and coloured races, but that it was also superior. Given the fact that white society was so clearly technically advanced and industrialized, with scientific thinking now also to its credit, the synthesis between three ideas – white skinned (race), superior and civilized – was complete by the end of the nineteenth century. Moreover, this view of the relationship between black and white society in the scheme of things was a conventional standard among social scientists as much as it was for the general, Western, public. While the eugenics movement debated ways of purifying the gene pool in the 1920s, anthropologists had already been out measuring heads;[27] and it would have to be acknowledged that much of the discourse on international politics, around this time, centred on something identified as race relations.[28]

In 1919, as Akira Iriye (1997:67) has pointed out, the *Journal of Race Development* quietly changed its name to the *Journal of International Relations*.[29] The editors did not think much of this event because they continued the volume sequence without any fuss and bother. Volume 10, the *Journal of International Relations*, simply followed on from where Volume 9, the *Journal of Race Development*, left off. From our contemporary standpoint, the name change, at least, seems quite incredible. The move from race to international relations would seem to represent both a qualitative and quantitative change in subject matter, yet, to the journal editors, the change was, obviously, less dramatic. The choices of the journal's title tells us something of what early IR scholars considered the subject of international relations to be about.

The original journal title tells us that the study of international relations was not simply the study of states and their foreign policy, it was also the study of people; and for turn of the century thinkers, people could be classified and discussed according to their 'race.' Naturally, then, the study of international relations would entail, in some form, the study of relations between the differing races and their development. However, although the change in the journal's title throws some light on the origins of one aspect of the subject matter in IR, it also tells us that the subject matter of 'race' was no longer considered appropriate by 1919. That 'race relations' no longer captured the idea of what international study was or should be about, indicates a shift in academic circles, especially in terms of the language employed to describe the subject matter. Scholars did not discard the language of their time completely. They did not abandon the concept of civilization, nor did they detract from the idea that the world consisted of different races, but they had undergone a change in their intellectual outlook by the end of the First World War, which signifies a further refinement of the concept of civilization. Effectively the concept of civilization was, to some extent, rescued from evolutionary theory and especially the biological determinists' ideas of it. To appreciate this transformation we need to look more carefully at the context of ideas that existed immediately prior to the First World War.

IR before the First World War

The main problem with studying people, and especially people on an international scale, is one of how to account for the vast array of differences between them. For early IR scholars, these differences were contained by the concept of civilization. What it meant to be civilized had become increasingly based in race theory in the latter part of the nineteenth century; and the formal study of 'race relations' was the inevitable outcome of this form of the civilization concept. Yet, the concept of civilization and its racial turn were not without their critics.

Two things stand out with respect to international politics around the turn of the century and the period that led up to the First World War.

First, the concept of civilization determined vertical relationships throughout the world. Not only were the upper classes seen (by themselves naturally) as more civilized than the lower classes, but the colonial powers saw themselves as more civilized than the colonies they administered. Even the lowliest of farm workers thought themselves superior to the 'primitives' in Africa. Race thinking made it easy to distinguish the savage natives from the sophisticated and pale-skinned tourists. It was the civilized world's mission, duty even, to bring the benefits of civilization to the natives.

Second, the idea of civilization affected international relations horizontally. Even within the so-called civilized world, there was a hierarchy of distinction that affected relations between states; Russia was clearly less civilized than Britain and France (although, there was clearly some dispute between the latter two as to which ranked higher than the other). Moreover, it was considered that only the civilized states engaged in proper international relations.

When China and Japan went to war in 1894, the incident was not seen as a proper war in the West as neither party could be counted as 'civilized' under the general terms of definition. Japan won the war and declared victory in the name of 'civilization' (Iriye 1997:36), ensuring (but not entirely securing) Japan a foothold in the civilization camp. When Japan was asked to contribute troops to the suppression of the Boxer Rebellion in 1900, it appeared that Japan's presence among the civilized states had become more acceptable. Of course, this was, largely, a superficial acceptance and did not amount to the genuine recognition of equal international status, for Japan still ranked at the bottom of the pile of civilized nations and the Japanese as racially inferior people.

When Japan defeated Russia in 1905, the shock was more than just a military one. Japan had graphically mounted a challenge to the contemporary understanding of who was civilized and what civilization meant, which suggested, by default, that the Japanese presented a racial challenge, although the West was not ready to accept that challenge, or deal with it, for some considerable time.[30] That Japan did not secure an equal footing among the civilized nations became readily apparent in the discussions that led to the establishment of the League of Nations on 20th January 1920 (a point discussed below), but the question of equal recognition of *others* would be a dominant problem in international relations for several decades after the First World War had been brought to a close by that same organization.[31]

If international relations proper were the province of the civilized states, then the role of war in these relations was additionally an affair for civilization. Nowhere in international relations is the coincidence between evolutionary thinking and the idea of civilization more dramatically evidenced than in attitudes towards war at the turn of the century period.

James Joll (1982) has noted 'a fundamental' change in attitudes towards international relations during the nineteenth century. This change was the result of economic problems and international rivalries, which were exacerbated because they:

> ... combined with the belief that Darwinian, or pseudo-Darwinian, ideas about the survival of species could be applied to human communities as to the animal kingdom. This in turn encouraged a new kind of nationalism in which the nation, now regarded as a living organism, was justified in taking any measures whatsoever which were thought necessary for its survival or expansion.
>
> (Joll 1982:213)

Where Baron von Clausewitz had told us, posthumously, in 1831 that 'war was the continuation of politics by other means' (which implied anyone conducting politics had access to the instrument of war), by the late nineteenth century, this instrument had taken a decidedly Darwinian turn. War was now the continuation of a specific kind of politics, those of the civilized people.

In 1871 Ernest Renan, the French philosopher–historian, declared that "[w]ar is one of the conditions of progress, the sting which prevents a country from going to sleep, and compels satisfied mediocrity itself to awaken from its apathy" (cited in Angell 1911/1972:139). And in 1910, ex-President Roosevelt said in London, "[w]e despise a nation just as we despise a man who submits to insult" (cited in Angell 1911/1972:139 and 175). War then, was seen as part of progress and a mark of 'manly pursuits.' Moreover, it was a way of weeding out nations less fit in terms of civilization, which reveals the extent of the association between the idea of civilization and evolutionary theory. The First World War would not only 'be over by Christmas,' but would also afford the civilized nations the opportunity to give the opposition a jolly good whipping. Whichever state emerged victorious from the process, they would have done civilization a good service, or this is how some of the British and French perceived things. The Germans, of course, saw it otherwise; it was the chance for kultur to put civilization in its place. Yet, even before the first shot was fired, critics were voicing contempt for this attitude towards war and questioning quite what the idea of civilization should really mean in the new twentieth century.

It is an obvious point that authors write about the subjects that concern them most, but a point easily overlooked or distorted when taken out of context. One of the things that authors comment on repeatedly in literature around the time of the First World War is how much the world has changed from the previous generation. It is a point we take for granted these days, but the growth in the number of international organizations "in the last quarter . . . of the nineteenth century and in the early years of the twentieth" (Lyons 1963:14) was staggering, especially when compared to the level of activity earlier in the nineteenth century. According to the historian F.S.L. Lyons, the number of international non-governmental organizations (NGOs) created between 1900 and 1914 was 304, while between 1880 and 1899 it had been 113, and in the period 1815 to 1849, only four NGOs had been created (Lyons 1963:14). Although there had been a steady increase in international activity throughout the century, it can be seen that this grew markedly in the first quarter of the twentieth century, both in volume and in the range of issues covered. There were now international organizations for regulating the postal service and petrol production, for transport, communication, labour and workers' rights, social and humanitarian issues, intellectual and religious cooperation, peace and even language.[32] The extent of cooperation required for regulation to be agreed to, let alone acted upon, is remarkable; all the more so, in view of the fact there was not an international body or comprehensive international governmental machinery, such as the United Nations system say, that might have been able, or have been expected, to facilitate this activity in any way.

It is easy for us today to take all of the international connections and organizations for granted, but they were a novelty in the nineteenth century, and therefore all the more reason to be admired for their existence in the early twentieth. Not surprising then that we find contemporaries believing that they lived in a new age – in a new world where flight, motorcars, telephones, radios and international communications, all things only talked about or marvelled at by the previous generation, were beginning to become features of everyday reality. Not surprising also, that for the contemporary generation, this new or 'modern civilization' as Alfred Zimmern described it, needed alternative ideas and new thinking to support it. The one thing that the critics agreed on before the First World War was that the idea of civilization needed to shed a few old-fashioned assumptions.

A major piece of IR literature from the pre-war period is Norman Angell's *The Great Illusion*. First published as the small pamphlet *Europe's Optical Illusion* in 1909, it was expanded into the volume in 1911. The book gained in popularity during the First World War and its aftermath, but as the work pre-dates the war, it covers a wide range of issues, not simply the prevention of war, and affords additional insight into the institutionalization of interest in that subject we now know as international relations.

Angell placed considerable emphasis in the text on the recognition of changes in lifestyle and social attitudes. He based the main points of his case on the fact that civilization had progressed and that this had profoundly altered global relations. He stressed the changes that had taken place in the economic sphere, for they had led to a greater interdependency between nations, but these changes had also effected a profound psychological change in human behaviour, in his view. Although he recognized the "survivals of the old temper" (Angell 1911/1972:237) as he called it, he remained convinced that the real changes occurring in the world, required, or would necessitate, a change in thinking sooner or later. It was the changing attitude towards war that he considered most pressing, especially in view of the substantive developments (the Anglo-German arms race) taking place at his time of writing. Under 'modern conditions,' according to Angell, it was no longer acceptable to link civilization to war as Theodore Roosevelt and his generation had done.

The fundamental aim of *The Great Illusion* was to rescue the idea of civilization from the "military conception" of it (Angell 1911/1972:186). The assumption of continued progress was an essential element in Angell's argument, his idea of progress was one tempered by environmental influence, not biology.[33] In this sense, his fundamental thesis remained Lamarckian. In every respect, the advance of civilization profoundly altered social life and Angell demonstrated this by way of numerous historical examples.[34] Quite simply, under civilization habits change and qualitatively so. Modern life was completely different from all past forms in every way; this was especially noticeable in terms of the quality of life among 'civilized' nations. Duels had been abandoned. 'Herbert Spencer does not have the same feelings as paleolithic man' and 'Lord Roberts does not drive his motorcar over the bodies of young girls in the manner old Northmen drove their wagons.'[35] "What was once deemed a mere truism," Angell argued, "would now be viewed with horror and indignation" (Angell 1911/1972:163).

The alleged 'truism' that early critical commentators of international relations viewed with 'horror and indignation' was the prevailing assumption that war was an acceptable component of the civilization concept. Many early IR thinkers, including Norman Angell, David Davies, Philip Noel Baker and Leonard Woolf, argued that this mentality was outdated and utterly disastrous. Not only did they fear it would inevitably lead to conflict, but they also thought the argument inappropriate for the age they found themselves inhabiting. The critics, however, did not seek to develop new concepts from scratch; they all remained well within the parameters of the dominant conventional assumptions of the time. This is to say that they all subscribed to the idea of civilization (which is indicative of the power the idea enjoyed). The British IR scholar Gilbert Murray provides us with a useful insight into what the idea of civilization meant to his generation:

> There was ... [he said, a] faith more universal and more deeply and unquestionably held ... a profound belief in the value and rightness of Western Civilization with its characteristic attributes – its faith in progress, its liberalized Christianity, its humanitarian ethics, its free democratic institutions, its common sense, its obedience to law, its triumphs of applied science, and its vast and ever-increasing wealth. To the men of my youth Western, and especially British, civilization was simply the right road of human progress: other civilizations, if one could call them civilizations at all, were just false roads or mistakes.
>
> (Murray 1948:20)

There was, then, no objection to the idea of civilization as such, but the content of the concept needed realignment. According to the critics, to be civilized was not to promote war but, in their view, to be peaceful. The serious differences and difficulties, between the critics, centred on how to guarantee and institutionalize 'modern' peaceful relations.[36]

This concern for a conceptual realignment in respect of the true nature of modern civilization, which all the early commentators held in common, would provide the founding disciplinary problem as the letter in which David Davies and his sisters proposed the establishment of the Woodrow Wilson Chair at Aberystwyth indicated. The Davies' wrote that the new Chair should be established "in memory of the fallen students of our University ... and for the encouragement of a truer understanding of civilization other than our own" (Aberystwyth 13th December 1918). The Davies' suggested, "[o]ld problems must be confronted in a new spirit ..." (Aberystwyth 13th December 1918). The fact that the Davies' believed 'a truer understanding of civilization' would be the key to a more peaceful future as well as provide the basis for the new discipline of IR is very revealing. It underscores the point that the meaning of civilization was an extremely important matter and one worth investing in – literally.

In 1916, Leonard Woolf argued that in its "broadest aspect the problem is to develop a whole system of international relationship in which public war shall be as impossible between civilised States as is private war in civilised States" (Woolf 1916:8). Woolf pointed out that the problem itself was not new, and elaborated that:

> It has for many centuries exercised the minds of those people who, because they were civilised, have at all times been contemptuously called theorists and Utopians by plain men, their contemporaries; but

periodically, when the world is swept by the cataclysm called war, plain men, amazed to find that they are not civilised, have themselves raised a cry for the instant solution of the problem.

(Woolf 1916:8)

It would be easy to read Woolf's objection to war in this statement as *idealist*, or, in his terms, 'utopian,' but the underlying focus is the distinction between those people who 'are civilized' and those who 'are amazed to find that they are not;' a distinction that carried considerable normative and intellectual weight at the time. The new generation of thinkers was clearly more civilized (had a truer understanding of civilization) than their plain predecessors.

We are familiar enough with Norman Angell's anti-war sentiments and 'idealism' within IR, but less well publicized are the arguments he constructed in his most famous work *The Great Illusion*, and why. It is little known, or insufficiently acknowledged, that *The Great Illusion* was a popularization of his arguments against biological determinism and that it was this, as much as, if not more than, his anti-war sentiments, that comprised the central component in his thinking. The 'great illusion' turns out to be all the manifestations of biological determinism, or the 'survival of the fittest,' in international politics.

Angell breaks his argument into numerous 'optical illusions;' the key ones are the illusion of successful military conquest, the transfer of wealth to the strongest parties, and an unchanging human nature. The assumption that the most powerful and the most aggressive states can conquer and inherit the earth, as well as profit by it, are dangerous illusions for Angell, since this form of IR relies on a conception of an unalterable human nature. It is this prevailing view (or 'conventional standard') of the 'nature' of human nature in international politics that the author sets about demolishing.

The Great Illusion took issue with views akin to those expressed by Professor Karl Pearson, for example, who said:

The path of progress is strewn with the wreck of nations; traces are everywhere to be seen of the hecatombs of inferior races, and of victims who found not the narrow way to the greater perfection. Yet these dead peoples are, in very truth, the stepping stones on which mankind has risen to the higher intellectual and deeper emotional life of to-day.

(Cited in Carr 1939/1995:48)

Much of Angell's argument was directed against those prominent commentators, politicians, militarists and clergymen who believed that 'war facilitated progress and was a significant factor in the development of civilization and humanity.'[37] Angell argued that 'warlike nations would not inherit the earth;' they may conquer territory but they would not reap the benefits that civilization has constructed because there was greater inter-national interconnectedness than in the past. War would injure everyone, which was why 'new' thinking was inevitable in Angell's view.[38] It was coop-eration not competition that provided the basis of civilization in the twen-tieth century. All that remained was to change the public's opinion and the mindset of a few aged generals who seemed to think that the only 'true patriot was the one who fought' and that stepping on human stones was the way to advancement.[39]

The need to understand and further civilization was at the heart of many intellectual problems, but since the dominant 'paradigm' was bio-logically determinist, this makes the early IR critics' work all the more important. By debating and questioning the idea of civilization and what it means to be civilized, Angell, Woolf, Davies and co. were contributing to, and participating in, the process of changing public perception on this matter. What the idea of civilization would mean after the war would be somewhat different to that which existed prior its outbreak. As *The Great Illusion* indicated, this process of redefinition began well before the League of Nations was established.[40]

All of the arguments against biological determinism in politics would have greater saliency once the atrocities of the Second World War had been revealed, but prior to the First World War the key challenge that the critics posed was over the question of what civilization was all about. Was the future of international relations determined by social and biological forces beyond human control, or was it more flexible and open to recon-struction? What would international relations be like if the determinists were right? Some frightening possible answers would come, in the 1920s and 1930s from the National Socialists in Germany, the eugenicists, and the segregationists in the United States, Australia and South Africa. In Britain, although race thinking remained a conventional standard and popular, by questioning the meaning of civilization (through campaign-ing, producing pamphlets, giving public lectures and writing newspaper articles) IR scholars took an active role in, and contributed to, the process that led to a shift in the understanding of what it meant to be civilized.

The larger challenge presented by the critics was whether or not the idea of civilization belonged to everyone and if it did, what should it look like? The early commentators continued to believe in the idea of civil-ization and to believe that the idea had universal relevance and saliency. They were not ready to discard the notion of civilization completely (this will come much later). Angell, along with his colleagues, was clear that civilization belonged to everyone and affected every aspect of inter-national relations, although it was equally clear to Angell that there were plenty of uncivilized areas that required 'civilizing,' but this much was true of most commentators at the time. The civilization concept was still hierar-chical – some people and states were clearly more advanced than others –

and it was still acceptable to write of different races and primitives. The concept of race remained the prevailing discourse for distinguishing between peoples around the time of the First World War. Angell retained the framework of civilization because it permitted him to offer a narrative of international relations in terms of progress, development, achievement and advancement. What he and his colleagues wanted to avoid was a deterministic or Social Darwinist, account of the future. It is an important point to recognize that a backlash against biological determinism was established in the founding of IR. Indeed, there would be little or no point studying international relations if everything was set within pre-ordained limits; but this backlash against Social Darwinism was also forming the factory conditions of the social sciences generally. Anti-biologically determinist arguments manifested themselves in other disciplinary areas, from the work of anthropologists in the United States, and in Britain, to Julian Huxley and A.C. Haddon's famous rejection of race in 1935. The idea that human society was set on some pre-determined path over which human beings had no control was being questioned and challenged from a variety of directions. In IR the argument that people could control their own destiny was about to be put into action (and to the test) with the instigation of the League of Nations. Yet, the debates over the establishment of the League of Nations at the time demonstrated how precarious the context and how delicately poised some of these arguments were (and further illustrate why one should be wary of writing history backwards).

Once the First World War started, it provided an obvious focal point of any discussion on civilization. Yet, by the end of that war, in the *idealist* sense and from an IR point of view, what it meant to be civilized had still not been conclusively decided. The founding of the League of Nations did not completely secure the meaning of civilization in the 'modern' sense; although it attracted wide support, the experience of the League, especially during the series of crises of the 1930s, would demonstrate that a considerable volume of the 'old temper' remained. As Gilbert Murray commented several years later, the early supporters of the idea of a League of Nations:

> were ridiculed as cranks with our new and fantastic 'League of Notions'; as unpatriotic, with no pride in the Empire and its achievements; as unpractical pacifists when advocating general disarmament, and as war-mongers when demanding the fulfilment of the obligations of the League against aggressors.
>
> (Murray 1948:2–3)

That the early supporters of the League 'were ridiculed as cranks' is very revealing. Public perception on this matter altered considerably during the course of the war and with the establishment of the League itself. If

the supporters of the League were seen as 'cranks' and 'traitors' before
and during the war, the experience of the war and the efforts of leading
intellectuals, including many in IR, served to sway public opinion considerably.[41] By contrast to the early days, the League became an extremely
popular organization, especially among the public and the smaller states.[42]
Although to be sure, public attitudes did not alter sufficiently in the
United States to enable that state to join the new fangled organization.
Although this had much to do with the Americans taking an isolationist
and a nativist turn in the first decade after the war, which demonstrated
the persistence of race theory and the determinists discourse in some
circles, as we shall see.

The change of public attitude towards the League of Nations and its
supporters should not be underrated, because it significantly affects the
course and mood of international politics in the years immediately following the war. On the one hand, there was the theoretical challenge that the
League, simply by coming into existence, presented to conventional
understandings of the concept of civilization. Whatever the later historical
verdict of the League (and I think calling it a failure is too simplistic), its
creation was a considerable achievement and the first of its kind. Its mere
presence demonstrated that other forms of civilized politics were possible,
even if they did not always turn out to be the success imagined or hoped
for. On the other hand, the debates concerning the organizational set up
of the League illustrated just how entrenched, not to mention global, race
theory and some of the underlying assumptions about civilization had
become.

Let us come back to the experience of Japan. The Japanese fought long
and hard at the Versailles conferences (1918–19) for the inclusion of a
racial equality clause in the constitution of the League. They did not get
it. The American President, Woodrow Wilson, was blamed for this, but
Alfred Zimmern tells us that it was an Australian delegate, William Morris
Hughes, who blocked the clause.[43] Moreover, it is Wilson who is remembered for his candid observation on the matter: "[h]ow can you treat on
its merits in this quiet room a question that will not be treated on its
merits when it gets out of this room?" (Zimmern 1936:262). He was quite
right. The world was not ready to embrace the concept of racial equality;
indeed the question of the relationship between the West and non-West
would remain unresolved for decades. What effect this had on the Japanese is open to debate. Akira Iriye seems to imply that the failure of Japan
to secure equal status amongst the civilized nations was a contributory
factor in the Japanese desire, during the Second World War, to establish
an alternative East Asian Civilization in opposition to the Western civilization. The Japanese it seems, at least, had accepted the idea of civilization, if not the Western version of it. What is more, the Japanese felt it
necessary to impose this civilization on their 'racially inferior' neighbours,
as they saw them – the Chinese, Philippinos and Koreans.

One can only speculate as to how things might have turned out had the Japanese and the other non-Western peoples obtained equal recognition and status in 1919. But considering how the non-Western states (Japan, China, Uruguay for example) viewed each other at the League and beyond, it suggests that perhaps it was not only the West that was not yet ready for racial equality. For example, there does not appear to have been much talk between the non-Western League states about extending rights to the non-League members, who included most African states and who were represented through the holders of Empire – the idea of racial equality had its limits it seems. As a powerful conventional standard, the assumptions of civilization extended and maintained its sense of hierarchical distinction throughout the world. The idea of civilization may have been wrested, in some quarters, from the biological determinists, but it was still going to be a hierarchical, patronizing and, somewhat, racist concept. Even if there were lots of civilizations and not just one common to all people, they were seemingly based on the same assumptions. All of which would change the shape and fortunes of the ideas of culture and kultur and, in turn, their relationship, in IR, to the concept of civilization. The refinement of the civilization concept in IR would, however, create a place for culture in international politics in the aftermath of the First World War.

Key points

- The idea of culture has its roots in cultivation – developing first of all, in the form of good manners and behaviour and then as an educated and enlightened self.
- The humanist concept of culture embodies the 'best of everything,' a sense of self-awareness, spiritual growth and improvement.
- The concept of culture took shape in opposition to the concept of civilization in Britain and Germany, albeit in different ways.
- In nineteenth century Britain, culture was thought to be the means for improving civilization.
- The discipline of Cultural Studies will eventually reject the elitist assumption that culture is 'the best of everything.'
- In Germany, the concept of kultur gradually becomes more nationalistic and exclusive.
- The concept of civilization changes – in the nineteenth century, becoming caught up with race theory and biological determinism.
- Early IR theorists reject the attachment of biological determinism to the concept of civilization. Peace not war is the hallmark of civilized behaviour.
- With the new international machinery of the League of Nations, the humanist concept gains a new lease of life in IR.

2   Cultural internationalism

One of the immediate and lasting effects of the First World War was that everyone worried about the nature of civilization. Faith in its durability and some of its characteristics had been severely shaken and there was a growing sense that civilization was not as robust or decent a process as had been previously believed. The possibility occurred that civilization might not progress as inevitably and naturally as Angell with his Lamarckian ideas made out. The idea arose that civilization might be a fragile structure and something that required effort to sustain; all of which contributed to the urgent need for a 'truer understanding of civilization,' necessitating the founding of a formal programme of study.

In the aftermath of the war, the confidence that we found informing Norman Angell's work in 1911 begins to evaporate. Nevertheless, the post-war era did open with an air of optimism and hope: optimism that a better, war-free, future was possible and hope that civilization was now firmly in the hands of a modern generation – a generation which hoped to establish a truer understanding of civilization than their predecessors. The idea of culture that emerged and flourished during the 1920s was in response to the problems confronting the civilization concept. Interest in culture during this inter-war period would elevate the humanist concept's status to the international stage and ensure that this idea of culture would continue to play a role in international politics until the present day; although this subsequent international role was not without difficulty.

The fragility of civilization

The war had proven the biological determinist view of international relations wrong, both substantively and morally. Angell had been right; war had not ensured 'the survival of the fittest' nor had it 'stung nations into progress.' It had only seen the fittest of Europeans suffer colossal losses and it had brought misery and despair on a mass scale. In this respect, Angell and his colleagues were seen to have been correct in their assessment of the pre-war mentality, but Angell had been wrong in his assessment of civilization in one crucial respect. He had taken the future progress of civilization for granted. The war had demonstrated that the future of civilization could not be taken for granted nor left to its own devices; it was something that had to be worked at. Angell had assumed that, under the new conditions of civilization, cooperation was inevitable, whereas the post-war generation of scholars argued that such cooperation in international relations could not be left to run a 'natural' course, it required management at every level.

The First World War generated two important and immediate developments. First, the concept of civilization was itself widely questioned, ensuring that the issue of what constituted the nature of civilized activity remained very much a matter for debate. Not only would contemporaries need to think differently about what constituted civilization, but they believed they would also require new mechanisms for guaranteeing its future survival. One of those mechanisms was the development of international machinery, which came in the form of the League of Nations. The argument, which began before the war, that peace not war was the more civilized activity continued, in earnest, in its wake. The founding of the institutions of the League of Nations substantively reflected the changing context and provided major new sources for discussion (Zimmern 1936:176).

The second development was that the means for preserving and/or disseminating civilization became 'modernized' and internationalized. This necessarily afforded the idea of 'culture' a greater instrumental role, but one that depended entirely on a new conceptualization generated by the debate over the nature of civilization itself. Together, these developments formed the 'factory conditions' against which IR theorists worked. It was only through opening up the notion of civilization to environmentally based definitions in the pre-war period, and, as a result of the war, questioning the assumption of civilization's continued progress in the post-war period, that 'culture' was able to attain international significance in the 1920s and 1930s in IR. This significance, however, would diminish over the course of the inter-war period, reflecting the changing context and the increasing number of international crises. Indeed, one of the things that people commented on during the inter-war period was the growing distinction in attitudes between the first and second decades following the war.[1]

When Angell criticized the dominant conceptions of civilization in 1911, he had not considered the possible demise of the whole structure and process. Yet, this issue would be uppermost in the inter-war theorists' minds. Feelings about the matter would gradually change across this inter-war period from one of hopeful optimism that civilization could be brought under control, to the more fearful view that civilization might collapse entirely. By 1935, the mood had changed to such an extent that Gilbert Murray was claiming, "there is something wrong. There is a loss of confidence, a loss of faith, an omnipresent, haunting fear. People speak, as they never spoke in Victorian days, of the possible collapse of civilization" (Murray 1948:23). This change in attitudes, from hope to fear concerning the concept of civilization, from enthusiasm for the future to increasing despair, marks the difference between the 1920s and the 1930s. The second inter-war decade found people discussing the nature of civilization in ways unimaginable prior to the outbreak of the First World War.

Where, during the 1920s, optimist faith in a new civilized order flourished, during the 1930s, there was a growing fear that civilization itself might be in peril; a fear that Oswald Spengler had anticipated in his *Decline of the West* (Spengler 1926/1939). Although Spengler had begun his project before the First World War and had begun to publish in 1918, his work seemed increasingly to capture (and reinforce) the mood of pessimism that developed across the inter-war period. Spengler believed civilization caused the death of culture. Culture represented, in Spengler's organic view, the flowering of human creativity. Culture had soul, whereas civilization was mechanical and artless. "Each Culture has," he said, "its own new possibilities of self-expression which arise, ripen, decay, and never return" (Spengler 1926/1939:21). All civilizations, in his view, went through a lifecycle of childhood, youth and flourishing growth (the period of culture), which were followed by age, decay and death (the era of civilization). The argument that civilization, the triumph of mechanical progress over the natural creativity of culture, was a degenerate form of progress was perhaps to be expected from a German scholar who favoured kultur. The questioning and pessimism that grew out of the First World War would, in the build up to the second, seem to justify Spengler's argument concerning civilization's eventual demise and it would feed the fears of people like Reinhold Niebuhr (1932 and 1944) who saw a darker side to humanity.

Arnold Toynbee, on the other hand, tried to be more upbeat about the survival prospects of Western civilization. As James Joll has pointed out, Toynbee could not, ultimately, accept the 'fatalism' that permeated Spengler's work (Joll 1985:95). In less pessimistic terms than Spengler, Toynbee began publishing his monumental *Study of History* in 1934, in which he traced and compared the development of some twenty-six civilizations, all of which were transitory, as he made amply clear (Toynbee 1934, 1947/1949, 1954a, 1954b, 1961). Western civilization, however, held out better prospects of continuing in Toynbee's view, because of its unique qualities.[2] Yet, generally speaking this cyclical view of civilization arrives on the scene *after* the brief period of optimism, which flowered in the wake of the First World War, had seemingly expired. As Murray revealed in 1935, during the 1920s Toynbee's *Study* "would have seemed to us at that time perverse and almost frivolous" (Murray 1948:20). Most other people, however, continued to think within the terms of civilization and believed the concept had utility and a future of sorts, albeit a future fraught with growing qualification. There was, still, an ongoing interest in civilization, but views differed on how to improve and then save civilization, if it could be saved at all. In the atmosphere of the 1930s, interest in culture seemed a trivial affair, but nonetheless it was an area that acquired a sense of importance as the urgency in the international situation, and the threat to civilization, grew. The humanist concept of culture became all the more important to those who still held out hope that another world war could be avoided.

The desire to improve civilization was an outlook ideally suited to the humanist concept of culture, committed as it was, in Britain at least, to 'polishing' the social aspect of civilization rather than allowing the varnish to develop by its own, uncontrolled, accord. Viewed from within the confines of IR, 'culture' appears to burst on to the international scene in the aftermath of the First World War with no prior history. Yet, it would be a mistake to think that its appearance was a sentimental response to the war itself and lacked theoretical grounding. The concept of culture that came to the fore during the inter-war period was much considered and was the outcome of debates surrounding the civilization concept, especially biologically determinist versions of the idea of civilization, which stretched back to the late nineteenth century. Interest in culture was not, then, simply a knee-jerk reaction to the First World War (although there is an element of response), nor was it a response born of blind idealism. Within the fears for civilization and the emphasis on environmental influence, not to mention control, the humanist idea of culture with its 'pursuit of perfection,' notions of conscious effort, and belief in its spiritual benefits, held obvious appeal. To apply this idea to international relations made good sense, especially when set in a context where biological determinism had to be proven discredited and the 'true' nature of civilization had to be entered into. There is some movement in the conventional conceptual standards of the age, but one should not overlook the element of continuity of ideas informing thinking about international politics at this time, including ideas about race.

Early inter-war scholars did not consider anything fundamentally wrong with the idea of civilization, on the contrary, civilization simply needed to be improved, not only to prevent war in the future but also to enhance the quality of international life. The major normative assumptions underpinning the idea of civilization remained intact; civilization was still accepted as a good thing, it was still progressive and naturally hierarchical. The word 'civilization' appears in all texts during this period and required no special indexing, because everyone knew what the word meant. Confidence in the fundamental idea remained high, but the comfortable assurance of its survival had been questioned. World War One had revealed civilization to be a more fragile structure than previously thought. As Alfred Zimmern made quite clear, there was a serious need to deliberately develop and promote mutual understanding between peoples, who in turn, it was hoped, would influence other aspects of international relations including their state's foreign policies. In other words, to change the civilized nature of international relations required something more than mere 'mechanical' contact, and, crucially, far more effort than Angell had imagined. As Alfred Zimmern pointed out in 1924, "[i]t is indeed one of the common fallacies of the age to believe that international understanding is brought about automatically, as a result of the play of impersonal forces" (Zimmern 1929:55). The distinction between what was once thought to be an 'automatic' outcome of other 'impersonal forces' (for example, economic interdependence), and 'real' understanding, is an important development in IR, and one that demarcates pre-war thinking from inter-war thinking on this matter. It was through the practical steps taken at the international level that the humanist idea of culture was able to realize a significant role in international politics.

Culture, certainly in British and French circles, remained 'the best of everything' and the 'pursuit of perfection.' The aim now was to pursue that perfection on an international scale and to spread the benefits of 'sweetness and light' globally by exchanging the 'best of everything.' The thinking behind the idea was quite straightforward and straightforwardly influenced by Matthew Arnold. If people became more cultured, then they would change their habits and behaviour; this would mean that they would become more civilized, which would, if all went to plan, affect the nature of international relations. In the short run, it could prevent war, and in the long run, it could lead to a whole new world order. Whereas Arnold had envisioned 'culture' performing a transformative role in English society, some people during the First World War saw no reason why this thinking could not be extended to the international level. Education would, inevitably, play a crucial part in effecting a global transformation, while the general approach comes under the broad descriptive heading of 'international cultural relations.'

The proposition that one comes to know oneself through engaging and exchanging with others, and is therefore likely to become a better person because of such activity, is the foundation stone of the idea of international cultural relations. Not only is this an idea that can be traced through Arnold back to Johann Herder, but during the inter-war period, this notion found expression in what Akira Iriye has described as 'cultural internationalism' (Iriye 1997). Iriye explains the basic propositions informing 'cultural internationalism' through a reinterpretation of Thomas Hobbes' statement on power in cultural terms. Whereas Hobbes told us that power was "man's present means to obtain some future apparent need" (Iriye 1997:11), Iriye suggests that 'cultural internationalists' have defined both the need and the means for achieving it in cultural, not power based, terms. This may be somewhat of an overstatement as far as much of the inter-war thinking is concerned because scholars did not overlook the place of power politics in favour of culture in their assessment of international relations. But Iriye's basic proposition that 'cultural internationalism' represents alternative means to 'brute force' is relevant, for it is clear that culture came to be considered as an important and non-aggressive tool in international politics during the inter-war period.[3] In short, the aspirations of Arnold were elevated to the international stage, placing high culture and education in starring roles in the 'pursuit of international perfection.'

One of the key principles behind 'cultural internationalism' was that through exchanging culture (or the best of everything) at the international level, people would not only learn about each other and themselves, but thereby overcome some of their differences. These differences, it was believed, had led to poor communication, misunderstanding and, ultimately, to disastrous foreign policies. By seeking to bridge the gaps in understanding and by making the *other* less foreign, culture could bring about major changes in attitudes between peoples and their states. The natives should be afforded every opportunity, and at every level, to engage with the tourists. By engaging in 'cultural interchange' (the exchange of culture) in the form of art, literature, exhibitions, concert tours and above all via the educational exchange of students, scholars and ideas, the natives and tourists would come to know and understand each other better. Although literature explicitly devoted to the subject of international cultural relations is quite limited, three phrases appear with extraordinary frequency in both the then contemporary literature and subsequent work on this subject. These phrases, 'fostering mutual understanding,' 'co-operation' and 'educating minds,' sum up the founding principle behind the humanist approach to international cultural relations or, in Iriye's words, 'cultural internationalism.'

Intellectual and cultural interchange

Gifts have always been exchanged between heads of states. The Hungarian ambassador to Turkey recorded the fabulous arrival of a gift of over 30 carpets in Istanbul, in 1553, to Suleyman the Magnificent from the Shah of Persia.[4] King George III (UK) received a cheetah from India in 1764, and George IV, a giraffe from Mehmet Ali, the Pasha of Egypt in 1827.[5] The government of the People's Republic of China was fond of sending 'friendly' furry ambassadors in the shape of the giant panda, as goodwill gestures to 'important states.'[6] The British Prime Minister, Edward Heath received two pandas from the People of China in 1974 – Ching-Ching and Chia-Chia – and they were housed in London Zoo, gaining them a measure of celebrity status with the public.

The diplomatic exchange of gifts is probably one of the oldest tools in the international relations box. It is an international activity probably as old as the existence of different communities and monarchs themselves. Exchanges of animals, books, carpets, textiles, military regalia, for example, are carried out for a number of reasons. They may be exchanged in the hope of promoting understanding between two states, of demonstrating friendship, as symbols of cementing relations and in the hope of securing future favours. They could also be returned or withdrawn with great effect, as the evidence of displeasure and lack of favour.

Gift exchange at the international level is a tricky business, deciding what to give and which message you wish the recipient to notice is very important. Maybe it is better to opt for a simple message as some of the American states did under President Carter's administration. When asked to produce a representative gift, Kentucky chose hand-woven woollen shawls.[7] Then again, perhaps it does pay to show off as Henry VIII of England and Francis I of France did in 1520 at the 'Field of the Cloth of Gold,' so named for the extraordinary display of wealth both sides exhibited. It depends on what the purpose of the gift is, and for whom it is intended; naturally, the aims, motives and message of a gift become quite central.

This general kind of gift exchange is sometimes referred to in IR as 'another way' in international relations; usually the fourth way in American literature and the third way in some British work.[8] After one has considered the political/diplomatic, economic and military ways of conducting international business, there is always culture. However, what may pass between two Heads of States on a personal basis, a giraffe or a pile of carpets say, is somewhat different from taking delivery of two pandas on behalf of a nation of people.

In effect, there are two faces to 'the other way' in international relations, no matter which way it is counted. The two forms appear as an extension either of national policy or of more general international activity and effort. In both cases the aim may be to increase understanding and knowledge, but the underlying motives and means of conducting this form of relationship differ somewhat.

There is a distinction to be drawn, therefore, between the official and state level exchange of gifts and the kinds of exchanges aimed at improving relations between peoples more generally. A former British diplomat, J.M. Mitchell, has drawn out the distinction between 'cultural diplomacy' and 'cultural relations' (Mitchell 1986). Where cultural diplomacy is a matter of state projection, international cultural relations require a state to 'present its best side,' in Mitchell's view. However, the idea of the state presenting 'the best side' does not go far enough in capturing the aims or spirit of the kind of international cultural relations practised during the 1920s, since presenting the best a state has to offer could still be seen as a matter of state level promotion or worse still, as the means for national propaganda as Mitchell acknowledges. Iriye's term 'cultural internationalism' is preferred because it captures the cosmopolitan spirit behind the idea of international cultural relations or 'cultural interchange' as the then contemporaries called it.

The idea that nations or states need to promote themselves like a pair of running shoes is an old one, and one where diplomatic gifts between heads of states become useful. The view of cultural gift exchange which emerged in the aftermath of the First World War, however, belonged to the internationalist spirit of the age. It had a much broader basis in terms of content, motives and purposes than that usually offered between states. The 'gift' was more broadly defined, and extended to the realm of ideas as well as to ordinary individuals, for want of a better term. It intended to deliberately foster mutual understanding between differing peoples, not just the elite or the state establishment, and to do so in a humanist way.

The exchange of 'culture' in the form of books, students and pandas can work wonders in the charm department and achieve what various officials, ministries and departments might be unable to – namely, to break down barriers in understanding. Indeed, 'tourism' in the very general sense, by promoting and sending 'gifts', may be the best a people have to offer to *others* around the world. 'Gifts,' like the tourist, step out beyond the boundaries of their existence and venture across divides. The inter-war theorists and activists offered a cosmopolitan narrative of international relations and explicitly appealed to the language of the mind and understanding common to the whole of humanity.

This cosmopolitan outlook recognized the need for a global language that could facilitate cross-national communication. It is, perhaps, not surprising that Esperanto became popular during this period, although it had been invented in 1887.[9] The differences which existed between races and nations were not thought to be a barrier to learning. Without difference acting as a restriction to cultural interchange, the interesting and egalitarian thing about international cultural relations or cultural internationalism (like Esperanto in principle) is that everyone can be involved in the activity in one way or another.

In international cultural relations, the personal encounter is the political, which in turn is the international encounter. It is not simply a case of recognizing the extent of such encounters and activity, it is to take this form of activity much further. It is, ideally, to institutionalize it and to make it a matter of policy, although not necessarily that of a specific government, but more the policy of aspirations and hopes which all human beings share. The cosmopolitan narrative is sustained by what humanity holds in common rather than by the differences that segregate people into distinct and isolated spheres of existence. Undoubtedly, we all engage in international cultural relations in our own small way when we have the opportunity to. I have been taken on personal tours in Australia, America and Europe by local people keen to show me the best their region has to offer, and I have reciprocated in my own locality. There is something personally gratifying in pointing out to visitors the best views, where the best monuments are located, the best beer can be drunk, or the best sausage is to be obtained. Indeed, we find Alfred Zimmern exhorting women to do their bit for international cultural relations by entertaining "a Dutchman or a Spaniard at tea" (Zimmern 1929:71). Patronizing to the contemporary woman's ears, the point is that this kind of international relations is not confined to the activities of state officials or VIPs; it is something with which all people can engage. We can all create forums for cultural interchange that will in turn foster mutual understanding – the tourists become potential ambassadors for culture. Easily dismissed and disregarded under more grandiose ideas of what international relations are about, namely the foreign and military policy of states, leaders and experts, these apparently small scale and insignificant encounters, of sharing information with strangers, might be more important than they seem. These personal international encounters might have more roles to play in terms of the impressions they create and the dispositions they lead to, rather than anything that can be achieved through an anonymous encounter with policy. Indeed, the more we consider this idea, the more we come to realize that there is a lot of this activity about, certainly in these globalized times, and it does affect the way we think about *others*, a point I return to in more detail in the concluding chapter. It was this kind of cultural internationalism that captured the inter-war theorists' and activists' attention, not that of 'cultural diplomacy' which was confined to the state level.

There is nothing sentimental or romantic in the cultural internationalist idea. "The problem," as Zimmern stressed, "is that of promoting international *understanding*, not that of promoting international *love*" (Zimmern 1929:54). As he explained, the problem was, at root, "one of knitting intellectual relations, not emotional relations, of developing acquaintanceship and mutual knowledge, not the warmer feelings of friendship and affection" (Zimmern 1929:55). We do not have to like each other, but we should make every effort to try to understand and know each other; although if friendship followed that would be welcomed. The main aim, then as now, is to strengthen intellectual understanding and 'mutual knowledge.' The emphasis on intellectual relations and developing mutual knowledge was a popular notion and in spite of our contemporary flinching, its elitist overtones would have passed largely unchallenged in the 1920s; although there were those sceptical of the impact this approach could effect, especially in IR (see below).

In the lecture delivered in 1924 on 'Education and International Goodwill,' Zimmern discussed the question of how 'international understanding and mutual self-respect might be promoted among nations with diverse personalities' (Zimmern 1929). Although the recognition of diversity among national personalities was a long standing one, and one Angell was aware of, the question of 'fostering international understanding and mutual respect' was an altogether newer development and one of the most pressing concerns in the aftermath of the First World War.[10] In his 1924 lecture however, Zimmern approached the problem somewhat differently than many might today. He was looking for a way of creating an 'organic relationship' between diverse nations at the international level; he was not concerned with 'celebrating diversity' in the manner in which we might be drawn nowadays to approach this issue. Indeed, one of the underlying points of his lecture was to advocate the 'obliteration of difference,' not to preserve or celebrate it; a suggestion likely to generate much discomfort these days.

Zimmern considered several forms of international contact in his lecture and assessed them for their potential to create the kind of organic relationships he envisaged. Primarily he was concerned with the institutionalized contact between states and the impact of contact brought about by trade, language, travel and information. What emerges from his lecture and other writings is the conviction that an international federation of states or governments, like the League of Nations, could not affect the kind of mutual understanding Zimmern and his colleagues were interested in (Zimmern 1929:56). At root, the problem was 'psychological.'

Where pre-war thinking had centred on biology and had tried to translate this into a determinist reading of international politics, the post-war generation was drawn to the intellect as the source of problems and the root for solutions. Even if people agreed to form a common international government, Zimmern doubted its effectiveness in 'obliterating differences,' he says:

> I wish I could believe this for, if it were true, we need only fold our arms and let the Covenant of the League of Nations – which is for many purposes a common instrument of government for the members of the League – do its obliterating work.
>
> (Zimmern 1929:57)

To even contemplate 'obliterating' difference, let alone stand up and lecture on the merits of such a proposition, appears a strong, if not offensive, suggestion today. Yet, Zimmern does not argue for the elimination of differences in nations, national personality (or of "starch" as he referred to these differences), and race, he makes plenty of references to both, indicating that he accepted these categories for the conventional standards they were.[11] Nor does he think that the world will merge into homogeneity, far from it; instead, he seems to think that these sources of differentiation, of race and nations, will remain. Rather, he objects to the politics of difference that these categories generate. Although Zimmern does not state this explicitly, he is arguing against 'fetishizing' difference as a basis for politics. He argued for a form of relationships that would make the most of difference and at the same time break down the barriers that prevent a meaningful and 'civilized' internationalism. In many ways, by recognizing the 'fact' of distinct national personalities and life, Zimmern was seeking to render real difference less *other*, for example, those that made the British different from the French. Therefore, it was distancing between peoples that required 'obliterating' not their substantive 'way of life.' This was no mere 'celebration of difference' for its own gratification, it was something of an altogether, more complex approach, and one in which cultural interchange would play a crucial role by spreading 'sweetness and light' around the world.

For Zimmern, the most effective means for creating international understanding from difference (personality and 'starch') were 'intellectual' and were those achievements and products that form the content of 'cultural interchange.' Zimmern, along with many of his contemporaries, argued for the need to exchange teachers, professors and students. We needed to introduce ourselves to other people and open our own minds to their worlds. He explicitly advocated that we should take "for our model not the specialism of the nineteenth century but rather the humanism of the sixteenth" (Zimmern 1929:70), while "[t]he most important thing of all is for our teachers to teach their students *how to open the windows of their minds* ..." (Zimmern 1929:67 – italics in original). Universities, and education in general, were to play a crucial role in international cultural relations, but even the tourists had a part to play.

Elsewhere, Zimmern made it clear that he was not interested in the "empty rhetoric of cosmopolitanism," but was seeking the common ground "of a uniting and reconciling human experience," upon which to build 'confidence and even friendship' (Zimmern 1922:161). He even wrote of the "law of greatest effort" (Zimmern 1929:72), which was, perhaps, best illustrated by his description of the 'lack of effort' exhibited in travel and tourism:

> The fact is travel is an art, an art of observation, of encountering new peoples and problems, of welcoming and enjoying the diversities of mankind. But the whole business of the modern tourist agency seems to be to preserve you from these thought-provoking encounters, to convey you, say, from Newcastle to Zermatt or Grindelwald with your national susceptibilities as unruffled and your comfort as undisturbed as if you were a parcel of eggs. The Englishman's shell must at all costs remain uncracked.
>
> (Zimmern 1929:65)

The remedy that would 'crack' the problem, he suggested, was to travel more intelligently in order to produce greater understanding of a people and their 'life' or personality (Zimmern 1929:65–6). It should be noted that he did not suggest we get to know a people's 'way of life' as the anthropologist might describe it. The problem, as he saw it, with the average English tourist was that s/he failed to experience or 'see' new peoples in a deep and meaningful sense. It was only by intelligent effort that the 'real' benefits of travel, reading and so on could begin to be felt in a humanist way, similar to Herder's experience of Shakespeare and of

Arnold's of German philosophy; knowledge of others opens up our world in incalculable ways. In creating opportunities and encounters with one another and forums where strangers were to be welcomed, Zimmern believed that more about each others' lives could be learned. Moreover, this should be "a contact between equals" – as in equal human beings (Zimmern 1929:72). "There is," he said, "no more deadly foe to international goodwill than patronage or condescension. How many a gift has been spoiled by the manner of its giving!" (Zimmern 1929:72).[12]

The exchange or interchange of cultural gifts in the humanist sense, as in the best of everything a people have to offer, has continued to hold appeal to this day. In the recent words of an Egyptian scholar, Dr Morsi Saad El Din, the humanist idea of "culture knows no boundaries."[13] Although the anthropological concept of culture had been invented by the inter-war period, it was not well known outside of the United States, and given the heritage of European scholars, it was the humanist concept of culture that attracted their attention. Cultural interchange would help to transform civilization, while the institutions of the League of Nations gave civilization a guiding hand, culture would work on the psychological and intellectual plane. The institution believed by the cultural internationalists to be the most useful for encouraging mutual understanding was the International Committee for Intellectual Cooperation. This organization was certainly an original development in the period and established a format that was replicated and expanded upon at the international and national levels throughout the remainder of the twentieth century.

Instituting cultural relations

In 1922, the League of Nations invited a group of intellectuals to discuss the establishment of a committee for intellectual cooperation. The result, the International Committee for Intellectual Cooperation (ICIC), was one of the first international institutions set up to further cultural internationalism and was an important institution with respect to 'cultural interchange.'[14] The aim of the Committee was to exchange academics, students, books and ideas to create greater understanding between peoples. The organization's central purpose was to encourage cultural interchange, as two early chroniclers explained:

> One of the great problems of the present time . . . is how to create in all peoples an understanding of the attitude of other countries. For this purpose not only the material interests, but also the culture and intellectual life of the different countries must be brought into contact.
> (Webster and Herbert 1933:291)

The ICIC was established precisely to fulfil the purpose of increasing intellectual and cultural contact between peoples.[15] Gilbert Murray described the basic idea behind the Committee as one of "making use of the artistic, scientific, and literary interests which are actually common to all cultivated nations as an instrument for achieving that goodwill and co-operation which was the aim of the League" (Murray 1948:4). What would pass under the term 'cultivated nations' was something the civilization concept still determined, since a hierarchical and elitist attitude remained within cultural interchange. This would be high art, not the popular mass literature F.R. Leavis loathed.

The Committee was based at Geneva, but received a considerable boost when the French government funded the International Institute for Intellectual Co-operation at Paris. The International Educational Cinematographic Institute quickly followed in Rome under the auspices of the ICIC. The Committee was involved in various artistic and intellectual activities. Its literary and musical events, advice on museum management and journalism, efforts to bring intellectuals and students together, and to regulate intellectual property and archaeological exploration, all met with mixed results. In his appraisal of the Committee, and in considering its achievements, Gilbert Murray thought "of the Goethe centenary in Frankfurt, the 'conversation' on the future of letters in Paris . . . [and] the discussion at Warsaw of the effects on philosophy of the recent discoveries in physical science" (Murray 1948:5). The Committee's inquiries into historical textbooks, and its recommendations for their revision along less nationalistic lines, and also its inquiry into the conditions of intellectual workers in Central and Eastern Europe, have been counted among its successes. Most important from the IR perspective is that the ICIC inaugurated an Annual Conference of Institutes for the Scientific Study of International Relations in 1928.

Inevitably the ICIC attracted interest in international educational matters, from the practical student exchanges and the establishment of libraries, to the general assumption that a broad, and international, educational outlook might undermine the parochial attitudes that led to misunderstanding. The focus on intellectual interchange was, in the words of Iriye, "unabashedly elitist" (Iriye 1997:65), and the Committee found it easier to deal with non-Western elites than the general masses. Nonetheless, by the 1930s, there were national Committees and affiliated bodies in forty-two countries.

The ICIC is often thought of as a less than successful organization, even by many of its contemporaries, and so it was not without its critics, as we shall see below. Yet, although the ICIC was seriously underfunded from the outset, certainly with respect to the tasks it had set itself, it should be remembered that the ambition to "reconcile the academies and learned societies" (Murray 1948:203), which had split as a result of the war, was an admirable one.[16] Moreover, the Committee attracted a number of prestigious members in its day. It was originally set up by a number of notable academics including Gilbert Murray, Marie Curie, Professors Millikan and

Henri Bergson, and attracted a glittering list of members including Albert Einstein, Béla Bartók and Paul Valery. Alfred Zimmern became the Deputy Director of the Paris Institute.

One of the main reasons that the ICIC was not particularly successful was that academics, on the whole, had their own mechanisms for international exchange including the International Research Institute and International Union of Academics, which necessarily tempered their involvement with the new organization. In spite of its limitations and failings, both the need for this kind of organization and its ideas continued, albeit with some modifications, with the founding of a successor organization after the Second World War, when the aims of the ICIC were reconstituted as The United Nations Education, Scientific and Cultural Organization (UNESCO). (UNESCO) and the plethora of similar organizations that followed in the wake of the ICIC, demonstrate the widely held belief that the cultural approach is capable of bringing much benefit to the world of international politics.

The purpose of UNESCO is "to contribute to peace and security by promoting collaboration among the nations through education, science and culture . . ." (cited in Goodrich *et al.* 1969:387). UNESCO follows on from the ICIC in spirit and aims; this much is apparent in the preamble to the organization's constitution, which holds:

> That since wars begin in the minds of men, it is in the minds of men that the defences of peace must be constructed;
>
> That ignorance of each other's ways and lives has been a common cause, throughout the history of mankind, of that suspicion and mistrust between the peoples of the world through which their differences have all too often broken into war . . .
>
> That the wide diffusion of culture, and the education of humanity for justice and liberty and peace are indispensable to the dignity of man and constitute a sacred duty which all the nations must fulfil in a spirit of mutual assistance and concern;
>
> . . . and that the peace must therefore be founded, if it is not to fail, upon the intellectual and moral solidarity of mankind.
>
> For these reasons, the States Parties to this Constitution, believing in full and equal opportunities for education for all, in the unrestricted pursuit of objective truth, and in the free exchange of ideas and knowledge, are agreed and determined to develop and to increase the means of communication between their peoples and to employ these means for the purposes of mutual understanding and a truer and more perfect knowledge of each other's lives . . .[17]

The central component in this preamble is the creation of mutual understanding between states and their peoples through communication, while education, shared knowledge and ideas are the principle means of creating this form of understanding.

UNESCO fulfils its remit through its various projects and programmes, development work, conferences and publications. The organization's Culture of Peace Programme commenced in 1998, and as the United Nations (UN) agency responsible for education and the reduction of illiteracy, it currently provides the co-ordinating role for the UN Decade for Literacy. Undoubtedly, the jewel in UNESCO's crown is its World Heritage Sites programme, which oversees the conservation and preservation of the world's cultural heritage. Currently, there are some 754 sites listed by UNESCO including, the Taj Mahal, India; Yellowstone National Park, United States of America; and Mir Castle, Belarus. The work of UNESCO has changed over the years in keeping with the international context. The organization has experienced the creeping influence of the anthropological concept; in 1995 UNESCO published its report, 'Our Creative Diversity,' which drew on the work of a number of anthropologists (see Wright 1998). Certainly, there is more emphasis today on cultural diversity than in the early days and 2001 saw this codified into the 'Universal Declaration on Cultural Diversity.' Although criticisms of 'cultural imperialism' made during the 1980s proved damaging to UNESCO, they have made the organization more sensitive to a broader definition of culture and education, and have made it less elitist. In spite of the fact that UNESCO has moved towards accepting the idea of culture in the anthropological sense (hence its interest in cultural diversity), as an organization it is still committed to exchanging culture to foster mutual understanding between peoples in the hope that greater understanding will render conflict less likely.

However, some of the criticisms made against the humanist concept by Cultural Studies critics, during the late 1970s and into the 1980s, manifested themselves at the international level and in UNESCO. A particular kind of elitism was seen to be a fault, not just the elitism of British cultural snobbery, or the 'unabashed intellectual elitism' which Iriye described among the cultural internationalists of the inter-war period. Coupled with the growing activity of international corporations, interest in dependency theory, and the seeming deliberate exploitation and underdevelopment of the Third World by the First World, a neo-Marxist argument made its way into UNESCO. This generated accusations of cultural imperialism; an argument that still finds voice in international relations today. During the 1980s, however, when American and British interest in the developing world diminished under the DIY political attitudes of the American President Reagan and British Prime Minister Thatcher, the problem came to a head.[18] Accusations of 'cultural imperialism' proved particularly damaging to the activities of UNESCO, since America and Britain (along with Singapore) withdrew from the organization citing financial waste and mismanagement, as well as anti-Western sentiment, as the reasons for withdrawal. To be fair UNESCO was not alone in this situation – the whole UN system suffered from US and British indifference during this period. Today, UNESCO enjoys greater support and is focusing on its broad remit of facilitating educational sharing and the exchange of culture.

The European Union (EU) was given a more active role in culture under Article 151 of the Maastricht Treaty, 1993. Like UNESCO, the EU has cultural programmes, notably (Culture 2000,) and annually designates a European City of Culture, which has nothing to do with a 'whole way of life' but is focused on 'the arts.' The EU also operates an educational exchange programme – Erasmus, which was first established in 1987 and developed into the Socrates programme in 1995. Erasmus sought to increase student mobility across Europe and broaden the educational horizons of European youth, while Socrates extends these aims to lifelong learning. In addition to the international organizations, many individual countries operate their own cultural relations programmes and organizations, which generally come under the authority of ministries responsible for foreign affairs.

The British Council, founded in 1934 by Sir Reginald Leeper of the Foreign and Commonwealth Office, was established to further 'cultural propaganda.' The British Council's original remit was to promote a global understanding of British culture, education, science and technology, and this aim of propagating Britain has ensured that the history of the Council has been inconsistent – reflecting the priority of interests (primarily those of the British government) in the context in which it has operated. The aims of the British Council have oscillated at various points in time between a cultural exchange organization, a development organization, and an English language organization. Nowadays the Council seems to be operating within a humanist remit of promoting British culture, i.e. the positive aspects of football culture, and tackling widely recognized human issues, such as racism for example, with British cultural resources.[19]

Unless one investigates each individual programme and organization separately, as well as assessing closely the aims of the respective state governments, it is impossible to generalize as to whether activities belong to the realm of cultural diplomacy or that of cultural internationalism; although many employ the language of cultural internationalism. The Indian Council for Cultural Relations, for example, has "[s]trengthening cultural relations and mutual understanding with other countries since 1950" as its slogan.[20] And The Japan Foundation, established in 1972, tells us, in clear humanist terms, that:

> The purposes of the Kokusai Koryu Kikin, the Japan Foundation, are to efficiently carry on activities for international cultural exchange and thereby to contribute to the enhancement of world culture and

the welfare of mankind, with a view to deepening other nations' understanding of Japan, promoting better mutual understanding among nations, and encouraging friendship and goodwill among the peoples of the world.[21]

Numerous bilateral cultural programmes and friendship societies support and maintain the Japanese concern with fostering mutual understanding – underscoring their interest in understanding both the natives and the tourists.

The French have always given a high priority to cultural relations and have a ministry of culture, the Ministère de la Culture et de la Communication. For the French though, their historical interest in the dissemination of French culture was closely tied to the administration of Empire. The 'mission civilisatrice' was always tightly allied to the French policy of colonial assimilation rather than administration. Colonies were viewed as an extension of France, but whether they were viewed as cultural equals can be debated. The French set much store on culture in this respect, as in making the natives cultured in the French way, rather than exchanging culture in the manner envisioned by Herder. In this respect, French cultural policy might be said to belong more to the realms of 'cultural diplomacy' (i.e. of furthering the cause of France) than to that of cultural internationalism. Having said this, however, the French have always been much more supportive and enthusiastic of cultural initiatives than their British and American counterparts.[22] French activities are wider than those of the British Council, and, perhaps more importantly, "expressions of national cultural pride . . . [have always been] backed by government finance" (Mitchell 1986:36).

In 1948, Representative Karl E. Mundt and Senator H. Alexander Smith sponsored a bill through the United States Congress – the Smith-Mundt Act. The act "established a statutory information agency for the first time in a period of peace with a mission to '*promote a better understanding of the United States in other countries, and to increase mutual understanding*' between Americans and foreigners."[23] Prior to 1948, cultural interchange had, largely, been the province of private initiatives and organizations such as the Carnegie Endowment for International Peace and the Rockefeller Foundation.[24] Although, the Office for War Information had been disbanded in 1946, remnants, including the Office for International Information and Cultural Affairs, remained. Smith-Mundt consolidated the remnants and confirmed the importance of both the educational exchange programmes and the dissemination of information (a dual role that was obviously problematic from the internationalist perspective). A number of reorganizations and several name changes followed, but finally, the exchange programmes came under the Bureau of Educational and Cultural Affairs (ECA), which was established with the Fulbright-Hays Act of 1961.

Smith-Mundt, like UNESCO, endorsed the humanist notion of increasing mutual understanding but it also saw the need for the continuation of an information programme, or state projection.[25] This duality was further emphasized in 1953 with the establishment of an independent information organization, the United States Information Agency (USIA), which took responsibility for the Voice of America radio broadcasts and then absorbed the educational and cultural exchanges bureau from the State Department in 1978. The USIA was an independent foreign affairs agency within the Executive branch of the government (reporting to the President) and was more closely connected with government policy than, perhaps, the humanists intended and certainly more so than many would have liked. But the humanist idea had not disappeared completely and the 1961 'Mutual Educational and Cultural Exchange Act,' otherwise known as Fulbright-Hays (famous for its Fulbright Scholarship programme), could be seen as a reassertion of humanist ideals, resistant of concurrent State developments that were more concerned with information and, under the conditions of the Cold War, of 'winning hearts and minds.' Other acts founding the Edward S. Muskie and Ron Brown Fellowship exchange programmes have followed in the spirit of Fulbright-Hays.

The United States Department of State's mission statement tells us that:

> The Bureau of Educational and Cultural Affairs (ECA) fosters mutual understanding between the United States and other countries through international educational and training programs. The bureau does so by promoting personal, professional, and institutional ties between private citizens and organizations in the United States and abroad, as well as by presenting U.S. history, society, art and culture in all of its diversity to overseas audiences.[26]

In similarity with the preamble to UNESCO's charter, the ECA seeks to foster mutual understanding through culture and educational exchanges, but like the British Council and UNESCO, the influence of particular (state) interests raises questions about the extent of humanist intentions behind the activities. This is especially pertinent to the ECA as it operated under the State Department rather than the Education Department, as some would have preferred.[27]

The fortunes and directions of these organizations, however, clearly reflected the tone set by, and developments occurring within, the broader national and international context; all of which present some difficulties at the operational and philosophical levels. Whether the agencies and organizations were primarily concerned with promoting mutual understanding or their particular state would depend on the national and international context. Whereas the British Council, in 1939, resisted being absorbed into the new Ministry of Information (for which read the war ministry of propaganda) and faced possible abolition in 1977, the American cultural and educational exchange programmes have moved between the State Department and USIA, which, at times, raised some doubt over their integrity.[28] However, the programmes appear to have adhered to, and remain within, the spirit of the humanist project in spite of the close relationship with the USIA with its information remit. The USIA was subsequently consolidated back under the umbrella of the State Department in 1999. In that same year, the ECA stated that it "maintains its authority under the Fulbright-Hays Act," which was testament to the humanist triumph in this area.[29]

The experience of the British Council and the American cultural programmes demonstrate the tension between 'cultural diplomacy' (including state propaganda) and 'cultural internationalism.' Crudely stated, it reflects the divergent interests between the state's need to communicate information and the people's desire to foster mutual understanding. Effectively it is a struggle between the humanist project and a state orientated one that is more concerned with national projection/propaganda.[30] During the Cold War this became also a struggle with the anthropological concept of culture (discussed in chapter four). This tension, between state projection and the higher aspiration of fostering mutual understanding between peoples, has dogged international cultural relations in both theory and practice. Yet, the aims of the humanist concept remain a persistent theme in international relations, as the work of UNESCO and the educational exchange programmes illustrate, although, within IR, many theoretical questions still hang over the approach.

Problems with cultural interchange

In spite of continued interest in 'the cultural way' in international relations, albeit by a small number of academics and activists, cultural interchange is seen, perhaps not unreasonably, as a peripheral matter when compared to the high diplomacy conducted between heads of states, or the topics discussed at major international conferences, or the pressing issues debated at the UN Security Council. This probably accounts for the fact that since the inter-war period, international cultural relations has been an under-investigated area of IR. We do not find much space allocated to the subject in the major textbooks, if indeed any mention appears at all. Although there have been some studies of bilateral cultural relations between states and the occasional paper, it is fair to say that, within IR, international cultural relations are a neglected matter. Since the end of the Cold War, there has been more interest in cultural policy, but this is obviously in the vein of cultural diplomacy rather than in the spirit of the inter-war cultural internationalism. Consequently, in view of the absence of consistent and coherent discussions, the humanist idea of culture in international relations has made little theoretical progress, which is not only regrettable, but also highly problematic. In short, the idea itself has not altered much in content since the League of Nations era and therefore, questions that have been easily dismissed across the years, but were considered central to the early theorists themselves, remain largely undeveloped and unaddressed.

The arguments for cultural interchange are based on several normative assumptions; that this kind of activity is a good thing, that it generates its own benefits, and that these benefits will foster mutual understanding. Repeatedly, reference is made to the twin notions of 'cultural exchange/interchange' and 'fostering mutual understanding.' These assumptions, problematic in themselves, additionally create three obvious difficulties with the idea of international cultural relations. The first difficulty involves substance, the second concerns effectiveness, whilst the third raises questions about the motives behind cultural interchange. There is very little certainty on how to approach these issues, although, to be sure, there are plenty of criticisms of the basic idea of cultural internationalism. The criticisms are prone to dismiss out of hand the notion of 'another way' of conducting international relations, which is unhelpful, especially considering the persistence and popularity of the activity.

The first problem is clearly a substantive issue; quite simply, what kind of culture is needed to foster mutual understanding? It is not at all clear what Matthew Arnold meant by perfection, although it was fairly clear what it was not – it was not Derby Day, for example. Nor is it apparent quite what kinds of things Zimmern recognized as 'culture,' apart from education and knowledgeable travellers. People who 'travel' may think themselves a cut above the average package holiday tourist, but what actually distinguishes the travellers from the tourists is not readily apparent. Aside from a test of knowledge, the characteristics that form an acceptable disposition are not specified by Zimmern. Yet, perhaps, we would all recognize that the culture of interchange should not involve football hooligans, although it probably does involve the works of Shakespeare, UNESCO's world heritage sites and the current examples of football culture promoted by the British Council. The problem is that extreme examples, namely those of hooligans and Shakespeare, are easy to identify. It is the middle range and between the extremes where the content is not specified, and where the traveller cannot be distinguished from the tourist say, that one usually finds the bulk of cultural interchange taking place. Inevitably, it is in this area that most difficulties seem to occur. Whether the British should send Shakespeare or rap DJs on tour depends entirely on what they hope to achieve and what one believes is achievable with either or both cultural products. In turn, this raises questions about what one can achieve, and why and how one recognizes the achievement. Indeed, the very idea of culture, in the humanist sense, alludes to some kind of exemplary behaviour and products, which would seem to omit 'undesirable' cultural elements altogether. Defining this kind of allusion centres on qualitative concerns. Whether, following

Arnold, F.R. Leavis or T.S. Eliot, rap DJs amount to something culturally undesirable or have done a good service on behalf of promoting under-standing of British youth, and have raised awareness on the race issue, is obviously a subjective matter.[31] This is an issue that the Cultural Studies scholar is likely to have an obvious interest in.

Take, for example, the vast amount of work involved in encouraging the teaching and learning of the English language. This can easily be criti-cized as a form of cultural imperialism, and clearly, the historical move-ment of the English language was synonymous with Empire.[32] Yet, the imperialist conspiracy argument loses considerable saliency when one considers both the motives behind the various agencies' work and those of the students who learn the language. Moreover, the distinctions between the use of a language for expedient purposes or pleasure and one which seeks to deliberately extinguish the native tongue, can be lost in an analy-sis that insists on viewing the acquisition of the English language as a form of imperialism. The natives may not see the world in those terms. Critical cries of 'cultural imperialism,' or of 'cultural invasion,' are probably, in the words of Saad El Din, "a reflection of uncertainty and of lack of confi-dence in one's own national culture" in any case.[33] Therefore, we need to be wary of arguments in which larger theoretical issues seem to be the overriding concerns. This is to say that a discussion seemingly based on culture may in actuality be more concerned with promoting other narra-tives based on power or imperialism in order to support arguments about a more generalized nature of international relations. Culture, in the form of an artifact like the English language for example, is called upon to provide a supporting role, as an example, in a narrative about exploitative and imperialist power relations in international relations. Culture is not the concept doing the work here – some notion of imperialism is. Although seemingly innocuous activities such as teaching the English lan-guage may generate a political response, and may even be written off in some circles as a form of politics, we still have no way of knowing and no means for identifying which kind of culture fosters mutual understanding, if it does so at all. The Cultural Studies style critique may take issue with particular examples of culture, e.g. English language teaching, but we are still left with the underlying problem of how to identify the substance of culture if, and it may be a big if, we accept that in principle the idea of cul-tural interchange is a sound and admirable one. Such criticism is inclined to pick at individual trees and not see the whole humanist wood, and this does not assist us in locating the positive substance of cultural inter-change.

The second problem, which has several component parts, concerns the effectiveness of international cultural relations. Cultural interchange is likely to be pooh-poohed by those whose attention is captured by the tan-gible aspects of international politics and, especially, those drawn to the manifestations of power politics (the 'Realists') in IR. Such criticisms abound and are easily made. C.K. Webster and Sidney Herbert, for example, made the obvious critical point in 1933 that a discussion on the role of poetry in binding nations together "is hardly likely to produce much effect on international relations" (Webster and Herbert 1933:295). Their comment concerned a discussion that took place between the British Poet Laureate and M. Paul Valery organized by the ICIC in 1930. Webster and Herbert may have been a little churlish, but they have a point; what can poetry do in the face of reducing the world stock of biological and chemical weapons? However, neither Zimmern, nor his colleagues at the ICIC, were much disturbed by such observations. Comments such as those made by Webster and Herbert simply demonstrated to the cultural internationalists the need for greater effort. But similar criticisms were made by subsequent commentators, as Akira Iriye has pointed out. According to Iriye, Nicholas Spykman said, rather sarcastically, in 1942, "[i]f the cooperation of our Latin neighbors is dependent on the popular appreciation of the rhumba in the United States, the future is indeed bright" (cited in Iriye 1997:145). In a similarly pithy and anti-international cultural relations vein, President Richard Nixon retorted in 1970, "some Americans think that we can rely on peace by sending a few Fulbright scholars abroad ... but that doesn't bring peace. We can avoid war if we are realistic and not soft-headed" (cited in Iriye 1997:160). What is particularly interesting about the views of Spykman and Nixon is that they express quite neatly the lack of (Realist) support for the whole idea of international cultural relations, yet, they both do so, ironically, at a time when the Americans and the Soviets were engaging in a different kind of international cultural relations during the Cold War. We will look at the cultural Cold War in the fourth chapter, but it is clear that both superpowers set some store by scoring 'cultural' points off their ideological opponent, so neither side could have considered the activity entirely fruitless.

Measuring the effectiveness of a policy is not a cut and dried matter. It is not possible to account, in quantitative terms, for the impact appreciation the rumba might have on American-Latino cooperation. There may be no obvious method for correlating between the volume of books sent, and rumbas danced, for example, and the numbers of minds won over or the amount of understandings generated. If there is any correlation between the two, it is unclear. Judging the effectiveness of cultural interchange is, in this respect, quite clearly a qualitative rather than a quantitative matter, so perhaps the criticisms themselves do not count for much. Indeed, it may be that in a vastly circuitous way, poetry might have some impact on the numbers of biological and chemical weapons in so much as poetry may contribute, in part, to more stable and peaceful relationships, which may render such weapons unnecessary. This said, we cannot rule out, entirely, a possible quantitative approach in evaluating the effectiveness of cultural interchange.

Creating positive impressions may have a tangible impact on international relations, so much so that such things may be accounted for by quantitative methods. The numbers of Japanese tourists to Britain, following the 2002 World Cup in football, had been predicted to increase due to an interest in David Beckham and the fact that the English football fans behaved themselves, contrary to the expectations of the Japanese before the tournament.[34] However, it is clear that judging the effectiveness of cultural interchange belongs, predominately, to the less tangible realm of qualitative and evaluative social science; which inevitably involves a considerable subjective element. To be sure, at the moment it is probably easier to identify the bad impressions, especially of Americans and Muslims for example, than it is to assess the volume of positive outcomes that the impact of cultural interchange generates.

Moreover, engaging in international cultural interchange rests upon the aforementioned normative assumptions that this activity will be beneficial and, further, that this will elicit the positive result of fostering mutual understanding. In fact, there is very little, or no, evidence in the relevant literature (including that from the inter-war period onwards) that this kind of activity creates greater understanding. One author, Charles Frankel, raised the question in 1966, but made no attempt to address it. Frankel pointed out that there was no ground for the common assumption that promoting international understanding led to the promotion of goodwill (Frankel 1966:83). Moreover, "the rhetoric that lumps 'goodwill' and 'understanding' together is dangerous ..." (Frankel 1966:83), and may prove an insufficient basis for action given the ambiguity of the terms. Even 'face to face' contact, he said, may not 'engender sympathy and mutual accord' (Frankel 1966:83): a point that American peacekeepers are probably all too familiar with in some parts of the world these days. The question of benefits and understanding is a serious matter and such an important one that it is surprising that no one has, seemingly, investigated the issue thoroughly, although the Realists have been apt to dismiss the matter out of hand entirely, of course.

In view of the lack of theoretical development, post-war literature is open to the same criticisms that were levelled at the inter-war theorists, namely that fostering mutual understanding through the medium of culture is 'wish-dreams,' woolly minded and idealist, which was President Nixon's view, and, therefore, a waste of resources. However, given the persistence of the theme and the fact that people do engage in international cultural relations on a vast scale, it does warrant taking seriously as an approach in IR, even if only for us to gain a more accurate insight into the impact of cultural exchange at the local level. It is all too easy to speculate and to be dismissive, but the fact is, we do not know very much about the impact which cultural interchange has on a locality, least of all from the native perspective. Yet, there is one development – globalization – that makes this subject more interesting for the current student. Globalization

has brought about a massive increase in 'unregulated' cultural interchange, but how we should approach this development is open to question and discussed further in the conclusion to this book.

The third problem is perhaps the most difficult of all and concerns the
question of motives. It is a serious theoretical problem, touched on by a
few commentators on international cultural relations and one that
demands careful thinking about the manner in which a gift is given. The
problem is revealed when one poses the question, at what point does cultural interchange become propaganda? Are these two the same, even
when an organization is not in the hands of a state?[35] The inter-war theorists believed that there was a distinction between the two, indeed they
deliberately set out to counter the propagandist uses of culture by making
appeal to a higher plane. In many ways, then, it is arguable that the
answer to the question depends on the nature of the intentions behind
the exchange of gifts. Pertinent here, also, is the question to what extent
there is a genuine interchange or two-way traffic in culture as opposed to
one-way movement (but that is to return to substantive issues). And additionally, the answer also, in part, depends on to what extent might the
state be involved and/or to what the extent the state might be using
culture as a means of policy promotion. This is an issue that arises over
the roles of the USIA and ECA in the United States for example, and
caused some unease among contemporaries at the time. (The role of the
state and the use of culture as a means for furthering state ambitions will
become a more transparent issue during the Cold War than it was during
the inter-war period.) However, the basic theoretical problem remains.
Mitchell attempts to draw out the problem when he makes the distinction
between 'cultural diplomacy,' which is explicitly a matter of state interest,
and 'cultural relations,' which appears to be something more generic.
There is something to be said for this distinction, and it may be that the
form of cultural interchange that remains closest to the humanist concept
in spirit belongs better to private initiatives and the work of NGOs than it
does to departments of state. However, the distinction, no matter how
valid (and I think that it is a valid distinction), remains an elusive one. So
long as there is an element of doubt over this activity, the suggestion that
participants and activists are promoting their view of the world or, worse
still, imposing it on others, rather than fostering mutual understanding,
will persist. And it is this doubt that allows the critics to contradict themselves in spectacular fashion. On the one hand, cultural interchange is
written off as ineffective when set against the impact of real power in international relations, while on the other hand, the activity is slated as a form
of 'colonialism, imperialism and propaganda,' which assumes a good
measure of power and effectiveness. A no-win situation for the humanist
concept it seems. Currently, believers in the power of cultural interchange
have no better tool than their faith to support themselves. Yet, no matter
how much our basic instincts may lead us to believe in the importance of

cultural interchange and no matter how strong our suspicions are that this is an effective tool in bridging gaps in our understanding of one another, the concrete evidence (whether that is produced quantitatively or qualitatively) and the supporting arguments remain vaguely stated.

In spite of these difficulties with the idea of international cultural interchange and irrespective of the kinds of questions which that activity generates, it is certain that the activity will continue to prosper in spite of the criticisms. The continuing and growing number of personal initiatives and the activities of NGOs are two examples in this area. As I write this chapter, a training ship, the *Stavros S. Niarchos* has sailed into Portsmouth harbour, UK, from Waterford, Eire, carrying young British and Indonesians, Christians and Muslims.[36] They have been brought together in the wake of the 2002 Bali bombings, for the explicit purpose of fostering mutual understanding. On the more formal level, it is good to know that the humanist notion of culture still has a place in international relations, functioning in the form of exchange programmes and in the continued presence of UNESCO, the British Council, the ECA and the other national organizations. The spirit of cultural internationalism that so captured the inter-war theorists' imagination persists, in spite of the fact that the Second World War had not been avoided, which, as a result, did serious harm to the spirit of cultural internationalism that pervaded the early part of the inter-war period. The war brought the humanist idea of culture, along with a number of other conventional standards from the period (notably race theory), into disrepute; a situation from which the humanist concept of culture has not fully recovered from within IR. The shift in thinking that actual world events precipitated became apparent among American scholars first of all, but it also influenced the sphere of cultural relations. In view of the changing attitude towards the idea of culture, it is all the more remarkable then that the spirit and aims of cultural internationalism still exist and that 'another way' of conducting international relations remains popular; which in no small way, indicates that the humanist concept continues to appeal to an important aspect of international and human relations.

Key points

- The First World War shook faith in the belief that civilization could survive unattended – a fear that grew during the 1930s.
- One of the means for improving civilization was the humanist concept of culture.
- Through the exchange of art, literature, ideas, students and scholars it was believed that mutual understanding between differing peoples could be achieved.
- Key international institutions include The International Committee for Intellectual Co-operation and its successor, UNESCO. Most states

have their own culture departments and programmes – The British Council, the American Bureau of Educational and Cultural Affairs, The Japan Foundation, for example.

- The humanist idea has persisted in international politics at the local level through individual efforts, the work of NGOs and local organizations.
- Separating the effectiveness, the motives and content of cultural interchange is problematic – the role of the state is a significant factor in this respect. Cultural interchange can easily be confused with imperialism and propaganda.
- The normative assumptions behind cultural interchange, (i) that it is a good thing, (ii) will bring benefits and (iii) foster mutual understanding, present theoretical difficulties. Even so, the activity cannot be dismissed out of hand.

3   The ever disappearing native

Around the time of the First World War, and as the humanist cultural project got underway in international relations, an alternative project, also based upon an idea of culture, was being established in the United States. This was the anthropological concept. In its infancy at the time of Norman Angell, this concept would be firmly in place by the time Gilbert Murray worried about the future of civilization in 1935. By the late 1940s, the 'modern' anthropological concept of culture was being described as "the foundation stone of the social sciences" (cited in Stocking 1968/82:302). Plainly, the idea of culture had travelled a long way since Matthew Arnold claimed culture was the 'best of everything.' It had become synonymous in American thinking with scientific study and a 'way of life.'

Few people nowadays dispute the observation that we all have 'culture' and that this is taken as a 'good thing.' In fact, the point is seen to be so obvious, it is taken to be true, which is where the problem lies; i.e. in the 'truthfulness' and usefulness of the observation. As a growing popular and intellectual industry, the 'truth' of culture as 'a way of life' finds wide ranging allegiance. This should be, or ought to be, a matter of concern. Simply put, it is strange to find a situation in which people who would normally disagree with one another on matters of importance, and fundamentally so, say on matters of politics, are in thorough agreement on the subject of culture. Culture might be applauded for its obvious universal success, in so much as it stands as one of the rare occasions in social science where an idea has managed to attract an unprecedented level of support. Yet, this feat alone ought to make us more suspicious than congratulatory, as the anthropologist Lila Abu-Lughod has advised (Abu-Lughod 1999:14). Suspicious, in the first instance, of the truthfulness and usefulness of an idea that draws in such a wide spectrum of people and who, in the second instance, seem to experience no obvious difficulty in accepting and agreeing that 'we are our culture.' The big questions then, concern how we came to believe in this concept and what, if anything, is wrong with thinking that culture somehow makes us what we are.

The rise of a new idea

As Norman Angell was arguing against biological determinism in international politics, a group of scholars in the United States were attacking evolutionary theory from an alternative direction within social science and with very different disciplinary aims in mind. Whereas Angell relied upon the inevitable progress of civilization and a change in human attitudes as the basis for his criticisms, American criticism rested upon the idea of kultur.

Late nineteenth century American Anthropology, as was the case elsewhere in the social sciences, had been dominated by evolutionary thinking and especially Lamarckian ideas. The British anthropologist Edward B. Tylor, very much a key scholar in the field, had strong working connections with prominent American scholars, including the head of the Bureau of American Ethnology, John Wesley Powell.[1] Tylor is frequently attributed with inventing the first major definition of the modern anthropological concept of culture in his 1871 volume, *Primitive Culture*. Tylor opened *Primitive Culture* with a much quoted and famous definitional statement: "Culture or Civilization, taken in its wide ethnographic sense, is that complex whole which includes knowledge, belief, art, morals, law, custom, and any other capabilities and habits acquired by man as a member of society" (Tylor 1871/1903:1). Tylor specifically acknowledged the work of the German scholar Gustav Klemm in his book, which led the anthropologists A.L. Kroeber and Clyde Kluckhohn to argue, in 1952, that Tylor deserved all the more credit for "his sharp and successful conceptualization of culture, and for beginning his greatest book with a definition of culture" (Kroeber and Kluckhohn 1952:46), since, in their view, Klemm had employed the term 'culture' ambiguously. In Kroeber and Kluckhohn's opinion, the key development was Tylor's foresight to link the notion of culture to a 'whole way of life.'[2] However, one can make too much of Tylor's definition of culture as marking the origins of the 'modern' concept and certainly his role in connecting the word culture to the idea of a 'whole way of life' can be easily exaggerated (see Stocking 1968/1982:chapter four). Kroeber and Kluckhohn 'wrote history backwards.' Their 'classic' volume of definitions was largely concerned with ethnographic definitions of culture, not humanist ones.[3]

Tylor was a contemporary of Matthew Arnold, yet where Arnold relied on the humanist concept, Tylor embraced the latest scientific thinking – evolutionary theory. In many ways, Tylor's definition of culture and civilization is not much of a departure from Arnolds' ideas – it is normative, hierarchical and singular.[4] The defining element of 'a whole way of life,' for which Tylor is famous, proves to be a bit of a red herring in the historiography of culture. As the anthropologist George Stocking indicates, it would be a mistake to think that Arnold's conception of culture did not include the idea of 'a way of life,' indeed, it was designed precisely for these purposes; a way of life ordered by culture was preferable to one determined by civilization according to Arnold. The differences between Arnold and Tylor are not as profound as some believe and that has led Stocking to go so far as to suggest that Tylor "simply took the contemporary humanist idea of culture and fitted it into the framework of progressive social evolutionism. One might say he made Matthew Arnold's culture evolutionary" (Stocking 1968/1982:87). According to Stocking, Tylor's definition "lacked certain elements crucial to the modern concept" (Stocking 1968/1982:200); these 'crucial elements' include, "historicity, plurality, integration, behavioural determinism, and relativity" (Stocking 1968/1982:200). These elements would form some of the defining features in the modern anthropological concept of culture which sought to capture 'whole ways of life' of people the world over. A more significant figure in the development of the modern anthropological concept, in Stocking's view, is Franz Boas, a German-Jewish émigré to the United States and in whose work these elements begin to be detected. The crucial conceptual break comes then, not with Tylor but with the work of Boas and, more importantly, with his students who further developed the idea. There is some dispute as to Boas's role in the development of kultur into the anthropological concept of culture, but he is commonly recognized as the founder of the discipline of Cultural Anthropology in the United States.[5]

Boas was raised in German kultur and trained in the scientific thinking and methods of the day.[6] Among his influences and teachers in Germany were Adolf Bastian, Wilhelm von Humboldt, Rudolf Virchow and Theobald Fischer, all of whom had themselves been influenced by German romantic philosophy, especially that of Herder.[7] Boas's conceptual departure from the German concept of kultur is not an obviously dramatic one. Indeed, Stocking discerns no sharp break in Boas, but suggests that his viewpoint developed slowly out of his "total life experience" (Stocking 1968/1982:157). Yet, the implications of this unfolding of the culture concept in scientific terms would prove profound for American anthropological work. It is important to note, however, that Boas did not invent the anthropological concept, rather he provides a crucial link in the chain of conceptual development between the German concept of kultur, which was becoming increasingly nationalistic in its native landscape, and the scientific study of people and their 'cultures' in American anthropology.

Where Arnold had attacked civilization from the humanist perspective at a time when most of his contemporaries were preoccupied with evolutionary thinking, Boas and his students attacked this dominant ideology from other perspectives – the 'scientific' and ethical. Shortly after permanently settling in the US in 1887, Boas attacked evolutionism; famously criticizing Otis T. Mason for his evolutionary layout of the U.S. National

Museum.[8] Boas not only considered the layout of the museum arbitrary, he also thought it 'bad science.' He did not simply reject the museum's display layout; he challenged the prevailing scientific paradigm. Boas did not think that explanations based on heredity were wholly capable of accounting for the differences between human communities; some space, he considered, must be allowed for environmental influence. As Joel Kahn has stated, in summarizing Stocking's work, "in breaking with evolutionism, Boas played a part in the invention of a new concept, albeit one with an old name" (Kahn 1989:6). The break with evolutionism, or more accurately biological determinism, is a significant development and it is worth emphasizing for the reader that this particular American conceptual break led to the formation of a 'new concept' with 'an old name.'[9] The word 'culture' now had two, distinct, theoretical bases.

Most commentators on Boas agree on two things. First, that he trained an extraordinary number of students, including many native scholars and some of the most notable anthropologists the United States has known, for example, Ruth Benedict, Margaret Mead, Alfred Kroeber, Edward Sapir and Melville Herskovits. Significantly, many of his students "revered" him as a "founder" of their discipline, and contextually speaking this is an important point, since it is illustrative of his influence (Stocking 1968/1982:196). Second, everyone agrees that Boas collected vast amounts of data, which has led to the misleading conclusion that he did not do much theorizing or make a significant contribution to anthropology.[10]

Whatever the view of Boas's contribution, it would have to be conceded that even at a minimum level, through the sheer number of students he trained and volume of data he collected, his contribution was a rich one. Therefore, it is plausible to suggest, as Stocking does, that much of Boas's thinking and influence might be observable through the work his students went on to produce. Certainly, most commentators agree that by the time one is considering the work of the second generation Boasians, so to speak, Benedict, Mead, Sapir and Herskovits for example, something quite distinctive is conceptually in place and is obviously distinguishable from the ideas espoused by the humanists. This group of anthropologists is clearly working with a conception of culture that is recognizable as the modern anthropological concept. 'Culture' was firmly established as a matter that relates to a whole community in a particular sense; it was relativist in so much as each community had its own culture; it included the qualities that Stocking has listed; and, more importantly, it was being studied scientifically.

All of the Boasians, students and mentor included, shared a commitment to cultural determinism and a belief in the primacy of 'culture' in human activity. This was driven, in part, by their ethical opposition to race thinking – thinking that dismissed indigenous peoples as 'primitive' and when placed in 'scientific' evolutionary schema, relegated their communities to the bottom of the civilized scale as an inferior species. Cast in different terms, this was an expression of the nurture argument in the nature–nurture debate, which, according to Derek Freeman, "had begun in earnest in about 1910, [and] was still very much alive" (Freeman 1983/1996:3) in the mid-1920s. Through this debate, the idea of 'culture' came to acquire a holistic influence over communities. The commitment to cultural determinism reflected Boas's ethical opposition to evolutionism, and specifically that brand of evolutionary thinking that Mason's museum layout, and Edward Tylor more obviously, had represented. Boas and his students were committed to countering racist argument and epistemology by promoting an egalitarian approach that valued all cultures.[11] With their environmental commitments, the Boasians confronted the biological determinists, evolutionary thinking and, especially in 1920s America, the popular eugenics movement.[12]

Boas launched his attack against biological determinism in 1916, and later, at his instigation, his students Alfred Kroeber and Robert Lowie issued "intellectual manifestos" (Freeman 1983/1996:6) in more strident tones in 1917.[13] The differences of opinion over nature and nurture became more extremely expressed and the debates increasingly acrimonious; the debate between the Boasians and the eugenics movement was especially bitter. However, thanks in no small part to the work of the Boasians, by the 1930s the controversy had been all but resolved – the idea of culture had captured the American imagination, although not quite in the same way as the anthropologists had envisioned. And the publication that is widely accepted as banging the final Boasian nail in the evolutionist's coffin, so to speak, was Margaret Mead's *Coming of Age in Samoa*, which appeared in 1928.

The idea that each community had a unique culture, and one that was to be appreciated in its own terms, readily lent itself to the charge of cultural relativism. Yet the cultural relativism identified in the work of some of the Boasian scholars requires contextualizing in respect of the racial thinking which was prevalent in American society. Ruth Benedict (1935), for example, expressed particularly strong views about the equal validity of all forms of local values and particular 'patterns of living,' which stood in sharp contrast to the unsympathetic ideology of 'civilized' superiority, developmental progress and racist hierarchical thinking. Understandably, in the aftermath of the Second World War, Benedict's egalitarianism, which advocated tolerance, was heavily criticized. Elgin Williams, for example, was quick off the mark in criticizing her argument in *Patterns of Culture* that all cultures were 'equally valid patterns of life,' since, as he pointed out, that would require "granting significance to Hitler's culture . . ." (Williams 1947:85).[14] Already, the new idea of culture was generating ethical problems of its own. Yet, when set against the dominance of early twentieth century racial and hierarchical thinking, the relativism which certain Boasians espoused ought to be read more sympathetically; it can be seen as premised on admirable intentions when set in the context in which it was constructed.

The 1920s in America was a particularly racist decade; membership of the Ku Klux Klan reached its height, restrictive immigration laws were passed and two of the most popular publications well into the 1920s, were Madison Grant's *The Passing of the Great Race* (1916) and Lothrop Stoddard's *The Rising Tide of Color* (1920).[15] There was a growing fear, which coincided with the questions hanging over the future of civilization, that the white race was in danger of being wiped out or overrun by the wrong kind of immigrants. Moreover, there was a perceived threat to the purity of white blood by the diluting influence of the other (inferior) races. Paradoxically, race thinking increased the public's interest in the anthropological idea of culture. Not only did America become isolationist internationally during the 1920s, but America took what can best be described as a culturally relativist turn, from a generic view of what America was, towards, what Walter Benn Michaels has described as, a nativist view of who could and could not become, or be counted, as American.[16]

Whereas America previously had been open to anyone and everyone, during the 1920s a parochial outlook took hold. There was great interest in defining who was a legitimate American, which meant distinguishing between different kinds of people – an interest that evolutionary theory had fuelled. Initially this was based on racial distinctions, but gradually this language gave way to that of culture. Placed against a background of racial and nativist views, the cultural determinists made convincing, if obviously more liberal, culture arguments. But, perhaps the reason for this concept of culture's popular acceptance had more to do with functional equivalence than with the demise of the race concept. Indeed, many a subsequent critic has made the connection to race theory, including Joel Kahn, who says that culture is little more than "a new kind of racism" (Kahn 1989:20) and Lila Abu-Lughod who recognizes that "the culture concept retains some of the tendencies to freeze difference possessed by concepts like race" (in Fox 1991:144), while Verena Stolcke (1995) claims that 'cultural' arguments merely create new boundaries and new rhetorics of exclusion.[17] The rhetoric of culture that came to the fore in America in the late 1920s certainly paralleled the rhetoric of race when it entered the public domain.

When Ruth Benedict published her popular *Patterns of Culture* in 1935, the atmosphere within the United States had changed considerably. In concluding her work, Benedict espoused one of the key tenets in the anthropological concept: cultures were, she said, "equally valid patterns of life" (1935/1952:201). This was very different from the idea that culture was universal and could be exchanged to foster mutual understanding and it is worth emphasizing some of the key differences between the two concepts. For the humanists and cultural internationalists in IR, 'culture' is a singular issue; it makes no sense to speak of 'cultures' as anthropologists do. Indeed, there are few uses of the term 'culture' in the plural sense before 1900 (after Tylor), and in the sense that provides 'the cornerstone' of anthropology, so to speak.[18] Stocking has usefully drawn out the distinction between the two concepts: "anthropological 'culture' is homeostatic, while humanist 'culture' is progressive; it is plural, while humanist 'culture' is singular. Traditional humanist usage distinguishes between degrees of 'culture;' for the anthropologist, all men are equally 'cultured'" (Stocking 1968/1982:200).

A further key distinction is that humanist culture requires effort and a level of awareness in ways that the anthropological concept does not allow, or at worst simply assumes. For the humanist, one cannot paint a masterpiece overnight, learn a new language, or appreciate Shakespeare, without considerable work. Alfred Zimmern's 'law of greatest effort' illustrates this aspect of the humanist concept in IR. The important thing is that we engage and create 'culture' because we are striving to achieve something better under the humanist conception. For the cultural anthropologist, 'culture' is simply acquired; it is something that happens to us whether we are aware of the process of acculturation, internalization, distribution, socialization (call it what you will), or not. And it is this process of acquiring culture and of identifying its influence, and demonstrating both in academic terms, which have proven highly controversial matters in anthropology.

The concept which the Boasians developed underwent many changes in the latter half of the twentieth century. The anthropological profession had remained a small, yet growing one, and its role in social science remained quite marginal until American interest in the Third World expanded the discipline after the Second World War.[19] First, there was a shift in emphasis from behaviour to ideas in the 1960s. During the 1960s and 1970s culture became a prominent issue, and a new generation of scholars became popular; notably, Clifford Geertz, Marshall Sahlins and David Schneider (see Kuper 1999). In the 1980s, there was an increase in interest in internal diversity and the idea that culture was a process became popular; while the impact of postmodernist thinking across the social sciences raised questions over the way anthropologists constructed the cultures they studied. In spite of the developments, the core assumptions laid down by the Boasians remained central to the concept.

Culture, in the anthropological sense, is about 'ways of life' and it is a distinguishing feature of every community, especially of a community's values. Subsequent generations of American anthropologists, particularly those associated with the concept's revival in the 1960s and 1970s, were critical of Cultural Anthropology's positivist tendencies but, as the anthropologist Joel Kahn has pointed out, they did not fundamentally reject the central proposition upon which their discipline had been founded.[20] Even if it was acknowledged, as it was by the late 1980s, that a culture could not be captured ethnographically and reproduced as a whole piece, most (but not all) cultural anthropologists have accepted the basic premises of the Boasian idea of culture despite advocating different methodologies for discerning it. Culture was thought to be a universal phenomenon – all human beings have culture(s) in some form or other (depending on how one defines the term 'culture' anthropologically and which methodology one employs to demonstrate its existence) – and most would agree with Mead's sentiment that culture helps make us what we are.[21]

The elusive native

The problem with this particular concept of culture is that, under examination, it does not appear to exist in the way it is spoken about or claimed. It is widely recognized that there is no such thing as 'a' or even '*the* Balinese culture' as in something that all the inhabitants of Bali do and share. Bali is too complex a society and its inhabitants too various to lend itself to such a homogeneous and totalizing abstraction. And what holds for Bali, is true of every society. There is no such empirical entity that is Balinese culture. Nor is there anything new or shocking in this observation. The British social anthropologist A.R. Radcliffe-Brown rejected the idea of culture as early as 1940 when he "objected that culture was not empirically real ... was not directly observable – 'since that word denotes, not any concrete reality, but an abstraction, and as it is commonly used a vague abstraction'" (Kuper 1996:185). The vagueness that Radcliffe-Brown identified as inherent in the concept did not inhibit its growing popularity in any way, although the vague nature of culture has proven a constant source of substantive and theoretical difficulty. The problem is that, even if we could identify Balinese culture, it would not remain an accurate depiction of reality for long – Balinese life changes and has always done so.

The fundamental attraction of the anthropological concept of culture, and the fundamental source of all its weaknesses, is its invocation of radical *otherness* as Roger Keesing and Joel Kahn among others have pointed out. Apparently, a culture, as anthropologically defined, is what a people have in common, and what they share collectively in distinction from *others*, which assumes a good deal of homogeneity and uniformity among a group of people.[22] This is why Americans are considered to be the way they are, why the British are considered to be the way they are, and why neither are like the Kayapo of Brazil nor the Tsimihety of Madagascar. Culture maintains the differences between the American, British, Brazilian and Madagascan native, although how this actually works in practice is extremely difficult to determine. Nonetheless the anthropological concept of culture is founded on the intellectual assumption that there always ought to be a 'distinctive way of doing things' or, that the natives have, in the words of P.G. Wilson an "ethnographic trademark."[23] Empirically it has always been difficult to isolate and identify this ethnographic trademark with any accuracy or certainty. As the ethnographic fieldworker George Hunt complained, in a letter to Franz Boas, "[y]ou know as well as I do that you or me cant find two Indians tell a storie alike" (cited in Stocking 1996:239 – spelling in original). If we cannot find two Indians to tell a story alike, we must wonder what the modern anthropological idea of culture refers to and how it is intellectually sustained.

Initially, it seems it was sustained with positivist zeal. Margaret Mead, for example, was highly confident that it was our "upbringing which determines all of . . . [our] ways of behaving" (Mead 1942/1943:19–20). She went on to say, "[i]t is necessary to learn how cultures hang together, what are the rules of coherence, unity and emphasis, as our grammar books used to say about our sentences" (Mead 1942/1943:238). For Mead, cultures were clearly discrete, homogeneous and coherent entities – or what has been referred to as the 'billiard ball model' of cultures (Wolf 1982/1997:6). She suggested that babies were culturally *tabula rasa* (a blank sheet), "[b]ut, as adolescents and adults, we do differ and we differ for good" (Mead 1942/1943:26). This assumption is refutable today; nonetheless, the modern anthropological idea of culture emerged as an extremely powerful and influential thing. It was the ethnographer's task to find culture and detail it in authoritative (scientific) terms.

The presumption of an ethnographic trademark is maintained through the further assumption that a culture is bounded and protected from other cultures in some way. Ruth Benedict famously opened her *Patterns of Culture* with a Digger Indian proverb about a cup: "[i]n the beginning God gave to every people a cup of clay, and from this cup they drank their life" (Benedict 1935/1952:facing page). The imagery of the cup is very striking, as the anthropologist Michael Carrithers has pointed out (Carrithers 1992:12–16). Cups clearly have hard edges and their content, as suggested in the proverb, is the 'culture' itself. Culture appears very much as a bounded, self-contained, autonomous, static and homogeneous entity in this image; 'every people' have their own cup, it is all of a piece and it remains, essentially unalterable. Even Kroeber, who appeared to adopt a more humanist approach than Benedict, noted, "that 'the container' of various distinctive cultures altered much less through time than the items, traits, and complexes that were 'contained'" (Kroeber and Kluckhohn 1952:360). The contents of a specific culture may vary over time, but the orthodox anthropological idea of culture conveys notions of communal integrity and saliency that are, somehow, 'all of a piece' and contained in a durable way, even if only in a loose sense.

No matter what shape this supposed 'culture' takes, or indeed, how porous the boundaries are or have been, 'something' still maintains its distinctiveness. Yet, societies have always been open to artifacts and ideas from outside – consider all the trade that has moved and continues to move around the world. No group of people is immune from this, least of all under the conditions of globalization, and it is doubtful whether any group has ever been immune from any outside influences even before the processes of globalization began impacting. Yet, the anthropological idea of culture insists that cultures are viewed somehow as discrete and self-contained to the outside – a billiard ball; and that they are homogeneous, coherent, uniform and 'all of a piece' on the inside. The distinctiveness of this form of culture is identified with a specific group of natives despite the array of diversity that exists within a community. The culture of the Tsimihety say, can only belong to the Tsimihety. Moreover, everyone who belongs to Tsimihety culture shares the same culture – it is not available to outsiders or interlopers – tourists for example. However, the reality of life is such that every society is full of internal diversity, disagreement, and different ways of doing things. So much so that it is seemingly impossible not only to identify a specific society's culture, but, in comparison to other cultures (or societies), it is extremely difficult to pin down any society's culture with any degree of confidence, even in theory. If we think about our own 'culture(s),' we recognize that we are unlikely to be able to describe it as if it were a single entity – for example, there seems to be no such agreed thing as 'British culture.' The British fundamentally disagree about its characteristics. We always find more exceptions than those which meet the rule, and more diversity than homogeneity. There are differences of class, of education, of politics, of gender, of religion, and between region, town and country, to be accounted for.

The incoherence of communities, or their level of internal diversity, has always caused difficulty. Bronislaw Malinowski struggled to find 'reliable informants' among the Melanesians he studied. He did manage, however, to write up a very coherent story about them (Malinowski 1922), in spite of the fact that his diary revealed he could not find two Melanesians to tell a story alike (Malinowski 1967).

A common solution to the problem of internal diversity is to nest cultures rather in the manner of a matroushka doll. It was T.S. Eliot's approach for example, to sit the (sub)culture of England, for example, in the larger culture of the British Isles (whatever that is) and then to situate this culture of the British Isles into a European one. However, as neat as this solution appears, it does not deal directly with the underlying problem; it merely postpones it. And the problem centres on what this 'thing' called culture is precisely, and how it works to make us all, eventually, what we are. At root, it is not a question of finding the 'right' characteristics or 'true' traits or even a better model of culture, it is of finding those things that we can all agree define (or touch) each single member of a society and in such a way that is sufficiently meaningful to distinguish the natives from the tourists. Even a cursory glance at society suggests that this appears impossible; an especially problematic matter when the reality of social life is constantly changing.

Another concern, from the standpoint of social theory, is that a fundamental 'something' of culture is believed to hold a society together no matter which point in time one cares to consider. This gives rise to the criticism of historicism, where the appeal of culture is based on the underlying assumption that culture endures irrespective of the volume of social change. So the British will always be British because of their culture and the Americans will always be Americans because of their culture, and so on. Culture has, as Lila Abu-Lughod pointed out, a timeless quality about it, which ensures the distinctiveness of a community of people in spite of all the changes that occur across time. As Roger Keesing pointed out, "'[a] culture' had a history, but it was the kind of history coral reefs have: the cumulated accretion of minute deposits, essentially unknowable, and irrelevant to the shapes they form" (Keesing in Borofsky 1994:301).

Grasping this history is problematic enough, but detailing the 'minute deposits' even more so. The problem is that most people's societies (or cultures if you prefer) are not bounded, homogeneous, static and self-contained – like coral reefs they change, and dramatically so. In addition, they change for an infinite number of reasons, which can be both internal and external. It is a mistake to think that *other* people's societies do not change very much; they change as much as our own. Even the Digger Indians whom Benedict described, managed to break their cup and lose their 'culture.'

Losing a culture is a problematic issue, but it is one of the most frequently cited fears in a cultural argument. However, to be without culture, a bit like being without history as Eric Wolf (1982/1997) cogently pointed out, is merely a matter of perspective, and one that tells us more about the normative assumptions of the claimant than it does about anything called 'culture.' As Michael Carrithers has said of Benedict's work, despite having 'broken their cup' the Digger Indians seemed to be getting along somehow. This may appear an unsympathetic comment, but one should not confuse the theoretical observation for an evaluation of the Digger Indian's circumstances, nor for the history that brought about the change. We all lose our culture in any case – consider life twenty or fifty years ago. America today, for example, is not the America of the 1960s, and 1990s Britain was nothing like that of the 1950s, the culture of the 1950s and 1960s has long gone.

Focusing on social and political change as though it represents a matter of 'cultural loss', as cultural theorists do, detracts from serious questions as to whether there has been injustice, a lack of power and control, and of whether or not one human being has abused another. Quite why the Digger Indians lost their cup is a serious matter, but what is certain is that issues of this order cannot be addressed on the grounds of culture; they can *only* be carried out because of political and normative theory, which needs to be disengaged from cultural theory. Evaluations cannot be made on cultural grounds because that issue rests entirely on one being able to identify the content of a culture (i.e. its ethnographic trademark) in extremely detailed and specific terms – namely, which values count as a part of which culture, and when and where they disappeared. Further, one must bear in mind that everyone must agree to this if 'culture' is a shared, homogeneous and continuous experience identifiable with a particular community that has lost something quite noticeable.[24] It is clear that no such level of agreement has ever been found among any community of people (and if it were, we ought to be highly suspicious of it). Moreover, an argument centred on cultural loss contains an inbuilt normative assumption – it is generally seen as a 'bad' thing, which, plainly, presents a conservative view of social change.

The anthropologist Colin Turnbull confronted the problem of social change head on. Over the course of several years, Turnbull made return trips to the Mbuti among whom he conducted his ethnographic research. To his irritation, he found that he had to continually re-write his findings because his ethnography did not correspond to Mbuti reality. Turnbull, apparently, blamed himself for the constant revisions, believing that he had repeatedly misconducted his research (cited in Carrithers 1992:22). However, as Carrithers has sympathetically pointed out, and Turnbull apparently "grudgingly" admitted, all that he, Turnbull, was witnessing was "change going on before his very eyes" (Carrithers 1992:22). This tells us much about the factory conditions Turnbull, like Malinowski before him, laboured under and the demands made by the profession to write up whole stories in a single ethnographic text.

The temptation to erase blots on the ethnographic landscape has been much criticized by a generation of anthropologists who came under the influence of postmodernism in the 1980s. Where Clifford Geertz had raised questions about methodology (how should we study culture?) and epistemology (what should we study?), a subsequent generation of scholars began to ask more searching disciplinary and ontological questions. Investigating the nature of the culture that past ethnographers detailed soon raised the question, 'whose culture is this?' The answer appeared to be, as Kahn has suggested, that the 'culture' described in some ethnographic texts was much more of the authors' making than had previously been acknowledged.[25] Geertz's post-positive successors, however, chose to focus their critical energies on specific acts of writing culture. James Clifford, George Marcus, Michael Fischer and Renato Rosaldo all complained in one way or another that the assumptions which past ethnographers had set out with had led them to subjectively re-write, or even totally write (invent if Clifford is to be believed), culture as they saw fit.[26] Clifford chastised Malinowski for writing up a very coherent story from the contradictory and 'unreliable' accounts he had obtained (Clifford 1988/1994: chapter three), while E.E. Evans-Pritchard was criticized by Rosaldo for telling an equally distorted story, one that conveniently ignored the brutal pacification programme the Nuer had been subjected to (Rosaldo 1989/1993:42–3).

Much of the criticism was exaggerated.[27] It is important to note that not every anthropologist has been guilty of the sins, say of homogenization, identified by many of the critics, and not all research was conducted in the manner that the post-positivist critics suggest. Franz Boas, for example, was well aware of the diversity within cultures and sought to capture as many examples as possible for future generations to contemplate. Granted, it is not obvious in *Patterns of Culture* that Ruth Benedict was describing the ideal conditions of three groups of Indians, but she makes it clear enough in her book *The Chrysanthemum and the Sword* that she is portraying an 'ideal conduct of life.'[28] The value of an ideal type is open to debate as is the value of the information contained in any ethnographic monologue, but these important theoretical questions were not engaged by the critics.[29] Intriguingly (and in spite of the alleged dishonesty of some ethnographies it seems), the latest generation of critical theorists' continues to work with the idea of culture and prefers to advocate the concept's reform rather than contemplate its complete rejection. Clifford was quite certain, for example, that culture is a concept he "cannot yet do without" (Clifford 1988/1994:10). Why this should be so is a matter dealt with in the final section.

Much of the information ethnographers gather is contradictory, while their actual experience in the field undermines the idea that people have anything distinctive in common in the first place. This, according to Andrew Vayda, was P.G. Wilson's verdict on the Tsimihety of Madagascar. Apparently, as Vayda has said of Wilson's work, "[a]lthough he [Wilson] found no distinctive Tsimihety way of doing things or, as he put it, no Tsimihety 'ethnographic trademark,' neither did he find the people to be living in chaos or anarchy" (Vayda in Borofsky 1994:321). This should come as welcome news to those who believe that to lose a culture, or to be without an original one, constitutes a social disaster – we all get by. The more insulting condition is to be accused of the cultural equivalent of 'suffering from false consciousness.' In this arrangement, cultures tainted by foreign influences are not what they ought to be – they have lost their authenticity – they are, in the colourful language of Kroeber, 'bastard cultures' (see Stocking 1996:291), although the more polite phrase these days is 'hybridity.'[30]

What all of these notions of otherness, coherence, homogeneity, historicity, loss and hybridity have in common is the larger assumption that culture exists in a meaningful way, that there is something out there that is exclusive, continuous and authentic, although, frequently, this tends to be hidden and employed in an unspoken manner. The problem with the natives is that we cannot find them with any certainty, or permanency; nor are they reducible to a single cultural type. The cultural native proves to be an elusive creature. The grounds upon which we continue to distinguish the natives from the tourists and the reason why we should even wish to do so become pertinent issues.

The essential problem

It is difficult to escape the widely accepted 'fact' that, in the words of Roy D'Andrade, "culture is a big thing that does things" (D'Andrade 1999:17). The problem is this has very little intellectual currency. As D'Andrade explains:

> If the term "culture" refers to what some group of people does, then we add nothing except confusion when we say that some group of people does what it does because of its culture. *In the "totality of behaviour" sense, the concept of culture has no explanatory value.*
>
> (D'Andrade 1999:16 – italics in original)

The concept of culture is indistinguishable from the claims made in its name. All too frequently, examples of difference are cited as evidence of culture, which by default are supposed to demonstrate culture's existence as the source of the differences. Of course, an argument of this order fails to demonstrate the merits of the concept, it merely provides us with a list of examples. To say that differences provide evidence of culture and that culture generates difference is tautological (and a well-known error in anthropology). We all know that the Chinese live differently from the Japanese, and in turn, they both live differently from the Americans and the English, but to say that they are different because of their culture demands more than the evidence of their differences. In fact the same evidence of difference, i.e. 'what people do,' can be convincingly interpreted under a variety of theoretical schemes, the least dramatic of which is to say that differences are the outcome of habitual practice and are wholly disconnected from anything a scholar might want to call 'culture.' Differences in eating habits, practices, world views, etc. might just as easily be attributed to politics, economics, religion, gender, class, or any number of social causes – it is not so obvious that they are a matter of culture.

To claim that culture is the source of differences though, is to suggest that there is something profound driving and determining these differences behind the scenes. In spite of the popularity of the practice, throwing more examples at the problem does not resolve it; besides it is well known in the social sciences that examples ought to embellish an argument, not substitute for it. For the cultural argument to work and to convince us 'culture' is the thing that did the deed, we need to know more about this thing called culture in the first place. We need to know more about how culture operates as an idea, *without* recourse to the infinite array of examples. The obvious distinctions between 'ways of life' count for nothing here – the evidence should come after the theoretical source has been accounted for.

Where that evidence is contradictory or vastly diverse, the theorist is presented with a problem. How does one account for a range of diversity and still claim that a culture is unique and exclusively belongs to a particular group of people? Initially the post-positivist critics looked like they had the answer. Scholars like Rosaldo and Clifford advocated a definition of culture that allowed for a multiplicity of interpretations not simply the ethnographer's reading, which, according to Clifford, had been Malinowski's mistake. Rosaldo suggested that "culture can arguably be conceived as a more porous array of intersections where distinct processes crisscross from within and beyond its borders" (Rosaldo 1989/1993:20). The retention of 'borders' within this definition is problematic for it is not clear how Rosaldo justifies their existence. Either, he invented them and imposed them on the criss-crossing processes, or they existed prior to this activity, which seems to be his implicit view. If they exist prior to the processes of criss-crossing, it more than suggests that this definition is not so far removed from the central assumptions behind the orthodox idea. That is to say, that the distinctiveness of a particular culture continues to be assumed as the basis around which boundaries are thought to form. 'Culture and its borders' appear as pre-existing in this definition, which then makes it possible to speak of Chicano culture separable from all the other 'tourists' based in the United States.

Talal Asad was among the first to identify the fundamental problem with the idea of culture and its essential conceptual component. Asad suggested that the crucial theoretical problem lay with "a notion of culture as an *a priori* totality of authentic meanings to which action and discourse must be related if they are to be properly understood and their integrity explained" (Asad 1979:608–9 – italics in original). The basic problem, shared by otherwise quite diverse theorists, was, in Asad's view, the 'emphasis on meaning,' which at his time of writing made social change difficult to conceptualize. 'Culture' is believed to belong 'somewhere' and do 'something' but it is only through accepting the presence of a mysterious 'thing' that our cooperation as readers can be secured in the agreement that this is the 'culture' of a community. As Andrew Vayda has said of Marshall Sahlins:

> Sahlins himself . . . claims that each society is ordered by a meaningful and essential cultural logic of which the society's members are more or less unaware and that the criterion by which the events in which members participate are to be judged important and worthy of anthropological attention is whether we can discern this cultural logic or order (or changes therein) in the events . . .
>
> (Vayda in Borofsky 1994:325)

However, what the job of an anthropologist or ethnographer is in the task of unmasking culture is a secondary issue. It is of greater concern how scholars conceive of culture, especially as the natives are blissfully unaware of it and the observer claims to know something they do not. The chief suspect behind what is thought to maintain distinction, or provides the mysterious source of cultural difference, has been identified as essentialism. In its simplest expression, essentialism, derived from an essence of culture, is a modern form of 'geist.' It is the hidden spirit of distinction operating behind the scenes of society. Although to be sure there is hardly anything 'simple' in the way essentialism manifests itself in culture theory, indeed, some of the covering arguments are highly sophisticated and distracting in their complexity. Yet, without doubt, the thread that holds all the conceptual manifestations of essentialism together is *meaning*, as Asad and Kahn have indicated. *Meaning* is the 'thing' that determines how people will react to, interpret, or deal with any event and force. The status of meaning in the culture concept is secured through its assumed ontological presence as a self-evident and really-existing phenomenon denoted, rather confusingly, by the idea of culture itself. Where it is believed that cultures have an enduring core of values, elements, ideas etc. (however the scholar chooses to identify such things) that belong exclusively to a particular community, then essentialist assumptions have entered the theoretical framework. Essentialist assumptions may operate by default on the grounds that a culture is what holds a community together in spite of the fact that the natives seem to think, and do things, differently.

It may be unkind, but it is certainly not unreasonable to suggest that any scholar who operates with the unspoken assumption that culture entails a pre-existing and enduring meaning has an essentialist conception of culture. The shift towards thinking about culture as a process, as was also the case with the shift from behaviour to ideas, does not, necessarily, denote a dramatic intellectual departure from the fundamental idea, particularly if *otherness* and the causal qualities of culture are retained in a less than specified way.[31] In short, the orthodox assumptions that lie behind the anthropological concept of culture remain in place even though the epistemology and methodology may alter greatly. Culture is still a 'big thing that does things' albeit in a more various way these days. Communities are believed to have an internal 'logic' or meaning that passes for 'culture.' This 'culture' may be unseen, working mysteriously behind the scenes a bit like gravity, but it is nonetheless a commonly held and pervasive, if not persuasive, belief that (like gravity) 'culture' exists everywhere and affects everything even if we cannot actually 'see' it. Yet, as Adam Kuper reminds us, these days "[f]ew anthropologists would claim that the notion of culture can be compared in 'explanatory importance' with gravity, disease, or evolution" (Kuper 1999:preface x). Nonetheless, plenty of commentators do carry on as though this were the case.

It may not be necessary to subscribe to a singular and homogeneous view of culture in the manner of Benedict or Malinowski, but it is inevitable that an essentialist conception will share with these scholars the view that there is a synthesis between community, difference and 'culture.'

The essentialist role of meaning becomes visible when scholars discuss what they believe 'culture' does. If a scholar believes that 'culture' makes us what we are, as Margaret Mead did, then s/he has entered the realms of essentialism. If it is assumed that culture keeps the natives separate from the tourists, again, essentialism is suspected. In this respect, even the critical cultural theorists (i.e. Clifford and Rosaldo) are not as radical as they seem – culture remains, for them, a concept that is still required to do some 'old' (essentialist) delineating work in a new guise. If there is not an essence of culture, how does it operate 'within and beyond' its borders in a manner that serves to keep the Chicano native separate from the average American tourist? Even the suggestion that we belong to a multiplicity of communities and therefore a multiplicity of cultures, only serves to complicate the picture, it does not elucidate the original idea.

The problem is not that communities share meanings and values, because clearly they do; the problem is attributing such things to 'culture' in a manner that more than suggests that these things are pre-existing and enduring (unless they happen to be lost). The crux of the matter is that culture is assumed to work behind the scenes of a community in a mysterious way; in short, it is an unspoken assumption that there is an 'essence' of culture. Essentialists do not invoke the idea of culture as a mere descriptive term, they invoke it, as Sahlins does, as an explanatory device and what this idea of culture is expected to convey is specific community meaning in a quite explicit sense. As an example, the meaning(s) that the Chinese community share, or the thing(s) that ultimately gives them their Chinese-ness, cannot belong to any other community. The problem here is not with essentialism as such, but with the belief that 'culture is a big thing that does things only for these people,' and that this idea of culture provides a scholar with a ready-made explanatory basis for everything that follows. In short, it is questionable whether some post-positivist conceptualizations of culture have really opened up the idea to the extent that it does correspond to a 'reality' which does not depend on radical *otherness* and exclusive meaning. The tourists still cannot be comfortably accommodated with the natives, even when it is appropriate to do so, as when for example, they interact with one another at resorts, or live together as neighbours.

In spite of the complaint that scholars have reified and essentialized culture, the basic charge may not be so disastrous. As D'Andrade points out, 'we reify and essentialize all sorts of things, but that does not necessarily undermine their conceptual utility.' Indeed, without some measure of reification and essentialism, "there is no way to explain things" (D'Andrade 1999:17). In IR, we refer regularly to 'states,' institutions and ideas like globalization that necessarily reify and essentialize the world. One needs to be very clear though, about the nature of one's concepts if they are to hold water and convince the audience. As D'Andrade has pointed out:

Most social scientists agree that . . . race as a biological construct does not have the causal properties that racists give it. On the basis of the preponderance of the evidence, it is an empirical error to essentialize race by giving it causal properties. But does *culture* have causal properties? Does it, *as a totality*, reproduce itself, give meaning to life, legitimate institutions, etc? Can we reasonably essentialize and reify culture?

(D'Andrade 1999:17 – italics in original)

Without better conceptual and theoretical clarification, culture may not be employable in the way that some scholars would like, meaning it may not be possible or indeed plausible to speak, for instance, of the culture of three hundred people. The question is not necessarily one of whether we have reified or essentialized the world of 'culture,' but whether 'reality' lends itself to this form of reification and essentialism and, moreover, whether 'culture' is a useful and appropriate concept in this respect.

It is a common assumption that tourists can never be genuine cultural natives. It is not so much that the *other* is separate from the *self*; it is that under the terms of the concept of culture the *other* must be intrinsically different and distinguishable from all other individuals or groups. Only in this way can the natives be inherently separable from the tourists. A seemingly innocent claim on behalf of British culture leads us to sorting out the British natives from the foreign tourists and resident guests. Inevitably, this becomes a question of who does and does not belong (or count) under the definition of what it means to be 'British.' Visiting asylum seekers, therefore, would be deemed not to belong, but second generation ethnic minorities are possibly more acceptable these days, especially as the asylum seekers present as a new group of impostors to focus on. Sorting out who does and does not belong, which is what the culture concept demands ultimately, necessarily raises some awkward questions about the continuity of culture and its relationship to history. In turn, this invokes uncomfortable assumptions about who can and who cannot claim this history – or put more bluntly, who can and who cannot belong to the culture.

The relationship between continuity and change is a difficult one to fathom, but the essentialist idea of culture makes a strong claim (or assumption) about this relationship. In spite of any obvious social change, the essence of culture must endure. Within the essentialist idea, the Chinese-ness of Chinese culture keeps the Chinese essentially the same, as does Balinese-ness, British-ness and so on. The connection between the past and the present (cultural continuity) is a crucial component in an essentialist conception of culture. The idea of culture explicitly commits people to a particular past (as tradition, cultural heritage, memory, etc.), or, alternatively, enables a group of people to claim a particular past exclusively as theirs and theirs alone. Refugees, immigrants and tourists cannot claim this past because they do not belong to the culture.

Walter Benn Michaels asks, 'why does it matter who we are?' and why does it matter that this is cast in continuous (historical) cultural terms? He says:

> The answer can't just be the epistemological truism that our account of the past may be partially determined by our own identity, for, of course, this description of the conditions under which we know the past makes no logical difference to the truth or falsity of what we know. It must be instead the ontological claim that we need to know who we are in order to know which past is ours. The real question, however, is not *which* past should count as ours but why *any* past should count as ours.
>
> (Michaels 1995:128 – italics in original)

Michaels is quite right, why should any past matter?[32] All history is dead and was not done by us, as Michaels goes on to point out, and in this way, what we know has no obvious direct linkage to the past. We may learn our history, but since learning is open to anyone, refugees and tourists included, this makes the past available to all comers. Yet, the principal claim of the idea of 'culture' is that 'our past' is not available to everyone and it is certainly not applicable to outsiders. The idea of culture forces us to address an awkward question: what is the barrier that prevents the New York Jew from becoming a Mashpee Indian, or the refugee from claiming a place in English culture?[33]

On the face of it the barrier is the culture itself, and since few people would dispute this notion, because it is obvious that foreigners are not part of the culture, the idea of culture justifies itself without complaint. Yet, if culture is a learned process in some way, there is nothing in theory that holds it together and prevents others from participating in it, and authentically so, because we are all capable of learning new things. Indeed, immigrants regularly prove that point. However, the claim made on behalf of the idea of culture is that it not only maintains its exclusivity but that this is passed down, somehow through history. The culture that 'belongs' to a particular community of people in a meaningful sense cannot simply be a matter of learning or epistemology, although it is believed to belong to (or is identified as belonging to) a particular community, it must be rooted, as Michaels argues, in other kinds of claims. Unless we allow 'geists' and mysterious essences into the frame, the only tangible alternative way in which we can justify a commitment to cultural identities and cultural exclusiveness is on the basis of blood-tie. Michaels demonstrates that the idea of culture is a continuation of race theory because it relies on an essentialist view of who people are and what is rightfully theirs. Therefore, "we are not Jews because we do Jewish things, we do Jewish things because we are Jews" (Michaels 1995:139).

In a cultural argument, it really does not matter what people actually do. The culture that determines a cultural identity, and keeps the natives from the tourists, derives explicitly from whom people are and to whom they were born. Michaels has demonstrated that the notions of exclusivity, continuity and authenticity, all crucial elements in the anthropological idea of culture, are falsely premised on the presumption of a 'cultural essence,' whereas they can only be based on blood-ties if, in actuality, they are to hold for an identifiable group of people. It is only in this way that exclusivity can be claimed, continuity maintained, and authenticity estab-lished. In short, the *meaning* of culture and the *otherness* it creates depend on biological descent and lineage, not 'culture;' irrespective of how 'culture' has been defined. One can see how this has led to the claim that 'culture' is functionally equivalent with race theory; culture does not replace race, it operates in similar theoretical terms. All of which helps to explain why the idea of culture became popular in the racial climate of 1920s America. The vocabulary changed but the basis for ideas of differentiation did not alter significantly.[34] The essentialist conception of culture does the same kind of delineating work as the idea of race – it keeps the pure native from the impure tourist.

Whether culturalists accept the criticism that the ontological basis of their idea is no different in theory from race thinking, and we can suspect that most will not, there are alternative and more interesting ways of thinking about culture other than those advocating essentialism. On the one hand, there is the humanist concept; but, as already discussed in the previous chapter, this approach requires theoretical expansion in IR. On the other hand, criticisms of the orthodox anthropological concept have generated an alternative conceptualization of culture that has been loosely termed, anti-essentialist.

The anti-essentialist approach seeks to grasp society in more realistic terms. As Keesing remarked:

> I have just come back from the Solomon Islands where dreadlocks in the style of Bob Marley and Kung Fu videos are the stuff of contemporary "culture." More than ever, the boundedness and the essentialism that motivate it must depart from observed "realities"; the gulf between what we see in the field and the ways we represent it widens by the minute.
>
> (Keesing in Borofsky 1994:302)

Closing the gap between 'reality' and theory remains a particularly urgent problem in the light of the criticisms. As Keesing goes on to say:

> ... attributing to "Balinese culture" a systematic coherence, a perva-sive sharedness, and an enduring quality – so that Bali remains Bali through the centuries, and from south to north, west to east (even nowadays, despite the tourists) – commits us to an essentialism of an

extreme kind. Balinese culture is the essence of Bali, the essence of Balineseness.

(Keesing in Borofsky 1994:302–3)

Where the reality of life makes it difficult to distinguish between 'the natives' and 'the tourists' and therefore makes it all the more necessary to remove that 'reality' to the realm of ideas, then, ironically, we have invoked a radical form of essentialism. This is not tenable, especially where the reality of lives is far removed from what we would like to see or think we ought to see in other people's cultures.

Recognizing that ethnographic research failed to account for the extent of debate and diversity within a community generated the question, as Vayda points out, as to "whether variations themselves, as much as, if not more than, any putative sociocultural patterns or norms, are to be made the objects of explanation and generalization" (Vayda in Borofsky 1994:322). Anti-essentialist scholarship "sees variations as [the] 'fundamental reality' ... and not as mere accidents about norms" (Vayda in Borofsky 1994:320). The problem with essentialist accounts of 'culture' is that they are 'biased' towards presenting an orderly and distinctive portrait of communities in their totality; a portrait that is almost impossible to sustain empirically and difficult to justify theoretically.

One useful development is to stop conceiving of culture as a noun (thing) as the essentialist does and to adopt Brian Street's suggestion that 'culture is a verb' (Street 1993). Culture does not make us what we are (or should not in the light of Michaels); the study of culture is concerned with accounting for the whys and wherefores of what people do and the context in which they do it. Indeed, it is one of the key anti-essentialist features that this approach is more concerned with doing than being. Street posits that:

> what culture does is precisely the work of 'defining words, ideas, things and groups' ... The job of studying culture is not of finding and then accepting its definitions but of 'discovering how and what definitions are made, under what circumstances and for what reasons.' ... Indeed, the very term 'culture' itself, like these other ideas and definitions, changes its meanings and serve different often competing purposes at different times. Culture is an active process of meaning making and contest over definition, including its own definition. This, then, is what I mean by arguing that *Culture is a verb*.
>
> (Street 1993:25 – italics in original)

The idea that culture is an active process of meaning making is far removed from the idea that culture is fixed and makes us what we are. It also challenges the very nature of cultural enquiry. Another scholar,

Michael Carrithers has argued that the point of enquiry is to pick up a strand in a "tangled knot of puzzles" (Carrithers 1992:3–4) and to follow where it leads. Cultural enquiry does not seek to establish or locate a standard of culture and then study a community by those terms, Carrithers' idea of culture, like Street's, is subtle and emergent. For Carrithers this leads into the study of inter-subjectivity and inter-sociality but in a limited way. Our view of culture as scholars is only ever partial in any case, but our role in the process is equally aspectival in Carrithers' thesis. These ideas move the concept of culture from being to doing and separate the critics of essentialist conceptions of culture who are still essentialists at heart, i.e. the James Cliffords and Renato Rosaldos of this world, from the anti-essentialists who think very differently about culture.

Terry Eagleton claims that: "[i]t would be odd to see three people as forming a culture, but not three hundred or three million" (Eagleton 2000:37), which sets him apart from anti-essentialist theorizing and provides us with a useful example to draw out the distinctions.[35] In order to envisage *a* culture of 'three hundred or three million people' some enormous generalities need to be reached and attained in a meaningful sense if one is not relying upon ideal-types, stereotypes or prejudiced assumptions. The methodological difficulties of capturing the attitudes, the values, the 'whole way of life' of a community of this size are considerable. Even if these problems were surmountable, what anthropological experience teaches us is that a study based on this proposition would only reveal debate and diversity. It would certainly not reveal the level of agreement and homogeneity that reference to 'a culture of three hundred people' implies. What permits this form of totalization is the assumption of communal cohesion or an underlying shared essence of community meaning. Anti-essentialists deny both the possibility of an underlying force or essence determining communal distinction *and* the possibility of methodologically essentializing large groups of people in this way. Therefore, Eagleton commits a fundamental error when he thinks he can speak of the culture of three hundred, let alone three million people.

Anti-essentialism is much more than a methodological shift; it is a profound epistemological and ontological shift. Anti-essentialists accept that there is no such thing as *the* culture, as in an underpinning essence or 'authentic set of exclusive/discrete meanings.' For these scholars, 'culture' is about strategies of interaction and intersubjectivity, which are necessarily open-ended, subject to a wide range of influences; none of which is predictable. *Otherness* and *meaning* are taken as constitutive elements in the same process; neither are presumed to be enduring – people can and regularly do learn new habits and tell new stories about themselves. In an anti-essentialist sense, we all have 'culture' no matter what has come and gone over the years and irrespective of where we actually are. Under anti-essentialism, 'the tourists' must be considered along with 'the natives,' and the breaking of cups, accepted as a daily occurrence.

Although these more intersubjective approaches have yet to make it to the mainstream, and have certainly not dented the popular conception of culture, one of the exciting implications of this kind of enquiry lies in its potential to liberate us from the synthesis between the concept of culture and the orthodox notions of difference and community that it has generated. No longer is it possible to say that the Chinese do what they do because of their Chinese-ness or culture; we need to examine very closely what makes a particular group of people behave and do things in the way that they do. The axiomatic connection between communities and 'culture' has been fundamentally questioned and broken. Where the orthodox and essentialist conception of culture supplies narratives that fetishes difference, the anti-essentialist approach shares with the humanist conception of culture an ability to transcend the orthodox boundaries of difference, albeit in very differing ways and through differing means.[36]

The underlying problem with the orthodox notion of culture as a way of life is not a question of modifying the concept so that it can capture 'ways of life' better or more faithfully. Ultimately, it is a question of moving our concepts out of the parameters set by nineteenth century social science. Of moving beyond the notion that there is a place and obvious space for everything and it can all be bottled, pickled, canned and put on a shelf forever marked 'culture.' We need to change our way of looking at the world and our way of thinking about the differences between people. The problem with essentialist conceptions of culture is not so much that 'one cannot find two Indians to tell a story alike,' because, clearly, on occasions one will be able to find several Indians who do; the serious difficulties concern the scholar who wants to keep two Indians together who may never tell a story alike. When real life suggests that it is better to place the Indian and the tourist together because they have more in common with one another, what are the grounds for keeping all 'the natives' together and apart from 'the tourists?' Anyone who claims that the grounds for distinction are obviously rooted in 'culture' has some serious theoretical explaining to do.

It is not obvious that we all have culture, nor that it makes us what we are. Certainly, we have differences but these might as easily be put down to habit (that changes) as to anything as vague as culture. Unless a scholar is prepared to tell us otherwise (and I stress this point because few are prepared to admit that they have abstracted the 'culture' they describe), the idea that a group of people share 'something' *meaningful* in common and are distinguishable on that basis leads to the suspicion that there is an 'essence' of culture supporting the theoretical claims made on behalf of the concept. If we are led to believe that 'we are our culture' or that 'culture makes us what we are' then we must know what this idea of 'culture' is that hides behind the claim. Actual examples are inconclusive; the fact that Americans are different from the Chinese tells us nothing worth knowing about the reasons for their differences. We learn nothing about culture as such (namely as a really existing force or as a depiction of reality) but what we do learn is what we already know and have always known about people – that they vary.

The idea of culture is an insufficient excuse for explaining the differences between us – we would be different even without the concept of culture. Imposing the concept of culture on our differences and as a means for explaining them does not enhance our understanding of the world in any way. Worse, the idea of culture creates unnecessary political problems as we shall see in the later chapters.[37] Perhaps more drastic measures are called for. Lila Abu-Lughod advises actively 'writing against culture' (in Fox 1991), while Joel Kahn hopes for the concept's immediate demise (Kahn 1989). The humanist concept indicates that we can live without the anthropological concept of culture, indeed we had to before it was invented and became popular; therefore, it is not inconceivable that we could live without the idea in the future.

Key points

- The anthropological concept of culture emerged in the United States during the 1910s and 1920s.
- It is synonymous with 'ways of life' – there is a presumed synthesis between community, difference and culture.
- The substantive and theoretical difficulties are considerable and numerous.
- The concept depends upon many unspoken assumptions – chiefly radical otherness, shared meaning and a continuous history.
- Ultimately, it relies on an essentialist ontology – an essence of culture – as spirit or blood-tie. Although non-essentialist conceptualizations are possible, they have not replaced the dominant essentialist ideology.
- Current debate is over reform or rejection of the concept.

4   The nationalization of culture

The orthodox anthropological concept of culture was fully constructed by the time the Second World War began. It exhibited the essential characteristics that would ensure the concept's success for the remainder of the twentieth century – culture was the totalizing concept that captured whole communities and enabled scholars to describe them. Although, it was an artificial construct, it had reflected the context, concerns and factory conditions within which the cultural anthropologists, as they were now called, worked. Once established in American social science, the anthropological concept of culture would take up a more prominent role in the factory conditions that IR scholars and practitioners operated under, becoming something of a conventional standard itself in the new post-war era.

The Second World War was proof that the inter-war humanist conception of culture had failed to generate sufficient mutual understanding to ensure world peace; worse than this, the humanist idea of culture had been perverted during the war to such an extent that the German experience of war-kultur did much to discredit and undermine the basic concept. Some of the theoretical weaknesses identified in chapter two, namely the inability to distinguish cultural relations from propaganda, were thoroughly exposed during the course of the Second World War. The theoretical problems would continue to weaken the humanist concept, but few scholars were interested in the approach after the second war – the world had moved on. Different concepts were required with which to meet the challenges of the unfolding Cold War era. In this climate, a new narrative of international relations took hold, Realism, which was suspicious of anything that did not involve national power, particularly military power, and which defended the national interest in some way.

One might think that the development of Realism would mark the death of culture in international relations, but in fact, the opposite was true. Indeed, in comparison to the inter-war period, culture continued to play as important a role in international affairs during the Cold War as it had between the wars. With the anthropological concept of culture popular in the American social and intellectual context, this provided additional impetus for the idea of culture to play its part during the Cold War. The anthropological concept of culture acquired a place in the thinking and practice of international relations that paralleled the significance which the humanist concept had enjoyed during the inter-war period. Yet, this anthropological concept was to be a very different form of culture in IR, both in theory and in practice.

The cultural Cold War

The Second World War marked a dark phase in the career of culture. In spite of the intellectual developments taking place among American anthropologists and their efforts to create an egalitarian concept and one tolerant of difference, culture (and kultur) had displayed an ugly side to its character during the war.

Kultur, increasingly nationalistic in Germany since before the First World War, had become thoroughly politicized under the Nazis and by the time of the second war was synonymous with the state. Joseph Goebbels took control of kultur in 1933 when he became Reich Minister for Public Enlightenment and Propaganda. Under his direction, every non-Germanic element in literature, film, music, theatre, art and the mass media was rooted out. Infamously, books were burned, music banned and anti-Semitic propaganda reached malevolent heights, while the 'pure' German folk were glorified and magnified.

The Nazi regime defined kultur for the Germanic peoples. Mendelssohn and Mahler were effectively banned, but Bach and Wagner were permitted; Madison Grant and Lothrop Stoddard were thoroughly acceptable, but Oswald Spengler was not. Race and kultur became intimately entwined and were at the disposal of the state. Although Adolph Hitler spoke in terms reminiscent of Spengler when he suggested that great cultures died, for Hitler this was the consequence of 'blood poisoning' rather than the loss of soul. Spengler, who found himself ostracized by the regime, did not draw the connection to race that underpinned National Socialist thinking and policies, and he died in 1936 before the full horror of state-controlled kultur was realized. In Italy, culture had also been co-opted to the Fascist cause, with that regime finally coming "to the frank assertion, 'Culture is Fascism' " (McMurry and Lee 1947:238).

In Japan, meanwhile, the concepts of culture and civilization continued to be deployed in tandem, but with an increasingly antagonist attitude towards Western civilization and neighbouring states. Akira Iriye indicates that the idea of a separate, but not yet confrontational, Asian identity appeared in Japan around the turn of the century and gained ground after the Russo-Japanese war of 1905. By the time of the Second World War, however, Japan was articulating the idea of a pan-Asian civilization, with its own values, united against Western civilization. According to this narrative, Western civilization was bankrupt and Japan, alone, could unite the five Asian races (Japanese, Chinese, Manchurian, Mongolian and Korean) to establish a new Eastern civilization that would stand in opposition to, and eventually supplant, the West. Inevitably, neighbouring Asians disagreed. When the Japanese 'liberated' some 800,000 books from libraries in Shanghai and Nanking they did so in the name of "cultural preservation" but the Chinese saw it as an act of 'barbarism' (Iriye 1997:119). The Japanese were not perturbed. The war against China was justified on the grounds of "the protection, promotion, and creation of a superior culture that promises mankind's just progress."[1] Eastern civilization was destined to progress and the Japanese increasingly employed the language of culture to justify their actions.

As with kultur, the Japanese idea of culture had become politicized and an extension of state politics, but unlike the Germans, the Japanese retained the concept of civilization in its generic, progressive and technical sense. Although, during the Second World War they saw this idea of civilization less in universal terms and defined it more as a specifically Asian (Japanese) issue.

The British and French, predictably enough, hung onto the old ideas of civilization and the humanist concept of culture; ignoring or little aware of the intellectual developments in the United States and avoiding the political developments, as best they could, that had taken place in the European continent. The ideas of culture and civilization that emerged out of the Second World War remained largely unchanged from those that had informed the British and French on the eve of its outbreak. Civilization was still the preferred concept for speaking of generic development and culture remained an individual matter, although both now demanded extra effort and vigilance if they were to continue to influence human affairs. In the meantime, a new force had emerged on the international stage that had to be reckoned with – the Soviet Union or USSR.

The Soviet Union had always been adept at using culture (in the form of artifacts and ideas) as the means for manipulating society. Arguably, theirs was a distorted application of the humanist idea, but there was nothing humanist in the deployment of the concept. Here too state cultural policy (or propaganda) was taken to the extreme. Culture had been harnessed to the service of the state since 1917, which was rather ironic in view of Marx's theory that culture was the kind of fluffy bourgeois stuff that belonged to the superstructure and was destined for extinction under communism. Far from disappearing, culture was one of the methods the communists used to manipulate and control mass behaviour from the cradle to the grave – brute force and terror being the alternative means.[2] Although the Soviets took great pride in their cultural achievements in the humanist sense, i.e. the Bolshoi and Kirov Ballets, the state circuses, the Red Army Ensemble, etc., there was no escaping the fact that culture had been politicized with communist rule. After the war, Soviet cultural policy continued as it had always done, but its international dimension acquired new meaning in the atmosphere of the Cold War where the USSR was locked in competition with their archrival, the capitalist United States.

The Americans had been a little slow in realizing the potential of culture in its politicized and state-controlled aspect, but they soon made up for lost time. In view of the intellectual and social popularity that the anthropological concept enjoyed by the time of the Second World War, it was to be expected that this idea would make an impression at the government level and find a place in American foreign policy. Unsurprisingly then, it was in the United States that the changes taking place in the meaning of culture could be dramatically observed, both in theory and in practice.

In practice, culture played its part for the Americans in the Cold War with the Soviet Union in a manner that also might be seen as a radical perversion of the humanist concept in its cultural diplomacy or propagandist role. In this sense, the USA would have had much in common with the USSR but for the fact that the theoretical context of the United States, and in which practice was grounded, was radically different from that of the Soviet Union.

The American theoretical and ideological context had changed dramatically in cultural terms from that which existed in Britain and France and had existed in the USA prior to the second war's outbreak. The 1940s had opened with Margaret Mead declaring 'we are our culture,' but by the end of that decade, culture was being proclaimed as the 'foundation stone of American social science.' In the American social context, the anthropological concept of culture sat comfortably alongside ideas about race and difference. The widespread articulation and knowledge of the anthropological concept would necessarily give any expression of 'international cultural relations' a distinctive edge. So much so that the culture of the Cold War would hardly have been recognizable by the inter-war theorists and would much less have met with their approval. Culture had gone native and what is more, it was nationalized in the American effort in the Cold War. In many respects, culture came to be an even more useful political tool during the Cold War from the American perspective than it had been for the League of Nations. Yet, theoretically speaking, it is arguable that the substantive role of culture had become impoverished, certainly this was the case when compared to the aspirations of the inter-war theorists, because the idea now seemed to be reduced to a sub-field of foreign policy. The concept was acutely associated with national ways of life and the culture of the natives.

When Louis Armstrong and the All Stars toured Eastern Europe in 1965 the battle lines in the cultural Cold War were already well entrenched. Armstrong was the first jazz musician to tour behind the 'iron curtain,' making his presence an historic event.[3] Armstrong was only there to play music, which under other circumstances would have been an admirable example of the humanist understanding of 'cultural inter-change,' but under the conditions of the Cold War, both sides viewed the tour differently. On the American side, the tour had been sponsored ulti-mately (when traced back through the United States Information Agency – USIA) by the Central Intelligence Agency (CIA). This was part of the CIA's campaign to win hearts and minds by selling the American way of life to the world.[4] On the communist side, it was an opportunity for the Soviet Union to exploit the fact that the United States of America did not treat its citizens equally as the communist system, allegedly, did. Black Americans did not enjoy equal rights, which made jazz music an accept-able and politically exploitable commodity for the communists. By all accounts Armstrong and the All Stars' tour was a roaring success and was later followed by Duke Ellington, Ella Fitzgerald and other American artists, but, in a contextual sense, these tours were a far cry from the era of cultural internationalism. The international cultural context had changed, and along with it, the American domestic context and the meaning of 'culture' had also changed. In spite of what the artists and those involved in organizing such events themselves believed, fostering mutual understanding was no longer the sole issue or even the main point of interchange; the meaning, motives and mere fact of the tour was a politicized matter from the perspective of the state.

Many of the artists and field operatives involved in cultural pro-grammes during this period seemed to be unaware of their role in the cul-tural Cold War in any case. Most artists, like Armstrong, simply wanted to perform or exhibit their work to an appreciative audience, while employees of the USIA wanted to engage with *others* on a mutual basis. In contextual terms, the innocence proclaimed by those involved in this aspect of the Cold War needs to be taken seriously rather than assumed as the further evidence of an international conspiracy conducted, largely, by the CIA.[5] To assess the role of officials and artists during this period, one needs to take into consideration the nature of both the international and the domestic contexts. And it is clear that in the American domestic context, a substantial change had taken place in the perception and purpose of cultural interchange, particularly from the point of view of the state, and that change had occurred during the course of the Second World War.

The American scholar Frank Ninkovich (1981) has identified two schools of thought and sets of policy makers that co-existed towards the end of the Second World War, and has detailed their changing levels of influence in the American government. One group, which he termed the 'culturalists,' he says, envisaged a limited role for government in cultural policy, or 'cultural interchange' as this group understood it, whereas the other group, which he referred to as the 'informationalists,' saw 'govern-ment as the central policy mechanism.' The competing views of the role of government that each side envisaged playing in 'cultural affairs' are revealing. For one side, 'culture' was too important an issue to be entrusted to the hands of particular governments. Culture was something that they believed a wider group of people (especially 'cultural' experts or connoisseurs and private organizations) must be involved in. Culture was, in the 'culturalists'' view, a matter with universal appeal; it should not be subjected to the specific whims of particular governments, while for the 'informationalists,' 'culture' was defined as a national issue and this school of thought considered that culture should be brought explicitly under governmental control. Crucially, Ninkovich indicates that these two groups were 'mutually exclusive' of each other (Ninkovich 1981:126). "The culturalists continued to hew," Ninkovich says, "to the reciprocity theorems of liberalism, whereas the informationalists were more congenial to what was an unashamedly nationalist approach" (Ninkovich 1981:126).

The problems between the two cultural approaches had become pronounced with the debates over the Smith-Mundt legislation. Those culturalists in the humanist camp expressed increasing concern over the dual role of fostering mutual understanding and providing information. George Zook of the American Council of Education, President Harold Dodds of Princeton, and Ben Cherrington, the first Director of the Division of Cultural Relations in the State Department, lobbied Congress for a separation of the cultural and information programmes (see Ninkovich 1981:chapter five especially). Cherrington wrote; "I have gone all out in advocating legislation that will divorce once and for all propaganda from cultural co-operation" (cited in Ninkovich 1981:126). In the end, as Ninkovich indicates, "Congress resolved the contradiction by creating a paradox masquerading as a compromise" (Ninkovich 1981:133). As the Cold War got under way and priorities changed, it became clear that humanist ambitions would be a secondary concern; every available resource would be committed to winning the struggle for hearts and minds, and saving Americans from the evils of communism.

The 'informationalists,' as Ninkovich has described them, were in the business of "selling America" to the world, whereas the 'culturalists,' whom he goes on to call the 'fundamentalists,' were interested in exchanging culture for humanist and universal benefit in the manner previously advocated by Alfred Zimmern and his colleagues (Ninkovich 1981 see chapter five).[6] Ninkovich's distinction between the 'fundamentalists and informationalists' is somewhat misleading from our point of view, but, without doubt, he has detected the differences between the humanist and the anthropological concepts of culture informing American policy makers' thinking, although he has not recognized it in these terms. Ninkovich employs his own descriptive terms of 'informationalist' and 'fundamentalist,' but what is noticeable is that he argues that these two schools of thought were incommensurable and were competing for influence in American foreign policy. Significantly, he says that before the Second World War "[w]hen Americans spoke of cultural relations, they actually meant intellectual relations – it would not have occurred to them that the two were not identical" (Ninkovich 1981:181).

From a current contextual view, it does not occur to us to transform these pre-war assumptions, as Ninkovich does, to claim 'that the two were not identical.' When IR scholars, Americans, and most other Westerners, spoke of intellectual relations they actually meant culture, which deserves to be taken seriously, rather than reinterpreted from the standpoint of a different conception of culture. What is clear is that the 'informationalists' (or those working closely with the anthropological concept) won the 'battle' for foreign policy and by 1950, according to Ninkovich, "American cultural programs of all kinds were deeply committed to waging Cold War" (Ninkovich 1981:139).

Culture during the Cold War was less something to be exchanged, least of all to foster mutual understanding, and more of a weapon in the battle to win hearts and minds. Moreover this battle was not entirely concerned with promoting a state's best side, the primary purpose was to win the competition between two, very different, 'ways of life' and this new development marks a significant departure from the kind of cultural policy that had existed before the Second World War. Further, in convincing the global populace of the rightness of one way of life (the American) over the other way of life (the Soviet), the cultural Cold War was necessarily preoccupied with establishing whose side everyone was on, and this was increasingly determined (by the Americans) under the terms of the anthropological concept. Whether one could be counted on one side or the other became a crucial question both internationally and domestically, as the persecution of dissidents in the Soviet Union and the McCarthy Senate hearings in the United States amply demonstrated, albeit in differing ways.[7] Within America the cultural Cold War went far beyond anything envisaged under cultural diplomacy; it touched every aspect of American life. It is these elements, of breadth and depth, which distinguish American cultural activity in the Cold War from anything that might fall under the usual remit of cultural diplomacy. The conventional standards (or ideology) informing the activities of the period differed greatly, and it was the anthropological concept that provided additional, if largely assumed, reasons for the 'rightness' of the approach.

Where cultural diplomacy might be described as the soft end of foreign policy activity in so far as it seeks to garner better relations with other states, or at least contribute to the creation of a favourable environment between states in which other policy areas, say trade for example, might flourish; yet, Cold War cultural activity, certainly in the early stages, was a deliberate and conscious attempt to engage in a battle between two competing value systems and their ways of life. Contrary to cultural diplomacy and the cultural interchange of the League era, it was not obvious what the 'gift' (i.e. a concert tour) was for; but as an example of American culture, indicative of the American 'way of life,' the 'gift' was presumed to speak volumes in itself. This activity has no resemblance to the representative 'gifts' openly chosen and knowingly given under Jimmy Carter's presidency, for example. In addition, and perhaps not surprisingly under the conditions of the Cold War, cultural activities during this period contained a secretive element – namely, many of the activities were financed by the CIA.[8] The role of the CIA in cultural diplomacy first emerged during the Vietnam War when it was revealed that the organization had funded the Congress for Cultural Freedom; this revelation caused a scandal at the time (see Kramer 1999:305–6). According to Frances Stonor Saunders (1999), the CIA deliberately focused on cultural products, jazz and expressionist art for example, for what they had to say about American life.

The secretive nature behind cultural activities such as art exhibitions and concert tours need not be taken, however, as evidence of sinister or immoral behaviour, especially when one considers the nature of the international context at the time.[9] Although it is clear that there were serious and unspoken motives behind the cultural activities, whether we chose to read this as evidence of a conscious conspiracy or not, is quite another matter. Indeed, this is an obvious situation where the underlying concepts (and normative assumptions) informing a narrative that accounts for cultural activities during the Cold War period require careful examination. However, it is clear that one of the distinctive features of the state's (and CIA's) attitude, especially during the early phase of the Cold War, was that the motives behind cultural activities plainly centred on the notion of a 'way of life' in every sense, and were not limited to the usual understanding of 'national interest' at the state level. All of which takes the idea of culture beyond an informative role (Ninkovich's terms), where dishing out information is the central purpose, and extends to culture a thoroughly politicized dimension in which national value systems were the crucial concern. 'The nation' has been more consciously defined and acquired a dimension that, perhaps although arguably always existent, had not been profited from to such an extent previously in foreign policy during peace-time. Certainly in the early stages of the Cold War, the cultural conflict was about determining the primacy of one value system over the opposing value system and of demonstrating that one way of life was superior to the other. Therefore, any assessment of the cultural activities of this period depends upon how we view the international context (the Cold War itself) and the domestic context (which conventional standards were informing policy makers' thinking) as well as the way in which we choose to define the idea of culture. The humanist concept still operated in the United States, but other motives had come to prevail, perhaps best illustrated by a remark made by Congressman John Davis Lodge

(R-Conn); "[t]he important thing is to bring the foreigners in here and work them over . . ." (cited in Ninkovich 1981:132). Not only were visitors to be 'worked over' in some way, but the CIA's agenda was to sell America to the world. Arguably, organizations such as the USIA and the exchange programmes found themselves caught between these two competing viewpoints (a reflection, in the USIA's case, of its dual role under Smith-Mundt), although none of this was too apparent at the time.

When we consider that the Cold War was a conflict between competing value systems and 'ways of life,' we have moved away from the humanist concept of culture and towards the anthropological concept of culture. This move was supported by the intellectual context in which the anthropological concept had, to a considerable extent, eclipsed the humanist concept of culture not only in American anthropology but also in American IR, a point discussed below. The deployment of artists and every kind of product was not simply a perversion of the humanist concept of culture but a deliberate (some might say cynical) attempt to convince people of the merits of the American way of life over the communist Soviet one. Sending a few Fulbright scholars abroad may not have contributed much to the cause of securing world peace but winning gold medals at the Olympic games certainly did help in the point scoring the Americans and Soviets were engaged in. Indeed, scoring points was the outward, and obvious, symbolic victories in a global game where success was measured in the defections of ballet dancers, the spectacular nature of shows put on in theatres and the numbers of bodies that passed through the exhibition halls. It was propaganda to be sure, but propaganda in which the stakes were highly placed – one in which the future of world order and the preservation of a 'way of life' were perceived to be at stake.

Realism and national characteristics

The credibility of the anthropological concept of culture had increased considerably during the 1930s. Cultural anthropologists had not only worked hard in the development of the new approach in social science but they had also done their bit for the war effort. Many of them had drawn portraits of 'national characteristics' for the American government. Margaret Mead sketched the American character and urged Americans to 'keep their powder dry' and to play to the strengths of their character to win the war. Her enquiry had been into the "quality of a people; their national character" (Mead 1942/1943:16) as she put it. In an obvious pitch against race theory, Mead argued that it is "not blood, but upbringing which determines all of . . . [our] ways of behaving" (Mead 1942/1943:19–20). She claimed that it was one of the advantages of cultural anthropology that it enabled one to examine 'culturally regular behaviour' and 'then to arrive at a systematic description of a people's culture.' Perhaps, the most well-known 'systematic description' in IR is

Ruth Benedict's *The Chrysanthemum and the Sword* (1946), which was a portrait of Japanese people and their culture.

It was an indication of the influence that the cultural anthropologists were beginning to enjoy as well as the impact that this particular culture concept was having at the government level that the Office of War Information commissioned much of this work. A number of anthropologists were employed by the department including Clyde Kluckhohn, Ruth Benedict and Nathan Leites. As Benedict explained, "[i]n June, 1944, I was assigned to the study of Japan. I was asked to use all the techniques I could as a cultural anthropologist to spell out what the Japanese were like" (Benedict 1946:3). 'Spelling out' what different people were like became a matter of national importance during the Second World War. As Mead pointed out, during wartime people were more interested to know the answer to the question, "[w]hat is an American, a German, an Englishman, or an Australian?" (Mead 1942/1943:17). Indeed, Ninkovich indicates that thinking in cultural terms had entered the highest echelon of American power during the war. President F.D. Roosevelt blamed German culture for the war: "[i]f ideology was rooted in culture, Germany was clearly a bad culture" (Ninkovich in Chay 1990:110). The distinction between good and bad cultures would continue to provide an important theoretical basis for thinking during the 1950s and 1960s.

The question of culture and character would remain a subject of great interest under the conditions of the Cold War where it became crucial to know 'what a Russian was like' and who could and could not be, potentially, counted on the American side. Sorting out the 'good cultures' from the 'bad' would provide an initial conventional standard in early Cold War thinking. Work on national characteristics became the vogue, and although not limited to the cultural anthropologists, it owed much to their concept of culture.[10] The assumption that communities could be reduced to type and systematically accounted for, even if this was in idealized terms as in the case of Benedict, was illustrative of the kind of work the essentialist concept of culture could produce.

The fact that it was believed that the characteristic traits of communities could be isolated and identified in cultural terms tells us that an essentialist conception of culture was the conventional intellectual tool for thinking about people and their differences during the Cold War. Today, we would as likely be interested in mapping discourses and chronicling variation as the Cold War theorists were in capturing national characteristics. Yet, the idea of a national character generated interest in the 1950s and 1960s, although much of this interest, it has to be said, was based upon prejudicial and stereo-typical assumptions, it does provide good insight into the thinking of the time. George Kennan, one of the key figures behind the American strategy of containment policy, was deeply interested in the Russian character. As a result of his diplomatic postings to the Soviet Union, Kennan was better experienced than most to shed light on Soviet attitudes and thinking. Although Kennan drew a distinction between the Russian people and their government, he did attribute certain problems to their national character. In his famous 'Long Telegram' to President Truman in 1946, he wrote; "[a]t bottom of Kremlin's neurotic view of world affairs is traditional and instinctive Russian sense of insecurity."[11]

Against this developing cultural background, a new form of IR theory begins to gain ground in the United States – Realism. Realism maintained a narrative about international politics that was state-centric, overly concerned with power and the pursuit of it in the name of the 'national interest.' It might be thought that Realism, the theoretical approach which dominated the discipline throughout the Cold War period, had nothing to say on cultural matters and, at first sight, its well known interest in power would appear to support the assumption. If we were in a less charitable mood, we might even 'blame' realism for the lack of interest in culture within IR, until recently, in view of its disciplinary dominance. However, this assessment would be misleading for not only was George Kennan influential in the practical policy aspects of the Cold War, which included the cultural dimension, but another prominent IR scholar of the time, Hans Morgenthau, was also busy working with the anthropological culture concept. Morgenthau's understanding of culture can be contrasted sharply with the inter-war theorists' conception and the humanist concept dominating British scholarship at the time (which we will examine in the next chapter).

Morgenthau clearly represented an intellectual departure from the pre-Second World War IR thinkers with respect to the concept of culture. This was, perhaps, not too surprising given Morgenthau's personal background and the intellectual climate in which he developed his ideas. Morgenthau, like Franz Boas some four decades before him, was a German-Jewish émigré to the United States, arriving there in 1937 via Geneva. Like Boas, Morgenthau was steeped in German kultur, but unlike Boas, he settled in the United States in a very different intellectual and social climate; one that Boas and his students had very much influenced. Morgenthau made his debut in the nativist atmosphere that was permeating the American social sciences and was beginning to make itself felt in foreign policy circles. We can witness the evidence of the 'new' concept at work in his most famous volume, *Politics Among Nations*, first published in 1948.

Politics Among Nations is counted among the classic Realist texts and is best remembered for the argument that international politics is better understood by way of "the concept of interest defined in terms of power" (Morgenthau 1948/1962:5), as well as detailing the 'six principles of political realism;' but it should also be considered as a landmark text in terms of the historical development of the concept of 'culture' in IR.

There were, in Morgenthau's view, perennial problems and persistent features in international politics; the most obvious were war and the balance of power. Morgenthau attempted to theorize these perennial features of international politics, although there was sufficient ambiguity in his approach for subsequent scholars to conclude that perhaps he did not achieve his theory of international politics to any great level of satisfaction.[12] Nonetheless, *Politics Among Nations* stands as a comprehensive survey of the problems and ideas affecting the international system as perceived by a thinker writing at, more or less, the mid-century point in time. In these terms, the book offers the contextualist some interesting insights into the assumptions, perceptions, concerns and thinking of the time.

As well as the usual subjects of diplomacy, law and, by now, the United Nations, Morgenthau also devoted a considerable portion of his book to discussing 'international politics as the struggle for power.' He discussed the various aspects of national power and its limitations, and the 'problem of peace' from different perspectives. Inevitably, in view of the time in which it was first written and revised (throughout the Cold War period), nationalism and ideology figure quite prominently. In many respects, the book represents a link between the issues coming out of the Second World War and those determining the Cold War. However, it is the frequent references to the term 'culture' throughout the work that are of most concern, for they are sufficient to make this, arguably, one of the key 'culture' texts in IR.

What is immediately important and certain is that the idea of 'culture' Morgenthau relied upon in his work was the anthropological concept. Unlike Alfred Zimmern who dismissed parochial expressions of culture, and especially that 'Continental' version of culture as he called it (meaning kultur), which the Germans had propagated during the First World War period,[13] Morgenthau was comfortable with a localized conception of culture. Moreover, it was clear from the outset that Morgenthau conceived of culture in a manner that encapsulated values in a relative and national way. Early on in the text, Morgenthau tells us, "theory and policy alike run counter to two trends in our culture which are not able to reconcile themselves to the assumptions and results of a rational, objective theory of politics" (Morgenthau 1948/1962:14–15). These two trends, which he despaired of, are first, the disparagement of the role of power in society and second, the opposition to 'realist theory and the practice of politics.' This opposition to political realism, he says, "stems from the very relationship that exists, and must exist, between the human mind and the political sphere … the human mind in its day-by-day operations cannot bear to look the truth of politics straight in the face" (Morgenthau 1948/1962:15).

That the 'relationship between the human mind and the political sphere' is said to be a 'trend of our culture' is revealing. It suggests that, for Morgenthau, 'culture' was more than the manifestation of artifacts or other products of intellectual and artistic achievement; it indicates that 'culture' was a matter of intellectual and social outlook itself. Aversion to 'the truth of politics' and being unable to look it 'straight in the face,' was fundamentally a serious issue. It was indicative of a general social attitude and the use of the term 'trends' more than supports this presumption. Of greater significance is Morgenthau's use of language. These are 'trends in *our* culture,' which suggests a possession of a very particular sort – culture has become a relative issue. To be able to distinguish between different types of culture (even to be able to ask the 'whose culture?' question and say that it is 'ours') represents a major departure from the humanist concept and inter-war thinking.

To speak of 'our' culture implies a certain measure of boundary and exclusivity that has not been detectable in IR theory, in cultural terms, until this point. Certainly, these qualities were detectable in the idea of civilization, particularly where references to 'Western' civilization and 'British' civilization occur, and notions of boundary and exclusivity were recognized in the form of racial and national differences as both Angell and Zimmern amply demonstrated. Yet, where these traits have been associated with the idea of civilization in British scholarship, in Morgenthau they are noticeably expressed in terms of 'culture,' which indicates a major shift in 'conventional standards.'[14] Morgenthau's use of culture was a novel development in IR; it marked the debut of an alternative frame of reference for culture in the discipline and formed the foundation for different kinds of narratives about international politics.

There are several sections in *Politics Among Nations* that deal explicitly with the subject of culture and confirm the presence of the anthropological concept in IR. First, Morgenthau discussed 'Cultural Imperialism' as part of his chapter on imperialism generally (Morgenthau 1948/ 1962:60–3). The problem of imperialism was, obviously, an ongoing and sensitive issue during the Cold War, particularly for the de-colonizing states, but it was the manner in which Morgenthau discussed this subject that provides us with excellent evidence of contextual influence in the form of the anthropological concept. In his section on the 'Cultural Approach,' Morgenthau tells us that there are some "primitive peoples" who are "receptive to the influence of foreign cultures to the point of suicide" (Morgenthau 1948/1962:521). This is obviously not a matter of cultural commonality but one of imposition, assimilation and loss and Morgenthau was clearly aware of the possibilities of this kind of cultural intrusion when he discussed the problem of imperialism. Cultural imperialism was, for Morgenthau, the deliberate "displacement of one culture by another" (Morgenthau 1948/1962:58 and 60), and potentially the more successful form of imperialism in view of its subtle and pernicious nature. Imperialism aside, the use of the terms 'displacement' and 'suicide' are particularly forceful in this context, because they demonstrated the existence of one of the key assumptions of an essentialist conception of culture; namely, that indigenous culture could be lost or eroded away by 'foreign' influences. That Morgenthau believed some communities were in danger of losing their 'culture' demonstrated his conceptual acceptance of the anthropological idea of culture and reveals to us where his normative instincts lay – losing 'culture' was a 'bad' thing.

Second, there is a larger section on 'National Characteristics' comprising three sub-sections on 'Its Existence,' 'The Russian National Character,' which is, perhaps, not too surprising in view of actual international developments, and finally, a sub-section on 'National Character and National Power.' That so much space is given over to the subject of 'national characteristics' tells us that this was an important and serious issue for Morgenthau, as it was for policy makers and anthropologists at the time. For Morgenthau, national characters are, plainly, an essential and cultural matter. According to him, the Americans exhibit "individual initiative and inventiveness," the British "undogmatic common sense," and the Germans "discipline and thoroughness" (Morgenthau 1948/ 1962:131). He goes on to tell us that the Russian character offers "striking proof of the persistence of certain intellectual and moral qualities" (Morgenthau 1948/1962:129), which is a large assumption in view of the tremendous social changes endured by the Russians. Remarkably, "the traits of the Russian national character emerged intact from the holocaust of ... [the communist] revolution" (Morgenthau 1948/1962:129), which also demonstrates the persistence of the essentialist theoretical assumption that 'ethnographic trademarks' remain unchanged. Counted among these 'persistent' Russian traits were 'a strong anti-foreign' attitude, 'secrecy,' 'spying,' 'elementary force and persistence' and a tendency towards the authoritarian policing of society. Whether this is an accurate or even meaningful portrayal of the Russian people across time and space is irrelevant, but it does provide us with an insight into the fears and perceptions of a Cold War thinker at the time. In this respect, we learn more about the context of the time, and the author's understanding of it, than we do about the Russians as real people.

The third way in which culture appears in this text, and, perhaps, of greater significance, is the substantial section he allocated to discussing 'The Cultural Approach' of UNESCO versus the 'The Functional Approach' of other international organizations and agencies. Morgenthau dissected the merits of each approach for its capacity to effect a peaceful transformation of the world community. Naturally, the Cultural Approach was dismissed since this turned out to be humanist culture and the stuff of interchange. Morgenthau was critical of the work of UNESCO, but this should not be mistaken for a rejection of the importance of 'culture' in his thinking generally, a point discussed below. Finally, there are a number of issues that might also be considered to be of 'cultural' significance, notably his discussion of 'world public opinion,' the sections on 'moral' questions, and the sub-section on 'propaganda,' obviously a subject of topical concern for those interested in promoting the 'American way of life' during the Cold War.[15]

Morgenthau's conviction that similar problems may occur with regularity and frequent patterning over time, led him to refer to such things as 'cultural patterning,' which indicated the influence of Ruth Benedict's work at least. When he discussed national character, he told us that:

> We are not concerned here with the question of what factors are responsible for the development of a national character. We are only interested in the fact – contested but (it seems to us) incontestable, especially in view of the anthropological concept of the "cultural pattern" – that certain qualities of intellect and character occur more frequently and are more highly valued in one nation than in another.
>
> (Morgenthau 1948/1962:126)

The 'fact' of national character and its 'existence' (the subheading for the section) may have been contested in some academic circles, but the obviousness of certain valued qualities, and therefore the 'incontestability' of national character, were reinforced, for Morgenthau, by the anthropological concept of 'cultural patterning.' Taken together, the empirical 'fact' of the matter and the weight of anthropological thinking, for Morgenthau, placed the notion of national character beyond dispute. The most pertinent critical observation to make is that the 'fact' of national character and of 'cultural patterning' remain largely instinctive and highly contestable forms of knowledge, despite the 'fact' that cultural anthropologists would have agreed with Morgenthau at the time. However, the anthropologists' idea of culture would appear less controversial and contestable for a scholar, such as Morgenthau, raised in kultur and striving for scientific explanations. Morgenthau quotes from Samuel Taylor Coleridge (Morgenthau 1948/1962:126–7) in order to affirm that nations have 'invisible spirits' that 'breathe through a whole people' making them distinct from one another, and further cites the differences between Immanuel Kant, René Descartes, Edmund Burke and John Dewey, as testimony of the "unmistakable distinctiveness" of each nation, and of its effects on 'intellectual qualities' (Morgenthau 1948/1962:127). When this is supported by the scientific enterprise of anthropology, culture becomes the undoubted source of differentiation and lends theoretical weight to the evidence of difference between national communities.[16]

There are several general comments to be made here with regard to the role of 'culture' in *Politics Among Nations*. First, 'culture' is a prevalent term throughout the text, and one requiring no special indexation, which tells us that this word is part of Morgenthau's everyday language. Second, the particular attention paid to 'culture,' and the subjects specifically discussed in relation with it, reveal the extent, and manner, to which he considered 'culture' to be a significant feature of international relations. For example, though crudely put, Morgenthau clearly believed that the 'culture' identified with UNESCO was ineffectual, while the 'culture' that gave rise to 'national characteristics' was unavoidable. Third, even through the various editions of, and additions to, the text, the notion of culture remained a persistent element of concern, confirming its continued importance in international affairs. Finally, the text seems to do two things; it offers us an expansion of ideas involving culture in IR (by, primarily, introducing the anthropological concept to the discipline) and it also supplies confirmation of the contextual significance of 'culture' in American discourse. The anthropological concept of culture was by 1948 informing narratives about international relations in a manner thoroughly disconnected from those informed by the humanist concept.

The tide turns against humanism

While the humanist concept lent support to narratives that promoted a cosmopolitan discourse, the anthropological concept was helping to shift the balance towards difference and particularity. Both concepts can be seen at work in American thinking during the Cold War, but each is accorded a differing normative value in international affairs. Where the humanist idea of culture was something to be either argued against at the international level or tolerated as a minor, individual, issue, the anthropological concept was being elevated to a significant role in the background of international relations.

In the manner in which Elgin Williams found it difficult to accept the equal validity of cultures posited by Ruth Benedict's thesis (since that would mean tolerating Hitler's regime), so some similar ethical difficulties of conceptual distinction emerged over cultural products in IR. On the one hand, American organizations and individuals seemingly had little difficulty in inviting German artistes and orchestral conductors to the United States in spite of their connections to the former Nazi regime (although Jewish organizations obviously objected to their presence); while on the other hand, communist equivalents were resisted on political grounds.[17] Although the separation of art from politics on this matter seemed arbitrary and spurious, contemporaries did not appear overly troubled by the distinction.

Kennan laid out the case for accepting cultural products:

> In recent years, there has grown up among us a most reprehensible habit, a totalitarian habit in fact, of judging the suitability of cultural contributions by whatever political coloration we conceive their creators to have acquired. I know of nothing sillier than this. A painting is not more or less valuable because the artist once belonged to this or that party or contributed to this or that group ... After all, cultural events are not political livestock exhibits in which we put forward

human figures to be admired for the purity of their ideological features.

(Cited in Saunders 1999:227)

In short, the value of an artistic product was to be measured by the humanist concept of culture.[18] Whereas in the ideological war with communism all products associated with that ideology were to be measured by the politics that spawned them. It may be a double standard, and, with hindsight, overtly hypocritical, to distinguish between politics and art in this way, but it should not be confusing.[19]

In the least, contemporaries did not admit to any confusion themselves and since, in contextual terms, we must allow some space for accepting that people have some idea of what they are referring to, our task as subsequent readers is to attempt an understanding. People like Kennan did not admit to theoretical confusion because they recognized the politics behind the Soviet cultural messages – the question generated by the contextual method is how could this distinction be maintained? A cynic might remark that the Americans recognized the difference because they were engaged in the same political strategy; selecting musicians, artists, and all manner of cultural artifacts for what they had to say about the American way of life rather than simply for what they had to contribute to the world of art. Yet, it is arguable that the distinction was being drawn between humanist categories of culture, i.e. all 'good' art is the same and valued on those terms, and the political ambitions of states. Products made on behalf of the state and seen to be glorifying it were to be viewed suspiciously.[20] Since the Soviet state controlled and directed every aspect of cultural life, everything attached to that system could only be viewed with suspicion. Conversely, Louis Armstrong did not make music for the state, nor was he compelled to do so (but he could be showcased on behalf of America).

The humanist idea of culture appeared to have been returned to the realm of the individual and removed from the international sphere and disassociated with the state. For Kennan humanist expressions of culture still had an appreciative value, but it was Morgenthau who explicitly declared that this form of cultural exchange had no value in international politics. What is clear is that, during the Cold War, cultural artifacts were not being put to political use in the way they used to be and certainly not in the way the inter-war theorists believed they ought to be. Art still could be accepted for its universal and aesthetic qualities, but that did not make it a valuable commodity when it came to conducting international politics. On the other hand, the culture that determined different ways of life, the anthropological concept, was not only capable of shaping the character of national politics it also and obviously affected the nature of international politics. Kennan was at the sharp end of this kind of politics in international affairs, pitting the American way of life, 'culture,' against that of the Soviets and using all available means. Indeed, he would congratulate the Congress of Cultural Freedom in 1959 for its work[21] and would, in 1967, say that the "flap about CIA money was quite unwarranted ... I never felt the slightest pangs of conscience about it" (cited in Saunders 1999:408). Like the Congress for Cultural Freedom, Kennan thought the CIA ought to have been praised for its work. Although the distinction between art, politics and culture appears contradictory, it makes better sense once the two concepts of culture have been disengaged from one another and we have considered the theoretical scheme which lies behind the argument.

For Realists, appreciation of the rumba was not going to make much of an impression on US–Latin American relations for example, but when it came to demonstrating the superiority of the American way of life over the communist one, jazz musicians could be called upon to do their bit in 'winning' the Cold War (or so it was believed at the time), not for what they actually did, but for what they represented, i.e. American values such as the freedom of expression. It is only by appreciating the distinction between the humanist concept that had been popular in international relations during the inter-war period and the context in which the anthropological concept experienced popularity in the aftermath of the Second World War, that some of the confusion and 'moral inconsistency' Frances Stonor Saunders has identified with this period can be accounted for (Saunders 1999:227). The confusion, seemingly, arises (for current writers) because the same or similar objects and artifacts, say jazz music or paintings for example, can be viewed in two distinct ways and produced within a number of narratives of international relations.

Under the humanist idea of culture, jazz music can be referred to as an example of the universal appeal of products within a cosmopolitan narrative, or it can be criticized as the evidence of some kind of elitist behaviour/attitude within a Cultural Studies type narrative. In addition, a jazz concert could be cited as an example of propagandist cultural policy, which, again, might fit better within a Cultural Studies narrative given its interest in power relationships. Alternatively, and this is unique to IR, examples of humanist culture, such as jazz music, can be rejected as irrelevant to international politics within a Realist narrative. Yet, it might be said that even to deny the value this kind of cultural artifact exerts in international politics is to acknowledge its significance (or at least that of its advocates) in no small way. Finally, under the anthropological concept, jazz music can appear as indicative of a way of life, which is taken for granted. This kind of culture is believed to account for the different kinds of politics which states produce and supports a particularist narrative (which does not, necessarily, have to be Realist).

It is only by carefully assessing the narratives in which 'objects' or products like jazz music, for example, appear that the meaning of them can be discerned in the context in which they are placed. This is to say, we need to know the thinking, the motives and the purposes behind an artifact's place in an individual scholar's and practitioner's scheme of things and we need to know this under their terms, not ours. This distinction (or difficulty) is clearly visible in Morgenthau's work, and serves to confirm the irrelevancy of the humanist concept to international relations and the growing importance of the anthropological concept to IR.

For Morgenthau, the political sphere was quite distinct from other spheres of 'life' namely the economic, legal and religious (Morgenthau 1948/1962:14). All of these things may have an international aspect but they did not constitute part of the political sphere in Morgenthau's view, nor did they constitute what he had in mind for the disciplinary activity of international relations. Any confusion that arises over the term 'culture' can be easily dealt with if we draw out the distinction between the humanist and anthropological conceptualizations. Morgenthau employed both concepts but placed a contrasting normative emphasis on each, which reveals to us the values and motives underpinning his thinking.

When discussing the sphere of international politics Morgenthau suggests that nations engage in varied forms of international activity with one another but these forms of engagement are not necessarily, nor are they always, political. Crucially, "a nation is not normally engaged in international politics when it . . . promotes the distribution of cultural achievements throughout the world" (Morgenthau 1948/1962:28). This stands in sharp contrast to the League era and those scholars who believed that 'promoting the distribution of cultural achievements' explicitly served an international political purpose. Here Morgenthau appeared to be disassociating the idea of cultural interchange as envisaged by the League era thinkers from international politics itself. The humanist expression of culture was, like religion, separable from the sphere of international politics in Morgenthau's thinking. Indeed the distinction between Morgenthau and the cultural internationalists (those involved with the ICIC, for example) becomes most obvious when he discussed the possibilities for building a 'world community' via the 'cultural approach' as exemplified by UNESCO (Morgenthau 1948/1962:chapter thirty). On this issue, Morgenthau demonstrated an opposition to 'international cultural relations' and the presumed effectiveness of the work of organizations like UNESCO in the same manner that fuelled C.K. Webster and Sidney Herbert's criticism of the poetry exchange organized by the ICIC. Morgenthau argued, "[t]hat an intellectual elite in the United States enjoys Russian music and literature and that Shakespeare has not been banned from the Russian stage has no relevance at all for the problem with which we are concerned" (Morgenthau 1948/1962:522). The problem that concerned him at this point in the text was the prospects for building a peaceful world community. This is similar to the criticisms of the effectiveness of 'international cultural relations' made by Nicholas Spykman and President Nixon. However, although Morgenthau was plainly hostile towards the idea of cultural interchange this was not simply on the grounds of effectiveness. In the light of his pessimistic view of human nature, his criticisms would seem to have an ontological basis nullifying the usefulness of cultural exchange from the outset. There is more than a simple 'realistic' rejection of the effectiveness of cultural interchange at work here. In order to discern what Morgenthau intended by his objections to the 'cultural approach' in international politics, it is necessary to separate out his political objections from his theoretical understanding. That is to say, we should not mistake the argument against the possibilities for creating a peaceful world community for an argument against the idea of culture itself, even though his objections were seemingly levelled against the value of culture and, especially, the international value of culture as something to be exchanged.

In his chapter on 'The World Community,' the humanist concept is instantly and easily detectable; here he writes "of educational and cultural activities aiming at the interchange of the products of national cultures" (Morgenthau 1948/1962:521–2). It is important to note that this interchange involves the products not simply of peoples and/or nations but of 'national cultures.' Zimmern would not have considered that nations had 'culture' in the same sense. Morgenthau rejected the idea of cultural interchange that derived from the humanist concept in this section, and it is clear that he was sceptical of the argument that this would lead, somehow, to mutual benefit. He doubts the effectiveness of culture as an instrument for creating a 'world community' in the manner that fuelled the thinking of Zimmern, for example. However, it is the second idea of culture that, although less obvious in this chapter (but located throughout the text), is fundamental to Morgenthau's thinking and marks the distinction between culture as a matter of 'achievement' from culture as 'a way of life,' or, 'our' culture as he referred to it. Indeed, his discussion of UNESCO focuses explicitly on the 'educational and intellectual' activities conducted by that organization, not on any life-forming, or nativist, aspects. Moreover, he wasted no energy in revealing and dismissing the assumptions upon which the work of that organization was founded. The 'assumption that nations go to war because they do not know each other well enough,' and that increased contact would 'foster mutual understanding' and lead to a more peaceful world order, represented a 'congenital defect' in the philosophy that generates cultural and educational interchange, he argued (Morgenthau 1948/1962:520). Morgenthau not only questioned the theoretical assumptions underpinning 'international cultural relations,' he rejected them outright.[22] In arguing against the humanist concept he was also acknowledging the influence it had enjoyed. Morgenthau's view of culture and its role in international relations was precisely the opposite to that of Zimmern; he dismissed the universal notion of culture in favour of that 'continental' version Zimmern so despised.

Morgenthau takes a few examples, apparently at 'random,' to:

> show that the quantity and quality of education and culture as such is obviously irrelevant to the issue of a world community. That issue hinges, not upon knowledge and the creation and appreciation of cultural values, but upon a moral and political transformation of unprecedented dimensions.
>
> (Morgenthau 1948/1962:521)

What is interesting about the above statement, as well as the examples that Morgenthau used to support it, is that it illustrates the influence of both the humanist and anthropological concepts of culture. The 'quality and quantity of education and culture' (the humanist expression) are dismissed as 'irrelevant to the issue of a world community' from an anthropological point of view. That this is so is revealed by the notion (assumption) that there were 'cultural values' of which we could have 'knowledge and appreciation,' and which were of 'local' relevance. Indeed their relevance was in shaping the national character and forming the context in which national politics were made. In the above statement, one conception of culture was being relied upon to undermine and refute the other idea of culture. The use of the phrase 'cultural values' was particularly revealing in this respect; in humanist terms culture was something to be valued and appreciated universally, it did not denote values of a specific 'cultural' type. For Morgenthau, the 'cultural values' that mattered and which influenced world politics were local and national, and were, therefore, quite specific.

In Morgenthau's view, humanist 'culture' was not an effective, reliable, or even useful, instrument of the state, or a conglomeration of states, capable of achieving political ends; although he was fully aware that states make full use of 'culture,' which he variously discussed as propaganda, ideology and nationalism.[23] Morgenthau was not interested in humanist culture or its cosmopolitan possibilities. Culture was, for him, seriously a matter of local community values not the superficiality of quantity and quality of education found in UNESCO and deployed, by that organization, for larger political purposes. In this way, culture played an intrinsic role in national political life, but it had no, effective, role in international life in terms of the deliberate and conscious deployment of certain artifacts or achievements deemed cultural. It should also be noted that Morgenthau's examples were always expressed in national terms, i.e. the Germans, the Chinese, the Russians etc., indicating, therefore, that the most conspicuous level at which the most salient understanding of culture manifested itself, in his theory, was local and national, not international. For Morgenthau, local culture came in the form of the nation-state, rather than any sub-national cultural identity, which would, arguably, be the most common association today.[24]

Within the first few pages of *Politics Among Nations*, Morgenthau tells us that, "the kind of interest determining political action in a particular period of history depends upon the political and cultural context within which foreign policy is formulated" (Morgenthau 1948/1962:9). More importantly, he tells us that "[t]he same observations [noted above in respect of foreign policy] apply to the concept of power. Its content and the manner of its use are determined by the political and cultural environment" (Morgenthau 1948/1962:9). From the outset, Morgenthau allocated to culture a significant and contingent role in his theory; both 'interests (formulated as foreign policy) and power' were culturally determined in some way or other. This aspect of his theory has been overlooked, given, as we commonly are, to focusing on 'power and interest' in his text, rather than the context in which he thought these things operate and are formulated. Yet, it was clear, given the number of references Morgenthau made to culture in *Politics Among Nations* that power and the pursuit of national interest were determined by the local habits, characteristics and traits that culture created. Ethnographic trademarks influenced manifestations of power and in turn, the foreign policy which a state generated. Political rationalism, then, was likely to vary with the cultural circumstance. No wonder there was so much interest in national characteristics at this time. If the natives could be reduced to type then it might shed some light on the way a nation-state behaved in international relations. Indeed interest in state behaviour was growing in IR during the 1960s.[25]

Morgenthau counted culture as one of the universal elements of human life, but fitting the community value of culture into a 'universal' theoretical framework proves problematic. It is a major assumption of Morgenthau that cultural differences divide us, that everyone has culture, and it makes us what we are, but unlike subsequent theorists who employ an essentialist version of the anthropological concept of culture (say Samuel Huntington for example) it is not clear how this notion of 'culture' manifests itself in international relations. At the basic level, Morgenthau clearly recognized that fundamental differences exist between communities and that these represent a serious difficulty in international relations; "[e]ven if the American, Russian, and Indian could speak to each other, they would speak with different tongues, and if they uttered the same words, those words would signify different objects, values, and aspirations to each of them" (Morgenthau 1948/1962:265). Unlike the cultural internationalists of the inter-war period, there are no grounds here for a common cultural discourse or interchange. As Margaret Mead suggested, Morgenthau takes the view that we are fundamentally shaped in our differences and fixed by them:

> The same item of information and the same idea mean something different to an American, a Russian, and an Indian; for that item of

information and that idea are perceived by, assimilated to, and filtered through minds conditioned by different experiences and molded by different conceptions of what is true, good, and politically desirable and expedient.

(Morgenthau 1948/1962:265)

People of different nations are fundamentally incommensurable and culture is the driving force behind their differences. All of these differences in understanding, attachment and meaning affect the way we understand, perceive and do business with one another at the international level. Although it is clear that Morgenthau recognized differences as problematic in international relations and that these differences are a matter of culture, it is not certain how these two conceptions fit together. Problematically, Morgenthau frequently fills the void between these essential differences and the perennial political problems they generate with the 'blanket' idea of psychological forces.[26] The presence of this 'psycho-sociological' strand in his work makes it all the more difficult to ascertain a precise role for culture in his theory generally, since some of these 'psycho-sociological' elements are conveyed by his use of culture and seem to substitute, at times, for the language of culture.[27] Yet, since Kennan was similarly interested in 'psychological' matters, particularly psychological warfare, it is fair to suggest that for IR scholars there was an overlap in their thinking between psychological and cultural issues when it came to international politics.

The difficult question centres on how far Morgenthau envisaged culture affecting international politics, particularly in view of his argument that political realism affords a truthful insight into the world of international relations and its perennial problems. Unfortunately for us it was largely the political effectiveness of culture at the international level and his arguments against 'cultural interchange' that concentrate his mind, rather than him thinking through the relationship between the ideas he is using. Nonetheless, culture is clearly an important concept in *Politics Among Nations*. Culture defines the national character, it informs the context in which power and foreign policy manifest themselves, and it is a universal matter – all communities have culture. This is 'our' culture, while the differences between communities are indicative of 'theirs.' Paraphrasing George Stocking from chapter two (this book), there is no 'progress' here; all nations are 'equally cultured.' Culture was taken by Morgenthau to be a universal phenomenon, manifesting itself in a multiplicity of forms, so much so that there was plenty of variety to be found in Realism and all of it is culturally based (anthropologically speaking).

Not only did Morgenthau consider culture the source of difference between people, but it was also plain that he conceived of culture as the particular expression of an unavoidable and necessary aspect of what it meant to be human. As he said, "[a]ll human beings want to be free, and, hence, want to have those opportunities for self-expression and self-development which *their particular culture* considers to be desirable" (Morgenthau 1948/1962:262 – my emphasis). All of which indicated that Morgenthau had a thorough appreciation of the anthropological concept in its essentialist guise. Differences entailed a 'way of life' and were fundamental to human existence. Culture was a complete communal entity/experience, which could be eroded under extreme circumstances, while in its purest expression it was discrete and exclusive. It belonged to a specific 'community;' was about *otherness*, invoked *meaning*, and depended upon a measure of environmental determinism; while national characters were accepted as the visible evidence of 'ethnographic trademarks.' Further, culture was spoken of in terms of consensus, homogeneity, unity and continuity. The appropriate level of application for culture was local and where the natives dwelt, and for Morgenthau this was most frequently expressed at the level of the nation as national culture. Where cultural commonality did not exist, as was the case within the modern states-system, it could not be made to prevail. All of this represented a fairly coherent and thorough appreciation of the main tenets of the anthropological concept of culture, as it existed during the Cold War period. This reading of Morgenthau assists our understanding of the Realist dismissal of 'culture' as an effective instrument in international relations and their promotion of 'culture' as a way of life at the international level. The humanist concept of culture had clashed with the anthropological concept during the early days of the Cold War, and seemingly had lost.

Morgenthau was, then, a typical example of an author labouring under contemporary 'factory conditions' and the prevailing conventional standards of his time and place – the anthropological concept of culture was taken-for-granted in his work. His criticisms of UNESCO, and the manner in which he dismissed the role of cultural exchange at the international level, serve to demonstrate that, fundamentally speaking, this is not the culture that mattered for Morgenthau; nor did it matter at the international level for Kennan either. Humanist culture had no place in the realm of international politics – it was an irrelevancy, although it may still be appreciated by individuals in the native setting, whereas the culture that determined ways of life obviously has a crucial role to play, especially in the make-up of nations. Given the theoretical significance of this kind of culture (the culture that shapes communities), inevitably, it was too important an issue to be ignored, especially if it could be employed in an exemplary capacity by the state. Once the 'way of life' had been identified, it could be put to political use at home and abroad. The substantive differences lay with the level of consciousness and certainty that a 'way of life' could be identified as part of a scientific programme of study. Morgenthau's work not only marks a turning point in IR literature, but also confirms that the anthropological concept had become a conventional standard in the American context. By the time these assumptions have become absorbed as conventional standards, the possibilities for its protection and deployment have become greatly extended in American thinking. The anthropological concept was informing the context in which culture could play a distinct role in national politics in a way quite distinct from the international cultural relations of the inter-war period. As Ninkovich points out, 'where once culture had formerly been the solution in American thinking, it had, during the Cold War, become the problem' (Ninkovich in Chay 1990:113). Culture was now clearly identified as the source of differences between nations. In *Politics Among Nations*, the natives trumped the tourists and their cosmopolitan ideas of culture. This trend was set to expand in both theory and practice. In IR, the transformation becomes visible in British scholarship through the work of international society theorists.

Key points

- The Second World War finds culture controlled and manipulated by the state.
- Cultural anthropological work continues to raise the profile of the anthropological concept in the American context.
- Interest in the humanist concept declines.
- This decline is confirmed in Morgenthau's theory of political realism and Kennan's interest in practical realism.
- Culture is used as a weapon in the Cold War – as indicative of American values and way of life rather than 'the best of everything' to foster mutual understanding.
- *Politics Among Nations* is hostile to humanist culture – the text relies on the anthropological concept and marks the debut of the idea in IR.
- *Politics Among Nations* supports the case for the anthropological concept and its influence in national and international affairs against the humanist concept.

5   International cultural society

During the early stages of the Cold War, and while American social science and the general public were busy embracing the anthropological concept of culture, the British retained the view that culture was 'the best of everything' in the humanist sense. In spite of the growing criticism in British literary studies that culture was more popular than exemplary, the humanist concept still dominated large areas of society and thinking. Gradually, however, under the growing influence of the anthropological concept, the British incorporated the idea that culture was a 'way of life' in their social and intellectual discourses. We can map the changing fortunes of the idea of culture and its meaning in Britain, to some extent, through the work of International Society theorists.

What is especially interesting about International Society theory, or the English school as it is sometimes called, is that this approach stands as one of the few areas in IR where the idea of 'culture' is allocated a specific place in a narrative of international relations. For scholars who adopt the International Society approach, international politics are more than just the relations between states. States form a society, with rules and norms, and the idea that supports this society is 'culture.' A key question then, is whether, or not, the term culture meant the same thing to all scholars in International Society, or in this chapter, whether it meant the same thing to the three key scholars, Martin Wight, Hedley Bull and R.J. Vincent.

A cultural basis for international society

International society has always been considered more than 'mere relations between states;' it entails international relations that are 'more or less permanent,' 'reciprocal,' and 'systematic' (Wight 1977:22).

When, in *Systems of States*, Martin Wight wrote, "[w]e must assume that a states-system will not come into being without a degree of cultural unity among its members" (Wight 1977:33), it was clear that he had a different conception of the nature of culture from that of the League of Nations thinkers. Although culture enjoyed a significant role in the international system for some inter-war theorists, it is Wight's notion of unity which implies that the place of culture is more substantial than the exchange of gifts between people, for the states-system (or international society as it will be subsequently called). Unlike the thinkers of the First World War period, for whom the concept of culture might be said to have played a peripheral role within the context of civilization theorizing, International Society theorists afforded the concept of culture a central and crucial role from the outset.

For the League era scholars, the idea of culture occupied a largely instrumental and narrowly stated place within their internationalist narrative – culture was the means for realizing a more civilized and peaceful form of cooperation in international relations; with International Society theory the concept of culture is a much broader notion and has a normative and social content. Culture was seen to be the basis of international society. It also seems very clear that this is not the possessive sense of 'culture' that Hans Morgenthau relied upon. This is not 'our' culture in the nationalized sense, it is something all states, party to the system, share.

At first sight then, it appears that the culture of international society is a greater substantial issue in international relations than that which operated under the humanist concept during the 1920s (i.e. it is more than the interchange of gifts) and it also seems to be something less parochial than the ideas which the anthropological concept was generating in American thinking during the Cold War (i.e. it is not limited to a specific national grouping).

The idea of culture has always been taken to be central to the International Society approach, yet when the complaint circulated the discipline, in the 1990s, that IR had neglected the subject of culture it necessarily had to be pointed out, as did Tim Dunne, that while some claimed 'the return of culture and identity to IR', "for the English School, questions of culture and identity never went away" (Dunne 1998:189). This is obviously so in view of the fact that a 'common culture' is the distinguishing feature of international society, but, given the centrality of the concept in this theory, it is somewhat surprising that no one, neither the International Society theorists themselves nor their critics, has considered closely what 'culture' means to this theory.[1] The basic assumption that international society is secured through the concept of culture has been left largely undisturbed; yet, such an acceptance is not quite as unproblematic as it seems. Although it is clear that the basic concept caused Hedley Bull and R.J. Vincent some difficulty, the actual idea of culture, its meaning and relationship to the idea of international society, has not been thoroughly interrogated.

In contextual terms, this lack of discussion over the meaning of 'culture' is revealing as it is elsewhere in the history of the discipline. It suggests that the idea of culture was sufficiently understood by the theory's scholars, readers and subsequent commentators to be taken for granted in all of its essentials. It also follows that if the culture of international society has been drawn upon as a conventional standard from the broader social and intellectual context, it is possible that the meaning of culture may have changed in that context. If this proves to be the case, then it might affect our understanding of culture in the theory, especially since work with this theory spans several decades of British history.

Two questions arise; first, what was the context in which this theory emerged and was subsequently worked? And second, how did individual scholars react to the context? The first question focuses on what it was reasonably possible for these theorists to know at a given point in time, while the second rests upon what they thought (as far as we can establish it) and how they used their ideas.[2] Was the idea of culture that helped to establish the theory in the 1960s, the same idea found informing scholars' thinking in the 1970s or 1980s?

International Society theory was established through the work of a small group of like-minded scholars who, in January 1959, "gathered to form a Committee to investigate the fundamental questions of 'international theory'" (Dunne 1998:xi). 'The British Committee,' as Dunne describes it, met regularly to present and discuss work on international relations; Martin Wight, principally an historian, was one of the founding members and an influential figure among the group.

Wight's idea of international society sought commonality amid diversity and, crucially, to locate that commonality at the international level. In his thinking, 'culture' denoted unity at the international level and was much more than simply *the means* for fostering mutual understanding. Wight, unlike the League scholars, did not rule out the possibility and presence of war within the international system, and therefore his idea of culture had little or no instrumental role in that capacity.[3] The terms of culture were more broadly conceived; 'culture' was, now, the foundation stone of society itself, which indicated an important theoretical expansion of the concept's role beyond that of intellectual exchange. In this respect, Wight took an innovative step with respect to the role of culture in IR, one that maintained a link with some of the international ideas and aspirations of the League of Nations era. Yet, beyond the simple definitional statement that 'culture' was unity and commonality, and distinguished international society from mere contact between states, there was a good deal of ambiguity in Wight's references to culture.

When Wight told us that "Western men are perhaps more various in their range of beliefs than the men of any other culture" (Butterfield and Wight 1966:89), he obviously assumed that there were other 'cultures' and values to be aware of. In *De systematibus civitatum* the three systems he considered "each arose within a single culture" (Wight 1977:33), which again implied that he was able to individuate 'cultures' in anthropological terms. Moreover, his work revealed a number of other parochial references to culture when, for example, he wrote of "other cultures" (Wight

1977:39), "cultural difference" (Wight 1977:85), "cultural grouping" (Wight 1977:128) as well as of the specific cultures of historical international societies. There were also references to what Wight termed "high" culture (Wight 1977:104–5), which also seemed to suggest that the primary culture concept was anthropological since it was only possible to identify a 'high' culture where a more pervasive and 'mass' culture was at work.

Yet, at other times, Wight spoke with a distinctly humanist voice. When he referred to "cultural interchange" (Wight 1977:26), "cultural interdependence" (Wight 1977:24) and medieval Europe's "unity of culture among intellectuals" (Butterfield and Wight 1966:93) it was clear that these were instances of 'culture' that cut across orthodox (and the anthropological definition of cultural) boundaries. Moreover, the Saracens and Frankish Crusaders, he said, engaged in "fruitful cultural exchange" (Wight 1977:121) in Spain and the Levant. These references to cultural interchange, cultural exchange, interdependence and the unity of intellectuals are all reminiscent of the humanist concept. There appeared to be some tension between the anthropological and humanist concepts of culture in Wight's work. Indeed, he recognized this difficulty in his re-reading of Grotius in 1971. Wight noted that Grotius "does not relate ... [the] variety of law that he glimpses to difference of culture" (Wight 1977:127). Grotius, according to Wight, defined international law " 'from the will of all nations, or of many,' " and this was not, as Wight recognized, "a multi-cultural or multi-civilizational international society" (Wight 1977:127). The use of language here is very interesting; to write of 'cultural differences' and 'multi-cultural' society indicates that anthropological thinking has seeped into the British context, but it was also clear that these ideas were being rejected by Wight in favour of an international conception of culture.

In view of the importance of Grotius to Wight's thinking, this abstraction and distinction from local culture acquires considerable significance. It is not simply the case that we must decide if culture at the international level is an either/or issue in International Society theory, as though it must be either anthropological or humanist (for Wight is, arguably, too subtle a creature for that kind of approach), it is more the case that we need to establish the contextual limitations and grasp Wight's intentions sensitively to establish what this international culture means in its *own* right. The concept of culture informing International Society appears to have its own unique qualities and mode of existence, above that of the concept of multi-culturalism. Whatever culture amounted to in Wight's work, it was clearly an ambiguous issue, yet a similar level of ambiguity (or confusion) was prevalent among the work of other British scholars during his time.

British scholars through the 1950s and 1960s appeared to operate with a complex, some might say confusing, tri-partite arrangement of concepts.

This is to say, some were still working with the civilization concept in conjunction with the humanist concept of culture, as British scholars had done since the nineteenth century. In addition there was growing awareness of the anthropological concept and we find phrases like 'their culture' creeping into literature. However, in spite of these instances, it can be suggested that British scholars could not have fully internalized the implications of the anthropological concept despite their increasing knowledge of it.

In Britain, Arnold Toynbee was aware of Alfred Kroeber and Ruth Benedict by 1961, yet he continued to employ the civilization concept and he still felt required to conduct a discussion as to whether culture should or should not include values (Toynbee 1961:272–80). If Toynbee had fully grasped the anthropological concept then the discussion would have been unnecessary because that notion absorbs values.

As late as 1975, the historian Norman Daniel was compelled to explain why, in his view, the civilization concept was no longer appropriate, and why he had borrowed the term 'culture' from anthropology to discuss differences between communities of people.[4] And in 1981, Raymond Williams distinguished three contemporary meanings of culture; first as a developed state of mind (being cultured), second as the processes of this development, and third as the means of these processes. Williams also recognized that these categories of culture co-existed "with the anthropological and extended sociological use to indicate the 'whole way of life' of a distinct people or other social group" (Williams 1981/1989:11). However, he went on to note, "[i]n our time," the third category (the means of process) was the "most common general meaning" of the word (Williams 1981/1989:11).

According to Williams, then, the conventional understanding of the term culture among the British, at least until the late 1970s, was as art, literature, opera and ballet – it was still predominately the humanist notion that informed most people's immediate thinking on this matter.

Martin Wight belonged to a generation of scholars working through the 1950s and 1960s for which the anthropological concept was not an obviously recognizable issue as it is today. Remembering that, as late as 1948, T.S. Eliot had struggled to define 'culture' in a qualitative form, from a European perspective. More importantly, although Eliot had noted the anthropological concept, in *Notes Towards A Definition of Culture*, he considered it only fit for 'primitive' societies. The distinction between culture as art etc. and the culture of 'primitives' appeared to have been common practice in British scholarship as Raymond Williams, Arnold Toynbee and Norman Daniel indicated. It is quite likely that Wight would have been aware of this practice, at least through his association with Toynbee, but more commonly as a British 'conventional standard.' The context here does not directly indicate that it is the anthropological concept informing Wight's work, least of all an essentialist version of it, although, clearly, the influence of this concept is growing and awareness of it increasing. Whatever culture means to Wight, it is not a straight-forward version of the humanist concept, nor is it obviously anthropological, as Ruth Benedict and Margaret Mead understood the term.

Two things are certain about international society in Wight's conception; first, that it is secured through a conception of culture at the international level, and second, it precedes society. Famously, Wight wrote "[a] states-system presupposes a common culture" (Wight 1977:46). This claim is so well known that its obvious problematic content has been obscured by the familiarity of the statement. That Wight insisted upon this order of relationship between culture and society tells us something about his concept of culture.[5] R.J. Vincent later commenting on Wight's suggestion 'that a states-system pre-supposes a common culture,' said, "[h]e [Wight] surely intended that this idea should have a content of its own, and not be the mere summation of the ingredients of a States-system" (Vincent 1980:256). Furthermore, Vincent tells us that he "take[s] Martin Wight's emphasis on a States-system's presupposition of a common culture to be an underlining of the importance of this point: culture might be, in Parsonian language, a prerequisite and not a mere requisite, and thus fundamental" (Vincent 1980:259). Whether Wight would have agreed with Talcott Parsons here is another matter, but it is clear that Vincent recognized the underlying importance of the idea of culture in Wight's work.

The difficulty is, how should we understand 'culture' as a prerequisite and as something that precedes society? At best it could be said today that culture co-exists with society, for it is difficult, in general theoretical terms, to imagine that people form 'culture' (as a 'way of life') prior to forming society; and there is no reason to think that international society is any different here, at least in principle.

An essentialist might argue that 'culture' is the product of society or belongs to a community of people, whereas an anti-essentialist might posit that 'culture' is something a society of people do or create on an emergent basis. The argument that people, or even states, form a culture before they form society is rather odd, unless of course it does not mean a 'way of life' in the anthropological sense, but something much less discrete, deterministic and coherent.

The culture of international society might be a more open issue in Wight's conception at least. When, for example, Wight enquired into 'how we could describe this international cultural community,' he raised certain questions:

> Does it consist essentially in a common morality and a common code, leading to agreed rules about warfare, hostages, diplomatic immunity, the right of asylum and so on? Does it require common assumptions of a deeper kind, religious or ideological?
>
> (Wight 1977:34)

That he asks these questions gives us some indication as to what the 'international cultural community' might (and might not) involve, but we should not draw the direct conclusion that 'international culture' does involve these things, for the international community may survive without them. That he did not address the issue with any certainty created some difficulty for subsequent readers. However, it was clear that a 'common morality and common code' were intended by Wight to be universally (within the states-system) accepted common goods, rather than a statement of ethnocentrisms. One may be able to accuse Wight of ethnocentrism (or as Hedley Bull did of eurocentrism), but Wight himself had his eyes on what was common to the international system as a whole, as well as all human beings.[6] Further, that Wight could even raise the question as to whether common culture 'required assumptions of a deeper kind' necessarily implied that the two might not belong together in his mind. Common assumptions of a deeper kind are, of course, taken-for-granted by the anthropological concept. Indeed, the essentialist conception only succeeds because it is believed that 'culture' invokes and defines 'deeper assumptions' in a unique and meaningful sense for the natives who have been identified as sharing 'the culture' in the first place. Wight was, clearly, still thinking about this association in the above statement, which suggests that he might not have conceived of culture in the same way. The idea of 'cultural unity' would seem to mean something very different to the author of *Systems of States* from that understood by the cultural anthropologist. Indeed, it might be a mistake to immediately assume that the culture of international society amounts to a distinctive way of life in the essentialist sense.

The essentialist version of the anthropological concept lays particular emphasis on parochial difference and rests upon the assumption that 'culture' operates in mysterious ways. This kind of culture effortlessly engages participants and in a manner that the participants are, frequently, blissfully unaware of. The humanist concept fails to recognize this condition and, more importantly, deliberately de-emphasizes difference to stress commonality. Clearly, 'culture' at the international society level is something that is carried out between certain international individuals (diplomats for example), and bodies (states, military organizations, etc.) and is conducted in a particular way (with 'civility' perhaps?). Whatever the 'cultural' activity is that is conducted at the international level it is clear that no participant was born to it in the essentialist sense. The 'culture' that diplomats are involved in, for example, does not seem to operate with the same measure of unconsciousness the anthropological concept invokes. There is an implicit suggestion of effort and awareness in Wight's idea of culture; diplomats consciously engage in diplomacy and militarists in war; one may even deliberately choose the career in the first place. There does seem to be a greater degree of consciousness in this form of international 'culture' than any essentialist harbouring 'the way of life' concept could permit. Moreover, it is highly significant that the 'culture' of international society, in Wight's view, transcends any parochial or nationalized sense of difference.

Although Wight toyed with the idea of values and deeper forms of understanding, overall, he did not convert international commonality into the language of 'ways of life' and ethnographic trademarks. Undeniably, some of the qualities that inform the anthropological concept, namely norms, values, ethos, habits and traits, are detectable in his theory. However, simply because Hedley Bull, for example, decided that society included 'common values' in a holistic sense, this should not directly lead us to assume that Wight thought along similar lines. The point is, it is possible to perceive the same object, for example international law, in a seemingly similar way, as the cultural evidence of international society, and even to use the same term, 'culture,' and yet, to understand that object very differently as either the evidence of agreed values and a 'way of life,' or, simply as common and habitual practice. Even Wight's reference to a common set of values may not imply that these are the same values, in an integrated and holistic sense. Indeed, Wight clearly indicated that international society was neither 'homogeneous nor uniform,' which would be the principal assumption behind an essentialist conception of culture (Butterfield and Wight 1966:113).

International society was, in Wight's view, a 'loose and incoherent' form of 'political organization' (Wight 1977:149). And it is significant that, up to 1972, we do not seem to find Wight employing the usual, contemporary, language of homogeneity, consensus or *otherness* with respect to international society itself, although he did recognize internal and external differentiation in cultural terms.[7] Moreover, it appears highly significant that he discussed homogeneity as a matter of politics and not as a matter of culture in *De systematibus civitatum*. Wight's use of language in his work supports the view that his understanding of culture was not primarily anthropological, since he did not refer to anthropological sources, unlike his successors or Hans Morgenthau before him. It is highly relevant that Wight did not 'speak' in anthropological terms, especially since he was a widely read scholar. When Wight did refer to shared commonality beyond functionality, and in normative terms, he describes this as "sociology" (Wight 1977:33).[8] According to Wight, international society "can be properly described only in historical and sociological depth" (Butterfield and Wight 1966:96). There was no suggestion that the culture of international society could be captured in a positivist sense and reproduced as an ethnographic monologue.

In Wight's "single most important paper" (according to Hedley Bull (Bull in Wight 1977:7)) on *Western Values*, it becomes apparent that Wight resisted thinking in deterministic and homogeneous terms. What is noticeable is that he resisted homogeneity as a defining feature of international society, leaving that notion, in this paper, to the revolutionists or

Kantians. Wight was looking for "a certain coherent pattern of ideas" (Butterfield and Wight 1966:90), but the "core of common standards and common custom" are, he says, "difficult to define" (Butterfield and Wight 1966:103). Invoking Suarez, he says that:

> Between the belief that the society of states is non-existent or at best a polite fiction, and the belief that it is the chrysalis for the community of mankind, lies a more complex conception of international society ... Such a conception lacks intellectual conciseness and emotional appeal. The language in which it is stated is necessarily full of qualifications and imprecision.
>
> (Butterfield and Wight 1966:95)

Wight claimed that a "certain unity" (Butterfield and Wight 1966:95) existed at the international level in spite of the differences between (at least Western) states. Following Grotius's lead, he suggested that in any attempt to describe this unity, "there is a fruitful imprecision" (Butterfield and Wight 1966:102). The unity that existed at the international level is a 'complex conception;' yet nonetheless, it was still one that transcended difference in some way. Transcending difference in practice was a notion reminiscent of the League era where culture was not thought to be the source of difference between communities but the means of overcoming differences alternatively defined, reminding the reader that differences were not defined in cultural terms, but rather in national, civilizational and racial ones.

Whatever the problems are in pinning down Wight's idea of culture within international society, the issue becomes a clearer matter for Wight's successors, Hedley Bull and R.J. Vincent, with whom it acquired a more obvious anthropological character.

The anthropological concept moves in

It could be said that Hedley Bull marks the end of the humanist cultural era and the beginning of the ascendancy of the anthropological concept in the discipline. Unlike Martin Wight, Bull is refreshingly coherent with respect to culture and presents as an almost archetypal essentialist scholar. For Bull, 'culture' involves homogeneity, consensus, uniformity, *otherness*, *meaning*, and environmental determinism. Above all, 'culture' is most salient at the local level and as a matter of 'ethnographic trademark.' In this respect, Bull's work more than reflects the changes that are taking place in the wider 'factory conditions;' it confirms that those changes are manifesting themselves within IR in quite specific ways.

Bull's most famous work, *The Anarchical Society: A Study of Order in World Politics* (Bull 1977/1995), similar to Morgenthau's *Politics Among Nations*, stands as a comprehensive survey of the things that the author considered relevant in respect of international politics. It begins by establishing the terms of analysis and moves on to discuss the 'bread and butter' topics in IR of diplomacy, war, great powers, law and the balance of power.

In his text, Bull attempted to clarify some of the ambiguities in International Society theory and his elucidation of the basic premise has proven an influential statement in IR. In a much-quoted passage, Bull wrote:

> A *system of states* (or international system) is formed when two or more states have sufficient contact between them, and have sufficient impact on one another's decisions, to cause them to behave – at least in some measure – as parts of a whole.
>
> (Bull 1977/1995:9 – italics in original)

Whereas:

> A *society of states* (or international society) exists when a group of states, conscious of certain common interests and common values, form a society in the sense that they conceive themselves to be bound by a common set of rules in their relations with one another, and share in the working of common institutions.
>
> (Bull 1977/1995:13 – italics in original)

Referring to A.H.L. Heeren, Bull told us that Heeren's definition of a states-system involved " 'the union of several contiguous states, resembling each other in their manners, religion and degree of social improvement, and cemented together by a reciprocity of interests' " (Bull 1977/1995:12). Bull interpreted this states-system "as involving common interests and common values and as resting upon a common culture or civilisation" (Bull 1977/1995:12). We can take it as read from this point onward, that any reference to commonality in respect of a more meaningful states-system is 'resting upon' the idea of a 'common culture or civilization' in some form or other.

However, Heeren's reference to 'manners, religion and social improvement' was defined by the eighteenth century concept of culture, not the nineteenth century concept of civilization or, even, the late twentieth century concept of culture, and so it is Bull's interpretation of Heeren that interests us most. Wight also relied on Heeren, but seemed to take his words in the spirit of common reciprocity which they invoked, whereas, for the most part, Bull focused on the issue of common interests and values as the means for undermining the notion of an 'international culture.' The question that disturbs Bull the most is the extent to which international culture is meaningful.

In the introductions that Bull wrote to the edited volumes of Wight's work, he repeatedly raised the question, which he acknowledged Wight did not address; "[t]he central question about the global states-system of our own times is perhaps whether – given the international fracture to which it is at present subject . . . – any sense of cultural unity can still be said to exist" (Wight 1977:18).[9] The question of cultural unity is clearly going to present a problem for a scholar thinking within the framework of the anthropological concept in its essentialist form. For Wight, 'cultural unity' was largely assumed to be self-evident if, and where, international society existed, but Bull has taken a step backwards and come to question its very existence. In this respect, Bull was also confronting the question of cultural effectiveness at the international level in a similar way to Morgenthau. Yet where Morgenthau faced a history in which the humanist concept had exerted some influence and therefore had to be addressed by him, Bull confronted a situation in which the anthropological concept was dominating the conversation. Morgenthau dismissed the humanist notion that culture could play a significant part in determining international politics, while Bull was dealing with the question of whether the idea of culture had as much meaning at the international level as it was presumed to have at the local level. The foregoing illustrates that different contexts generate different questions that in turn lead to differing narratives about international relations – yet all of them invoke the idea of culture.

In many ways, *The Anarchical Society* confirms that by 1977 the civilization concept is falling out of intellectual and popular favour and is being replaced with the anthropological idea of culture. It became apparent as Bull's work unfolded that 'culture,' and the increased number of references to it in a variety of settings, was the term that predominately occupied his interest. The distinction between a system and a society rests upon commonality, for which 'culture' is often the describing term. For Bull, 'culture' belonged to community, while the question that appeared to bother him the most was whether or not that community could be international in the similarly meaningful terms that he obviously believed existed at the local level. Of course, even raising the question depends on how one has, initially, conceptualized the idea of culture. If Bull had defined culture in anti-essentialist terms, or the structuralist and world polity terms as John Boli and George Thomas (1999) do, then he might have identified far more 'international culture' than he thought possible. Further, this might have enabled Bull to have approached the question of normative depth in international politics somewhat differently.

It seems clear that Bull subscribed to the idea of meaningful international society determined by common values, rules, institutions and interests, distinguishable from mere contact between states, in much the same way as Wight. However, Bull was not merely clarifying the distinction between a system and society in *The Anarchical Society*; he was also contributing to the theory in terms of commonality. Wight also thought in terms of 'common values,' yet, the crucial question for us centres on how both Wight and Bull conceived of these 'common values' and what they imagined they entailed. In short, what meanings did each scholar attach to this phrase and intend to mean by it? Whereas in Wight there is ground to suspect an admixture of both the humanist and anthropological concepts, in Bull, there is, arguably, less ambiguity. This becomes apparent in the kinds of questions he asks and the kinds of problems he believed the idea of culture generates for international society. Just how 'international' or 'common' the 'international culture' of international society was in the post-colonial era proved a prominent question in his thinking, and one that presented profound problems for Bull.

Bull referred to "the lack of consensus" (Bull 1983:13) in modern international society, to the "contraction of consensus" (Bull 1977/1995:154), the "decline in consensus" (Bull 1977/1995:248) and to international society's "precarious foothold" (Bull 1977/1995:248) in view of the fact that the "area of consensus ... has shrunk" (Bull 1977/1995:154). It would not be unreasonable to say that Bull was fairly obsessed with the notion of consensus, which makes one wonder what it was that he was searching for in international relations (complete coherence, uniformity and something more than shared practice?). What is particularly noticeable is the frame of reference within which the difficulties over consensus are discussed, for on the whole they are cultural. However, 'culture' and 'cultural unity,' in Bull's terms, was not the same 'culture' or 'unity' that it had been in Wight's understanding. For Wight unity was signified by historical and contemporary practice; for Bull it has become, thoroughly, a matter of *meaningful* consensus and this more than suggests that the anthropological concept, in its essentialist guise, is framing the latter scholar's terms of reference.

International culture was being undermined by local culture and the most significant challenges, in Bull's view, came from the differing concerns of the decolonized and/or Third World states, which formed the focal discussion point in the *Hagey Lectures* (Bull 1983).

In the first of these papers, Bull identified five demands for justice; of the last demand, he said, "Third World countries have put forward a demand for justice in matters of the spirit of the mind: they have asserted a right of cultural liberation and issued a protest against the intellectual or cultural ascendancy of the West ..." (Bull 1983:4–5). That culture was now associated with 'matters of the spirit of the mind' more than confirms a shift of emphasis away from 'doing;' culture now included less tangible qualities and was something that manifested at the local (native) level. Further, the idea of 'cultural liberation' could only make sense in essentialist, 'way of life,' terms; and terms that assumed there was *a* culture to be liberated in the first place. Opposite to the idea of cultural loss, the notion of cultural liberation presumed that there was an ethnographic trademark that could be rescued and saved. Clearly, and substantively speaking, under the terms of reference of this conceptual scheme some natives had come a long way since Morgenthau feared for their 'cultural suicide.' Although, this view of culture was strongly articulated in the *Hagey Lectures*, it was an issue that also appeared in *The Anarchical Society*.

In Bull's view, the problem was that, in the past, international society was predicated on a homogeneous, European, culture, but as this developed across the globe, its homogeneity had been increasingly challenged. The initial presumption of European homogeneity was a strong one; eventually, Bull was forced to question whether, "the bonds of this society [were] stretched and ultimately broken as the system expanded and became world-wide?" (Bull 1977/1995:39). He was less convinced of the global acceptance of the original international society than Wight, and Bull's answer to this question was not completely affirmative, but close enough. Bull may have held out some hope that 'international culture' clung on, but it was certainly not as meaningful as it had been, because it was not as cosmopolitan as it needed to be to solve some of the more difficult issues of world politics, notably justice claims.

Under the terms of Bull's understanding of 'culture,' difference was, plainly, obstructive at the international level. What was certain was that for 'culture' to be both effective and meaningful it needed to be consensual and homogeneous – or, in the words of Ruth Benedict, 'all of a piece.' That Bull also conceived of culture as 'all of a piece' is betrayed by the way he expressed his interest in cultural unity. Under his contemporaneous international conditions (with large numbers of states gaining independence), and because of the expansion of international society, the 'bonds' that held international society together had become weakened. Wight had acknowledged the dilution of these bonds, but they still seemed to serve his theory sufficiently well, but for Bull this difficulty raised a different set of questions and concerns. "It is important to bear in mind," he said, "however, that if contemporary international society does have any cultural basis, this is not any genuinely global culture, but is rather the culture of so-called 'modernity'" (Bull 1977/1995:37). The simple notion of 'common culture' was undermined in this statement by the fact that 'if' international society did have a cultural basis then 'this was not any genuinely global culture.' Of course, what counts as 'global culture,' or was believed could count as 'genuinely global,' derived exclusively from the initial conception of culture and did not depend on evidence of global manifestations to confirm its absence or presence. Put more succinctly, if Bull could rule out the presence of a 'genuinely global culture,' then it was because he was working with a distinct view of culture (what it is and how it works etc.) in order to tell us that it might not exist within international society. It is only in this way that he is able to draw the distinction with 'the culture of modernity.'

That Bull could doubt and dismiss the notion of 'global culture' more than implied that he was defining culture in seemingly differing terms from Wight. If international society did not have a 'genuinely global culture' other than the culture (or commonality) that modernity brought, then what kind of culture concept was this? Overtly stated, it was not that Bull was attempting to add precision to an already incomprehensible idea, far from it; he was looking for quite specific qualities in 'culture' – qualities that he suspected were lacking, or absent, at the international level.

In the quest for certain qualities or his confirmation of their absence, Bull could be said to be redefining the idea of culture in international society theory itself. He was not carrying out this redefinition in a deliberate and self-conscious way, but rather, he was working with an alternative set of 'conventional standards' and under different 'factory conditions' which led him to approach the whole subject of 'international culture' in terms that had been unavailable to Wight.

In the *Hagey Lectures,* Bull tells "Western countries to stand firm in dealing with Third World demands for change . . . without being false to their own values and weakening their own integrity" (Bull 1983:33). This appeal to notions such as 'their own values' and 'their own integrity' conveys a message with a particularly potent force under the anthropological concept. Values and integrity must belong, and be identifiable as belonging, 'somewhere,' and to specific people. Like the cultural anthropologist, Bull could identify a seemingly endless array of cultures, so long as they appeared coherent and discrete to the observer and could be identified in particular terms. In the space of two pages, towards the end of *The Anarchical Society,* we find references to 'cosmopolitan culture; common culture; common intellectual culture; diplomatic culture; international political culture; elite culture; a common moral culture; cultural particularisms and the dominant cultures of the West' – some of which appeared more than once (Bull 1977/1995:304–5). Apparently, this all demonstrated that the world of international culture had become much more heterogeneous than even Wight could have imagined, but it also illustrated just how complex the *academic* world of culture had become.

We might, today, call into question the multiplicity of culture and the value of the introduction of such a plethora of categories into IR theory. However, the main point to draw the reader's attention to at this stage is that all of these cultural categories are based on the same unspoken assumptions about the nature of culture. Ontologically this is all the same culture – anthropological – reconfigured under varying terms, some of which, to Bull, appeared more creditable than others.

What is clear is that Bull may have acquired some measure of conceptual precision for 'culture as consensus,' but this was achieved at the expense of the original idea of an 'international culture.' Without consensus, the culture that was believed to underpin international society could be doubted and even dismissed. 'Culture' was now a matter for the natives not the tourists. Bull's idea of culture seemed to have lost its sense of the international.

Perhaps, more than any other International Society theorist, Bull conceived of culture as a discrete entity. As he said, "[b]y a society's culture we mean its basic system of values, the premises from which its thought and action derive" (Bull 1977/1995:61). 'Culture' had been reduced to a 'basic system of values,' or, in the words of Talal Asad, an 'integrated set of *a priori* meanings' and assumptions from which everything about a people could be explained. The 'ethnographic trademark' of culture was an axiomatic principle to Bull. In the *Hagey Lectures*, where Bull discussed different conceptions of justice, consensus was also his pre-eminent concern. Nowhere in these papers did he mention the idea of 'international culture;' instead, he raised the issue of "world common good" (Bull 1983:13), and the extent of consensus at the international level. These papers were written in the spirit of 'pluralism and solidarism,' terms which appeared in both the *Hagey Lectures* and *The Anarchical Society* and acquire greater significance when considered contextually and in conjunction with Bull's 'intentions.' Nicholas J. Wheeler has affirmed the significance of this language when he noted, "Bull's writings are characterised by a tension between pluralist and solidarist conceptions of international society" (Wheeler 1992:468).[10] This tension, as well as Bull's seeming growing preference for the ideas of 'solidarism and pluralism,' all seems to reflect his difficulties with the notion of 'international culture' and his diminishing references to it; all of which are especially noticeable in the *Hagey Lectures*. Arguably, this change of terminology and shift of emphasis from 'international culture' to 'pluralism and solidarism' would seem to both challenge Wight's conception of an international common culture and to confirm Bull's underlying suspicion that culture at the international level was, increasingly, a redundant concept.[11]

Bull was quite convinced that Third World countries had undergone something of a 'psychological and spiritual awakening,' to such an extent that they needed to assert their culture rights (Bull 1983:27). Parochial culture rights and values plainly transcended any notion of international common culture. That Bull viewed local communities in solidarist terms was self-evident; he saw nothing erroneous in the argument that Third World countries needed to claim their right to 'cultural liberation,' which was a key idea in his papers. He even pointed to the importance held by these countries in "the attempt to preserve cultural identity and some element of continuity with traditional modes of life against the inroads made upon them . . ." (Bull 1983:23) by the dramatic changes taking place in, for example, the global economy. To accept 'cultural liberation' as a salient issue and to be able to link culture to identity, let alone to believe in the preservation of cultural identity in the first instance, clearly demonstrated the presence of an essentialist conception of culture underpinning Bull's particular theory of community.

In his discussion of 'order in primitive stateless societies' (Bull 1977/1995:57–62), the essentialist aspects of culture became readily

apparent. The politics of 'primitive' societies were attractive for their possible comparison to international society as far as they lacked government.
The parallel between 'primitive' society and international society was one
that can be traced back to the civilization concept, and it was a connection
meeting Bull's approval, since it was repeated in the *Hagey Lectures*.[12] In an
especially revealing passage in *The Anarchical Society*, Bull tells us:

> whereas modern international society, especially at the present time,
> is culturally heterogeneous, primitive stateless societies are marked by
> a high degree of cultural homogeneity. By a society's culture we mean
> its basic system of values, the premises from which its thought and
> action derive. All primitive societies appear to depend upon a
> common culture; stateless societies appear to depend upon it to a
> special degree. Fortes and Evans-Pritchard came to the tentative con-
> clusion … that a high degree of common culture was a necessary con-
> dition of anarchical structures, while only a central authority could
> weld together peoples of heterogeneous culture. But the society of
> sovereign states – or, as it has sometimes been called, the inclusive
> society, today a political fabric that embraces the whole of mankind –
> *is par excellence* a society that is culturally heterogeneous.
>
> (Bull 1977/1995:61 – italics in original)

It is interesting to note that heterogeneity and homogeneity are explicit
'cultural' concerns in Bull's view. Compare this view to the early IR scholars for whom issues of homogeneity and heterogeneity were racial,
national and civilizational, not cultural, and one begins to see the conceptual transformation within IR more clearly. What makes the heterogeneous nature of international society a cultural issue, and a problematic
cultural issue, was never entered into by Bull. The presumption and
'taken-for-grantedness' of 'culture' speak volumes of the force of an essentialist anthropological influence in this respect. Of course, most, if not all,
of the assumptions concerning culture in Bull's statement have been discredited, or at least questioned, by recent debate. 'A high degree of cultural homogeneity,' even among so-called 'primitives,' is recognized as
something of a myth. Yet, Bull seemingly subscribed to the view that
culture invoked difference either within or between communities with
apparent ease; all of which served to illustrate how far the idea of culture
had travelled since the days when it was held to be the 'best of everything
that was thought and said in the world.'

Local versus global culture

R.J. Vincent is the most interesting scholar from our point of view, since
he is one of the few theorists in IR who explicitly discussed the problems
associated with the anthropological concept of culture in relation to

International Society theory. Against an IR background overly occupied with power relationships, national and security interests, Vincent explored some of the issues that have come to prominence in the post-Cold War period. Like Hedley Bull, Vincent is best remembered for his interest in normative issues, and especially his work on human rights. What is particularly significant in terms of our interests is that Vincent defined culture in obviously anthropological and essentialist terms. Like Morgenthau, he was openly and obviously influenced by certain American cultural anthropologist's ideas. In addition to his papers on cultural relativism, race and Western conceptions of morality, and his book on human rights, Vincent explicitly discussed the problems of local expressions of culture in comparison with something he called 'global culture.'

In his most famous work, *Human Rights and International Relations* (Vincent 1986/1995), Vincent unravelled the different views of human rights and argued for a minimum of subsistence rights before all other forms of rights. Again, the overriding problem seemed to be the level of effective consensus in international affairs, but the most awkward problem as it presented itself to Vincent, was that of cultural difference. If Bull relied very heavily upon the assumption that culture presented a barrier between 'the West and the rest' over justice, Vincent explicitly named it as such in his work. Like Bull, he remained optimistic that international society could overcome its differences and create a new climate of understanding and common global culture; one that was based on human beings and their welfare rather than the security and preservation of boundaries. Yet, it was clear, given his discussions, that culture was an idea that caused Vincent considerable conceptual difficulty.

What is immediately noticeable in Vincent's work is that he reinstated the idea of an international 'common culture' that originally found articulation in Wight's work as the evidence of international society. Vincent referred to this common culture as 'global/cosmopolitan culture.' Whereas Bull struggled to find depth within the idea of an international culture, frequently questioning its content and transforming the language of culture into that of solidarism and pluralism, Vincent explored in theoretical detail what might constitute international culture. Vincent's work restated the underlying significance of the idea of culture at the international level for this theoretical approach, while also, amply demonstrating the difficulties of labouring under the restrictions of the anthropological concept. Vincent did not follow the cultural anthropologists easily, although he accepted their framework for thinking about culture, but it was clear that this generated specific difficulties for this IR theorist.

The influence of culture was evident throughout *Human Rights*, but was especially obvious in his chapter on 'human rights and cultural relativism.' That cultural relativism was a topic to be discussed, illustrated the extensive reach of the anthropological concept. Here Vincent attempted to overcome the arguments for cultural relativism with the evidence of a 'global cosmopolitan culture' that formed 'part of the world social process' of modernity. We are less concerned with Vincent's actual arguments here, but are more interested in the manner in which he framed his discussion.

Vincent discussed three positions that a possible common culture of modernity had generated with respect to cultural relativism and global culture (Vincent 1986/1995:50–7). The first position held that there was "not one single animal" (Vincent 1986/1995:50) as a single 'global culture,' that there were, instead, three 'international' cultural worlds.[13] The second position held that there was a multiplicity of cultures, which ruled out the very possibility of an effective global culture (this was a statement of the classic essentialist view). Finally, the third position conceded a global culture but would question its "pedigree" (Vincent 1986/1995:51), i.e. whether or not the Western origins of global culture amounted to cultural dominance, or whether a universal perspective was possible. This last is the equivalent of the 'whose culture' question that is prevalent today.

Vincent carefully unpacked the assumptions of each position and exposed the weaknesses in order to demonstrate that a modicum of global culture did already exist in international relations. In many ways, this view rested upon the basic assumptions of International Society theory expressed elsewhere; that the evidence of commonality was culturally meaningful at the international level. Vincent interpreted international law as inter-cultural law to support his case. However, in spite of the sophistication of Vincent's theorizing these, supposedly, different positions all turn out to be based on the same concept of culture. His discussions could be said to amount to similar lines of argument, differently stated, within the confines of the same idea. The basic difficulty lay with the assumption that culture was a singular, homogeneous and consensual issue, irrespective of whether or not it manifested itself as either one global culture, three worlds of culture or a multiplicity of local cultures. It was in short, all the same culture, namely, the anthropological concept of culture that caused him most difficulty and therefore ensured that the problem of relativism remained a prominent issue.

That Vincent attached importance to the idea of culture was an indication of the influence of the wider 'factory conditions,' but that he should have been so easily persuaded by American thinking on this matter was a further demonstration of the demise of the humanist concept in British understandings of culture in IR. The influence of a changed and changing set of 'factory conditions' was especially noticeable on a scholar whose critical talents were forcefully demonstrated in other areas of his work; this is, arguably, particularly evident in his paper on *Race* (Vincent 1982). Vincent acknowledged that race was a contested category and even nonexistent in biological terms, but he also recognized that for certain groups of people race was an issue that featured as part of their everyday language and lives, and as such, had the potential to impact on international politics. That Vincent was aware of the politics deriving from an otherwise questionable idea was illustrated by his discussion of the subject of race as a serious, yet political and politicized matter impinging on international relations. In his view, race was a category with social saliency, strategic significance and one in which the "subjective element is crucial" (Vincent 1982:661). It is intriguing then, that Vincent did not consider the question of the culture concept in similar terms to the race concept, especially in view of the difficulties it generated for IR. Similar to the manner in which Morgenthau found the fact of national character incontestable, so Vincent appeared to accept the idea of culture as a conventional and unquestionable standard; placing the concept beyond fundamental critique. Indeed, what difficulties Vincent had with the culture concept, he did not see them in similarly political or politicized terms as he did the race concept, rather, he argued that culture was an important element in international politics. In short, he accommodated his narrative of international politics to the demands of the essentialist concept.

"There is, first," Vincent said, "the fact of the plurality of cultures in world politics" (Vincent 1980:252). Today, the 'fact' of a plurality of cultures is open to doubt. However, the 'fact' that Vincent accepted the 'fact' of culture, spoke volumes in itself, especially since this was not a generic notion of culture, but one that enabled a 'plurality' of cultures to exist – each with its own significant difference. As he pointed out in *Human Rights*:

> the emergence of a good part of the world from the dominance of European imperialism has carried with it a new emphasis on the plurality of values in world politics and on the rediscovery of the deep roots of indigenous culture.
>
> (Vincent 1986/1995:37)

Like Bull, Vincent accepted that decolonization had profoundly altered the nature of international politics and with it the nature of international society. Further, in conjunction with Bull, he had little difficulty accepting that the 'deep roots of indigenous culture' presented a serious challenge to international society; a challenge that he continued to tackle throughout his work. However, this notion of a resurgence or rediscovery of indigenous culture would prove a popular 'cultural' image as we shall see in the following chapter with respect to Samuel Huntington, but it is also one fraught with theoretical difficulty as was indicated in chapter three.[14]

Vincent's paper on *The Factor of Culture in the Global International Order* (Vincent 1980) discussed some of the key problems which the anthropological concept, as he understood it, generated from an IR perspective. It is important to acknowledge from our IR perspective that Vincent was not able to let go of the possibility that, as Wight had argued before him, there was something of a deeper relationship at the international level. However, what was curious in this paper were the terms under which Vincent considered the possibility of a meaningful international culture, which he believed was in the manner Wight originally intended.

There was a brief discussion of an international political culture, which shows the influence of Gabriel Almond and Sidney Verba (1963) and the popularity of their idea of 'political culture' at the time. Interestingly, Vincent argued for a move away from 'international political culture' to his notion of 'world culture' in order to discern any meaningful unity within the states system. His primary difficulty seemed to be that the concept of political culture was focused on moderation and the via media of international relations, whereas he was fully aware that the politics at the state level were much more various and precarious and therefore required a different kind of theorizing from that advocated by Almond and Verba (and by implication, presumably Bull also, since he too had referred to Almond and Verba).

If anything held international society together, Vincent said, then "we should look . . . to the unity of culture for the real source of world order" (Vincent 1980:257). In addition to 'stability and order,' issues that preoccupied Bull, Vincent also discussed the significance of culture in connection to 'justice and liberty' or what he described as the 'quality of civilization,' and he also considered the 'question of cultural engineering.' All of these issues offer insight into the then contemporary debates; they reveal not only how far British scholars (and British based scholars) have accepted the American definition of culture, but are also significant for telling us about the nature of the culture concept as it was understood during the 1980s.

Discussing whether or not an international culture was ethnocentric, or Western, and the possibility of an international or global culture eroding other local cultures, tells us that culture was being conceived of in an essentialist and ethnographic trademark sense. Primarily, it seems that the natives can only have one culture. Like Bull, Vincent appeared to accept this most essentialist of propositions. Vincent even wrote of the politics involved in the "preservation of the integrity or authenticity of a local culture" (Vincent 1980:255). Whatever problems politics generated, they did little to undermine the theoretical existence of such a thing as culture and merely served to highlight the significance of essentialism in international politics. For Vincent, culture mattered in IR because the "[r]ecognition of a distinct Soviet, or Chinese, or Islamic, or even African, approach to world politics may be more a reflection of the power of these cultures than of a new enlightenment in the West" (Vincent 1980:252). Recognizing the power of these cultures and their impact on international processes and the idea of common unity was what concerned Vincent the most, and caused the most difficulty.

The problem with the idea of culture, Vincent noted elsewhere, was that it was not 'a precise concept' – "as is revealed by the acceptability of our using it to describe a continent (Africa), a country (China) and a religion (Islam)" (Vincent 1986/1995:48). Awareness of the conceptual problems set Vincent apart from Bull. Similar problems did not appear in Bull's work; indeed Bull did not seem to have many conceptual difficulties with culture, only practical ones. Since Vincent found 'culture' to lack conceptual precision, it is perhaps all the more remarkable then that he not only stood by the concept but that he continued to attempt to work anthropological ideas into his narrative of international relations. His effort to weave together an explicitly international problem, that of 'global culture,' with that of cultural theory, and to tackle the significance of local culture and relativism, illustrated his sensitivity to the concept of culture. By suggesting that there was a transcending global or cosmopolitan culture, he not only reinforced the idea of culture in its homogeneous and consensual sense but also implied a matroushka-like-doll nesting of culture; which necessarily invoked a descending order of significance, so that local culture was more visible and meaningful than global culture. But what was interesting, and in keeping with Wight's approach, was that even though Vincent conceded that there was a "shallowness of the global culture of rootless cosmopolitanism" (Vincent 1980:263–4), he was not prepared to abandon the idea of international culture so easily.

Vincent was so convinced, when writing from an IR perspective, that his idea of global culture was likely to cause anthropologists some discomfort, that, in deference to them, he felt the need to explain their objections to the reader in the introduction to *Human Rights*. Vincent outlined the basic premises of cultural anthropology as he understood it, when he said:

> Before embarking on this enterprise, I should note the anthropologists' objection to it: namely, that people are interesting, both generally and in point of the rights they ought to and do enjoy, not for what unites them but for what sets them apart. The utility of the concept of culture is to distinguish one society from another, not to describe what they have in common. According to this view the quest for a global culture of human rights is not only dull but also pointless.
>
> (Vincent 1986/1995:3)

Culture was, then, firmly fixed in Vincent's mind, at least as far as his understanding of anthropology was concerned, as a matter of differentiation between communities. Not only did communal difference come under the category of 'culture,' but this was now the recognized project of anthropology. The inter-war theorists would have had no such similar difficulty in linking what was common to all societies to culture and would not have been embarrassed by the idea of global culture. That Vincent associated the utility of the culture concept initially with anthropologists *and* difference, rather than with sociologists or political culturalists and commonality, was an important indication of the extent of change that had occurred in the British context. It revealed that the extent of power the anthropological concept of culture exerted was such, that any commentator who tried to apply the idea of culture in a manner that included both the natives and the tourists would, now, be compelled to apologize for distorting the anthropologist's worldview.

We are inclined to ask what kind of anthropology Vincent had in mind and which anthropologists? On the whole these turn out to be a particular type of anthropologist and a specific form of anthropology – predominately American cultural anthropologists and notably Ruth Benedict, Margaret Mead and Clifford Geertz.[15] The degree to which Vincent accepted the authority of cultural anthropology is demonstrated when he described what anthropologists more generally do. "The idea that conceptions of rights vary according to culture," he said, "is an anthropological commonplace. If it were not true, doing anthropology would lose much of its point" (Vincent 1986/1995:48). Many British Social Anthropologists and more than quite a few of today's anthropologists on both sides of the Atlantic would have difficulty in recognizing this description of their activities. Nevertheless, it is interesting to note that Vincent seemed to think that the whole anthropological enterprise was concerned with exposing cultural differences – this is the point of what anthropologists *do* in Vincent's view. The influence of Geertz on Vincent is heavily noticeable in this respect. Even Vincent's implicit asides to the Javanese, as well as his direct references to Geertz, betray the influence of this cultural scholar on Vincent's thinking.[16] The most obvious point to make is that Geertz, like any other scholar, had his own specific epistemic take on the world and did not represent the sum total of anthropological thought, or indeed even cultural anthropological thought.[17] Where Vincent did draw upon British social anthropologists in the form of Meyer Fortes and E.E. Evans-Pritchard (like Bull before him), he did so, in keeping with Bull, only for what these scholars had to say about politics in the absence of the state. He did not rely on them for what they had to say about the nature of communities more generally; on this matter Vincent relied wholly on the American cultural anthropologists.[18]

What is particularly important, with respect to Vincent's qualification of anthropological thinking as mentioned above, is that he clearly believed that not only was the idea of culture useful and meaningful in some form or other, but that as an IR theorist he could overcome parochial expressions of culture at the risk of being 'dull and pointless' from the anthropological point of view. In this sense, Vincent had, arguably, tapped into one of the theoretical advantages of the discipline; the possibility of exploring alternative levels of cultural analysis to those limited to the local and/or national levels.

Whether he was aware of it or not, Vincent was in keeping with the earlier cosmopolitan conviction that culture could play an international role. Despite the respect Vincent may have held for the anthropological idea of culture, he needed to take this concept to new heights and to new regions of application, because from his perspective there was a normative imperative to do so. The question of universal rights and of the quality of human well-being was, and remains, a pressing one in IR. It is arguable that Vincent would have done well to have persisted with the IR perspective, as the inter-war scholars had before him. Instead, he found himself trying to accommodate the problems generated by anthropological theory, namely local relativism, into his work. But therein probably lies the influence of 'factory conditions'.

By the 1980s, the language of culture and cultural differences was coming into prominence. The weight of cultural anthropological thinking and conceptual definitions was to be found forcibly bearing down on Vincent's thinking about culture. This not only gave the idea of culture a more coherent status in his work, more so than one can identify in Wight's work, but it necessarily impinged on his understanding of international society. Whereas Bull attempted to accommodate the differences of newly decolonized states into a theory of international politics based on common consensus, Vincent was specifically drawn to the challenge that cultural differences presented to the underlying unity of international society.

There was clearly some overlap in Bull and Vincent's interests but their frames of reference, the manner in which they defined the problems facing international society in cultural terms, as well as their general levels of acceptance and understanding of the culture concept, were all subtly different. This led to a difference in emphasis on culture within each scholar's work. Bull's scepticism of the meaningful depth of culture directed him to qualify his thinking in cultural terms and even to seek alternative modes of discussion, from thinking in terms of 'genuine' global culture to that involving the language of solidarism. Similarly, Vincent qualified his terms, for example, with the language of a 'global cosmopolitan culture,' but he did seem more prepared than Bull to argue the case for international culture within a framework supplied by the basic assumptions of the anthropological concept.[19] Vincent was better able to support that role by critically analyzing the idea of culture with which he worked. In short, because he was more familiar with the tenets of the anthropological concept than Bull, he seemed less inclined to accept them at face value. Vincent's attempt to establish universal appeal for the idea of culture was an important element in IR theory. It was indicative of an attitude that stretched back to the League era scholars and had some similarity with what they were trying to achieve in so far as it was possible to conceive of culture as constructed, mutualist and internationalist.

Undoubtedly, Vincent's thinking would have benefited from some of the reformist cultural arguments that have been expressed within anthropology and were mentioned in chapter three; especially since Tim Dunne has suggested that "the essence of international society ... exists in the activities of state leaders, and is reproduced in the treaties they sign, friendships they form, customs they observe, and laws they comply with" (Dunne 1998:99). The 'culture' of international society theory then, might be said to reside in 'doing' rather than 'being.' Indeed, Wight's 'historical and sociological' interests very much focused on 'what states and their leaders, etc. have done.' It becomes a fascinating proposition as to whether this theory could be read in anti-essentialist terms, say, for example, by employing Brian Street's argument that 'culture is a verb.'

Speculation aside, it is clear that the idea of culture had acquired a more coherent status with Vincent, who exhibited greater awareness of the problems that the anthropological concept entailed. Yet, in spite of supporting Wight's original proposition that international culture was a meaningful concept in its own right, the pursuit of conceptual clarity brought its own difficulties. Vincent was compelled to deal with the subject of cultural relativism and to acknowledge the significance of culture in its parochial form.[20] He found himself discussing the nature of international culture in terms that had been decided for him elsewhere by cultural anthropology. Arguing the case for a 'global culture' was an act of deference to the power of anthropological assumptions. That he, Vincent, remained within the realms of basic anthropological assumptions tells us a good deal about the 'factory conditions' and prevailing political concerns of the time; it does not imply his failure as a theorist to overcome these difficulties. Indeed, many of the difficulties were inherent in the essentialist conception of culture and there would have been little opportunity to avoid them at the time. As the idea of culture in International Society theory acquired an increasingly anthropological character, so new difficulties were generated; difficulties that had more to do with the anthropological concept of culture than they did with the idea of an international society.

However, IR needed to establish (and still does) whether or not global culture existed, and if it did, how important was this in the scheme of things. Since, in view of the anthropological idea of culture, it was not so obvious that an international culture existed, least of all in the terms that Wight described it, international culture had to be justified against and argued for in recognition of (and maybe even in spite of) other, more significant, cultural ideas – namely, those stemming from cultural anthropology. At which point in thinking and time, probably around the time *The Anarchical Society* was published, it was confirmed that scholars on both sides of the Atlantic were speaking the same language of culture and adhering to the same assumptions and a uniformly agreed frame of reference. The essentialist, anthropological, conception of culture was being taken for granted as a conventional intellectual standard in IR. The concept of culture was now clearly identified with specific communities and their differences – the natives were everywhere, while the tourists were nowhere to be seen.

Key points

- International Society theory rests upon the idea that international society shares a common culture.
- British scholars in the 1950s and 1960s operated with the civilization concept, the humanist concept and began to incorporate the anthropological concept into their work.
- Martin Wight's idea of culture was ambiguous – it appeared to be both humanist and anthropological.
- Hedley Bull came to question how meaningful the culture of international society was. The idea of international culture was undermined by the presence and claims of local cultures in his view.
- In *The Anarchical Society*, Bull's concerns were noticeably anthropological, suggesting that the shift in conventional standards was well under way in the British context.
- R.J. Vincent argued that international culture, as global culture, did exist – but he had to take issue with the anthropological concept. Cultural relativism remained a central problem for Vincent.
- The questions which these theorists asked and the problems which they confronted – demonstrate how the initial conception of culture can determine theoretical interests and the outcome of narratives.

6 Strategies, civilizations and difference

Where, by the 1980s, the work of R.J. Vincent and Hedley Bull in International Society theory illustrated that the anthropological concept of culture had eclipsed the humanist concept in IR; the 1990s witnessed a considerable expansion of this trend. With the end of the Cold War interest in culture, in its anthropological sense, appeared to be everywhere. However, given that the idea of culture generally relied upon was drawn into IR as a conventional standard, it was not surprising to find that most commentaries employing the concept invoked (albeit unwittingly so) the essentialist version. As an unspoken assumption, it was clear that culture made us what we were and that the very idea of culture now embodied, or represented in some short-hand form, the idea of difference. Where the concept was incorporated from anthropology with little regard for the debates and difficulties associated with the idea, essentialism was not only self-evident, it was rife. Undoubtedly, many scholars will be uncomfortable with this assessment, but where there was an absence of detailed conceptual explication (how culture worked for example), and indeed where the significance of culture was simply assumed, then the contextual method indicates that essentialism must have informed the underlying basis of the idea. No one, it seemed, saw any point in arguing against the existence of culture, nor was much doubt expressed over culture's alleged pervasive influence; all of which confirmed that this particular conventional standard was exerting an extraordinary level of power and enjoying high intellectual status.

It had become widely accepted that communities were different and the concept that best captured their differences was culture. The synthesis between notions of community, difference and culture, now an almost orthodox assumption, could be applied to a variety of fields and subject areas in IR. Two developments stood out in the discipline; the increase in work on strategic culture and the impact of Samuel Huntington's 'Clash of Civilizations' thesis. Both developments confirmed the extensive reach of the anthropological concept in IR, although Huntington has proven especially problematic and is discussed in more detail here. At the same time, these developments demonstrated that nearly every aspect of international politics was potentially a cultural matter. The implications of this situation in IR were that narratives tended to reinforce the theoretical entrenchment of the natives, while the tourists appeared to be somewhat irrelevant. There was no denying the 'fact' that culture, as a way of life belonging to a specific group of natives, had become a popular idea.

Strategic culture

A growing area of cultural activity in IR, from the 1970s, could be found in the field of strategic studies.[1] In many ways, the study of strategic culture grew out of the interest in state behaviour that had developed across the discipline in the 1950s and 1960s. In Britain, until the 1960s, the small yet growing discipline of IR had been dominated by historical and diplomatic studies, whereas in the United States the new spirit of scientific study was making considerable academic progress and expanding vigorously. Whether states behaved in accordance with a 'truthful' and scientifically discernible pattern of behaviour as Hans Morgenthau and the Realists had argued, or whether states had their own collective personalities, or were subject to those of their leading individuals, was the source of considerable debate during the period well into the 1970s.

International behaviour, how to study it, how to look for patterns within it, how to make predictions based on assessments of it, had become the central and dominant intellectual concerns. The extent to which anthropological work on national characteristics fed the interest in state behaviour is unclear, but certainly the interest in national character reflected the wave of behavioural studies that swept across the social sciences, which had implications for the nature of the discipline. Leaning towards the arts and history produced a very different kind of international theory (and different kinds of narratives as International Society theory illustrated) from that which aimed to approach international relations scientifically. Although interest in national characteristics was replaced by a general interest in state behaviour and the place of the state in thinking about international relations, it did not disappear entirely from the scene. However, under the conditions of the maturing Cold War, interest in more generalized forms of theory came to the fore, notably those surrounding notions of deterrence in strategic studies.

Orthodoxy quickly established itself, one that was rational and material based – meaning, states were thought to act in a 'sensible' manner in accordance with their resources and the pursuit of their national interests. National interests as well as the states' capacity to act were to be judged in terms of their material constraints. Crudely stated, for the Realist narrative of international politics, this came down to how much military might a state could muster and how far this was off-set, or balanced, by other states. Obviously some states were more powerful than others in view of the fact that they had greater material resources, i.e. military and economic power, and were therefore able to do more things at the international level. The Soviet Union and United States were certainly ahead of other states in terms of having greater material resources – as the epithet 'superpower' illustrated.

One of the assumptions behind the study of international relations during this period, and one clearly driven by the scientific factory conditions of the time, was that all states were, more or less, the same, and therefore could be expected (or be predicted) to act in similar ways. This rational assumption extended to the strategic sphere, where 'rational strategic man' provided the basis for thinking about military behaviour.

Although curiosity about the nature of the Soviet character remained, it had become assumed that, given the nature of states and international politics, the Soviets would act in the same way as all other states. And since most of the theorizing over state behaviour came out of American institutions, it was perhaps inevitable that state behaviour was modelled on the American perception of these issues. It was, therefore, assumed, unsurprisingly, that the Soviets acted and thought as the Americans did.

The Cuban Missile Crisis, or rather Graham Allison's assessment of it in 1971, changed the perception that there was a single and rational course of action that lent itself to scientific analysis. Allison's study explored three models or ways of looking at the Cuban crisis, with the net result that there was more than one 'truthful' way of accounting for this event.[2] The question arose as to whether or not the Soviet Union thought and behaved in the same way as the American state – there was a growing recognition and fear that the Soviet leadership and military machine might not behave in such a predictable manner. With the world living under the threat of 'mutually assured destruction' the possibility that the Soviet superpower might not only think but also act differently from the US, became a major concern.

Jack Snyder first explored the differences between the American and Soviet military machinery in 1977. In *The Soviet Strategic Culture: Implications for Nuclear Options* (Snyder 1977) he not only challenged the notion that decision makers in the Soviet Union thought similarly to those in the United States about nuclear strategy, but he is also accredited with first employing the phrase 'strategic culture.' Snyder suggested that the historical experience of the Soviet Union contributed to a distinct Soviet point of view; a conclusion that George Kennan had, also, in part reached about the Russian character.

Then in 1979, Ken Booth seriously challenged the ethnocentric assumptions prevalent in strategic thinking of the time. Booth (1979) criticized the orthodox thinking that did not allow space for local differences in his ground-breaking work, *Strategy and Ethnocentrism*. In this text, Booth argued against the prevailing view that there could be a single rational actor model of the state and he criticized the belief that strategy could be objectively determined without reference to cultural differences.

Once the presumption of state similarity in the military sphere and in strategic thinking had been brushed aside, the question of differences between organizations and their operational stances became acute. Suddenly the question of 'national style' was firmly back on the agenda. 'National style' was the preferred term to national characteristics because, as Booth pointed out in 1979, the phrase national characteristics had become tainted and "associated in some minds with extreme stereotyping" (Booth 1979:16); although how far the conceptual assumptions concerning national styles differed from those informing the idea of national characteristics is open to debate. The inter-war theorists had also acknowledged the presence of national differences but they had believed that these could be overcome, to an extent, with cultural interchange and the influence of global institutions. Under the Cold War and the threat of nuclear annihilation, however, the question of national difference acquired a more significant place in academic thinking on military matters. The world of cultural relativism was to be opened up in strategic terms in a context in which the idea of culture was, as Ninkovich has pointed out, "assuming a sacredness that it had not before possessed ..." (Ninkovich in Chay 1990:115). Due to the influence of certain anthropologists, notably Clifford Geertz,[3] "cultures were no longer good or bad, merely different ... " (Ninkovich in Chay 1990:115), and it was differences in strategic policy and style that captured these theorists' attention in strategic studies.

During the 1970s, the focus of academic activity was the Soviet Union, but from the mid-1980s onwards, other country specific and regional work began to be appear.[4] The 1990s witnessed an expansion of this work both empirically and theoretically, and the sub-field of strategic culture acquired a greater measure of respectability, especially as the disciplinary influence of Realism began to wane.

It has been said that work on strategic culture has been generational.[5] Where the first generation of scholars such as Jack Snyder and Colin Gray focused on the Soviet Union and the second generation, notably Bradley Klein, looked for intellectual hegemonies (the Cultural Studies approach), the third generation has been seeking greater conceptual clarity. The need for conceptual clarity was great, since as Ken Booth and Russell Trood pointed out, the notion of strategic culture was a "contested" (Booth and Trood 1999:vii) one. "It is contested," they said, "because, so far, it has largely been asserted rather than demonstrated" (Booth and Trood 1999:vii). Nonetheless, they were convinced (as is every scholar in this field) that culture was a vital component of any study of strategic issues, although no one went so far as to claim that it was the only factor that mattered in this area.

The underlying questions driving interest in strategic culture are undoubtedly important ones: how do we account for the differences between national strategic preferences and those that exist between differing military organizations? The subject area is a broad church; but in short, since it became apparent that not all states are the same, the initial crucial problems centred on explaining or understanding the anomalies.[6] As Elizabeth Kier (1997) inquired, why do some states adopt offensive military doctrines and others defensive ones? Why have some states chosen a nuclear policy, while others, Sweden and Australia for example, have not in spite of having the resources to do so (Poore 2000). Alastair Iain Johnston was intrigued by the persistent realpolitik attitude among the Chinese, especially since it had been sustained "across vastly different interstate systems, regime types, levels of technology, and types of threats" (Johnston in Katzenstein 1996b:217). In terms of Japanese national security, including the police and the military, Peter Katzenstein asked how we could account for the fact that American law enforcement officers "killed 375 felons each year between 1988 and 1992 ... [while] [b]etween 1985 and 1994 Japanese police officers killed a *total* of 6" (Katzenstein 1996a:1 – italics in original). The approach has also been considered useful for obtaining a broader understanding of a state's security outlook and interests overall. Ken Booth and Russell Trood hoped that by understanding the nature of strategic culture it would help to "open up strategic attitudes to more pacific possibilities" (Booth and Trood 1999:22).

Issues and questions of this order are vitally important and have generated interesting case studies. Scholars agree, contrary to the Realists, that ideas count and their studies have made a significant contribution in generating a more sensitive approach towards the strategic *other*. However, in spite of the success of the project, there are some major underlying conceptual problems concerning the cultural approach. Not only has the value of the approach been contested within security studies, but also debate has been generated between the strategic culturalists themselves over the nature of the project. Some of the questions raised over strategic culture resonate with the problems associated with essentialism and expose the difficulties that a cultural approach entails.

There were two problems confronting the strategic culturalists; first, how did culture relate to social action and outcomes, and second, how did the idea of culture work? It is fair to say that discussions within strategic studies have dealt more adequately with the first issue than the second; indeed what little has been said on how culture works has generally been incorporated into the discussions from anthropology and sociology.

John Duffield (1999) has suggested that strategic culturalists share three common points: first, that culture belongs to collectivities; second, that cultures are distinct and the differences are held to be profound; and third, that cultures are relatively stable and change only gradually, if at all. All in all, it seems, following Duffield, strategic culturalists subscribe, at the basic level, to an essentialist conception of culture in the anthropological sense. With considerable regularity, scholars in this field define culture as a matter of the 'values, attitudes, norms and beliefs, of a specific group of people.'

Ken Booth defines strategic culture as "a nation's traditions, values, attitudes, patterns of behaviour, habits, symbols, achievements and particular ways of adapting to the environment and solving problems with respect to the threat or use of force" (Booth in Jacobsen 1990:121). For Snyder, strategic culture is "the sum total of ideas, conditioned emotional responses and patterns of habitual behaviour that members of a national strategic community have achieved through instruction and imitation with each other with regard to nuclear strategy" (Snyder 1977:8). Moreover, it is accepted that culture "is one of the key factors determining *who* is *whom* in the social universe" (Booth 1979:14 – italics in original), that it "has an independent causal role in the formation of preferences" (Kier 1997:5) and that basically, "[c]ulture is as culture does" (Gray 1999:69).

The underlying belief held in common by this group of scholars is that what is shared by a collective is meaningful for the collective, it is distinctive, exclusive, bounded to some extent and makes people what they are, which in turn has implications for what they do. Indeed, more than one scholar has argued that culture affects everything. Colin Gray has said:

> culture is literally everywhere: it is too pervasive, yet elusive, for its influence to be isolated for rigorous assessment [by the falsifiable method] . . . it has long been clear to me that everything with strategic significance is chosen, employed, or interpreted, according to some particular ideational set that we can call cultural.
>
> (Gray 2003:294)

The pervasive nature of culture that affects everything and exists everywhere is, as was discussed in chapter three, a problematic proposition, especially when it is abstracted to the realm of ideas (in which case its causal role has become even more essentialized because we are, arguably, unable to demonstrate its presence with any certainty). In the light of the assumed pervasiveness of culture, inevitably, the problem of delineating the subject matter has been a prominent issue in strategic culture.

Quite clearly, as Johnston pointed out, the notion that culture shapes everything ran the risk of opening up a bottomless pit in IR, in which everything including the kitchen sink would have to be examined in order to account for the behaviour and attitudes of a specific organization, or accounting for a particular policy outcome. Johnston has argued for greater methodological rigour, subjecting the concept to testable criteria. As he pointed out, it made no sense to speak of "Germans thinking this way, Chinese thinking that way, and Americans thinking another way about war and peace" (Johnston 1999:522) unless there was a way of demonstrating and proving the point that they all do think in different terms. In the absence of clarity, Johnston argued that the way lay open to criticisms of essentialism and the kind of accusations that were levelled at "the old, discredited . . . national character studies of the past" (Johnston 1999:522). Johnston was obviously aware of the empirical problems attending the anthropological concept, and had identified the essentialist undercurrent in Gray's work, but whether he, Johnston, can succeed in an endeavour that other anthropologists have abandoned, remains to be seen. The problem of methodological rigour and conceptual clarity has been, as was discussed in chapter three, a major stumbling point for the anthropological concept.

However, one of the outcomes of the criticisms and complaints concerning a cultural approach might be said to be that scholars did have to carefully detail what their specific studies entailed and what they would, and would not, focus on. In this sense, scholars working on strategic culture have been forced to be more reflexive about the subject matter and, by default, more transparent over what they expected the concept of culture to do, more so than their contemporary Samuel Huntington for example, as we shall see below. By restricting the subject matter and by accepting that everything is cultural but required narrowing down to a manageable project, the strategic culture debate has exhibited an element which is lacking in Huntington, namely some recognition that the idea of culture could not, so easily, be taken for granted when applied to a substantive case study. There appeared to be wide acknowledgement that the concept did require some theoretical justification. Indeed, the strategic culturalists have devoted considerable energy in accounting for their preferred approach.[7]

Yet, at the same time, by consciously defining the parameters of their studies these scholars could be said to have exposed themselves to the similar observations made, in anthropology, by Joel Kahn of Clifford Geertz and by James Clifford of Bronislaw Malinowski; notably, that since the scholar limited the subject matter and then wrote up the culture accordingly, this is something they themselves have created/invented. Was the strategic culture something that really existed, or was it something the scholar had abstracted? Whichever the case may be, the question of whether or not this constitutes a problem is a separate issue and one that, so far, does not seem to have been recognized in strategic culture.[8] To address this issue would be to deal with an ontological question, i.e. in what way does culture exist – a matter that has been, plainly, taken for granted.

It is a striking feature that strategic culturalists define culture as an ideational matter, and as something to be interpreted in some way, but the influence of the idea of political culture is also strongly evident. In strategic culture, Almond and Verba meet Geertz it seems. The tendency to sub-divide culture in a matroushka-like-doll manner has been noticeable and much discussion has been given over to the question of what kind of variable culture was. Yet, it is arguable that much of this methodological discussion has been, to a considerable extent, self-serving: it has justified (or explained) the culture that has been identified, but it has not accounted for the fundamental idea of culture as such. The question of whether culture was an independent or dependent variable was an issue that stemmed directly from how much influence one believed culture exerted and whether or not culture could be isolated sufficiently to form the basis of study. There was some difficulty within strategic culture literature as to whether the culture of a military organization could be studied in isolation or had to be taken in conjunction with the wider social context in which it was situated. Isolating the subject matter (or referent group) was arguably one of the most contentious areas for strategic culture. In short, were scholars to study the culture of the military machine, or did they have to factor in the national culture (if they could determine it) as well?

For those focusing on military organizations, the subject matter was more easily and obviously limited; but their approach does raise some interesting questions for the essentialist conception of culture. Some of this kind of work has drawn its ideas from work on organizational culture (see Kier for example). Although it should, perhaps, be noted that Susan Wright (1998) has pointed out that some of the literature on organizational culture derived inspiration for its thinking from anthropology, so many of the theoretical difficulties over culture remain with concepts of organizational culture, albeit implicitly. However, since an organization might be said to operate in different and limited terms from those of society in general – a new recruit is deliberately trained and schooled in an organization's ways of behaviour and company ethos for example – then this may be one area where the essentialist concept of culture might prove useful. Indeed, Kier stresses the point that, unlike other forms of society, military organizations are "total" institutions, and "are well equipped to inculcate a common culture. Contact with outsiders is relatively limited, and members work, play, and often sleep in the same place. The organization defines its members' status, identity, and interactions with others" (Kier 1997:29). As the essentialist concept of culture depends on notions of homogeneity, coherence and shared meaning, all of which are thought to manifest themselves in an enduring, if not timeless way, then one place to look for this kind of culture might be in a totalizing organization like the military where uniformity is expected. Indeed, it is arguably an easier and more straightforward task to abstract this kind of culture from a military organization, in the manner of Ruth Benedict's patterning for example, than it obviously is from a whole society, which is diverse in its complexity.

However, one of the notable weaknesses of essentialism lies in its reliance upon notions of fixity and durability. It would be a mistake to think that even an essentialist conception of culture was not liable to change, reminding the reader once again of Colin Turnbull's Mbuti experience as discussed in chapter three. Although an essentialist conception of culture might tell us a good deal about current organizational conditions as well as of those in the past, one ought, perhaps, to be wary about taking any condition for granted. Indeed, even under conditions of the essentialist concept of culture, the place of change as well as the role of individuals, must be accounted for – a matter that the essentialist concept has persistently struggled to deal with. Although strategic culturalists are well aware of the changes taking place within the organizations they study, they still seem to need to spell out explicitly how a concept that depends on a good measure of homogeneity, exclusivity and continuity, changes in theory. All of which returns us to the problems inherent in this concept of culture and the question of whether or not this will prove, in actuality, a useful way of approaching the problem of differences between military organizations.

Strategic culturalists have been sensitive to internal change and variation in their studies. Yet, conceptually speaking, there is considerable tension here between some anti-essentialist concerns, namely the recognition of cultural change and internal diversity, and the underlying essentialist assumption that culture is an unavoidable aspect of life making people what they are and is therefore the source of distinction. These two viewpoints do not fit comfortably together. Indeed, the question of whether culture is a "cause or a context" (Farrell 1998:408) is the direct result of the confusion over the initial conceptualization of culture in this respect. To address the problem of what culture does, one would have to be quite specific about what it is and how it works.

This problem is perhaps better revealed when the relationship of history to culture is considered. Many of the studies make a connection to past experiences; indeed it was one of the criteria of Booth and Alan Macmillan's framework for analysis that historical experiences be considered (in Booth and Trood 1999:Appendix). Why it was necessary to inject more history into studies was not fully explained. Although there might be good reasons for assuming that a military organization or national strategy is defined in the light of past experience, it is not obvious that we are what we are because of what we have done. Although strategic culturalists have discussed the problem of historical determinism, the connection between history and culture needs to be made explicit, especially since this is one of the noted weaknesses in essentialist accounts of culture. The danger is that culture is equated with tradition, and in terms that are assumed to be continuous in an ambiguous sense (the notion of continuity merely appears plausible because the essentialist concept of culture demands this relationship).

In recognition of the problem of historicism, Katzenstein, rather refreshingly, stated that he "did not view culture as a child of deep continuities in history" (Katzenstein 1996a:2). He argued, "we should be able to point to political processes by which norms are contested and contingent, politically made and unmade in history" (Katzenstein 1996a:2). In a move that seemed to echo anti-essentialism, Katzenstein focused on the "contested and contingent" nature of norms and their construction. In spite of producing an interesting insight into the changing perceptions and outlook of security organizations in Japan, and one that was sensitive to the changing context in which they operated, it was not clear what additional value the idea of culture was expected to contribute to his study. Notions of norms and identity seem quite capable of surviving without the idea of culture to support them.

Much of the literature on strategic culture has engaged with Realism and the Realist argument that material interests/constraints are the dominant issues for states. These were important matters and there is no doubt that, contrary to the Realists and their interest in material issues, ideas and discourses count. The question was, and still is, whether or not it was worthwhile turning these two factors, of ideas and discourse, into a matter of culture? Ironically, while the culturalists criticized the Realists for their assumptions about material factors, they failed to consider that they too relied upon a major assumption – the existence of culture. As Gray put it, 'strategy is made by people who cannot help but be cultural.' The important question is what does being cultural mean. Such a broad sweep of ideas was problematic. Although it undoubtedly opened up new avenues for research and presented important questions about how groups thought and behaved, the real difficulties were not so much methodological (how to identify such things) or epistemological (which values, etc. counted and how they were identified), but ontological (what was the nature of these values, beliefs, systems, etc. that enabled a scholar to abstract them so completely). This is especially problematic since all of these things, values, beliefs, etc. have been assumed to be part of the 'culture' because the idea of culture has already been assumed to exist as a pre-given and *a priori* set of integrated meanings.

The central difficulty is that the idea of culture is taken for granted from the outset, and this is a stance attributable to culture as a conventional standard. It is taken as given that culture is about being (i.e. it makes us what we are), rather than it embodying something that we do and that it is employed as a noun, not a verb.[9] For strategic culture, it is a basic assumption that culture shapes particular military organizations or strategic preferences into what they are. Culture is believed to be an important conceptual tool in helping us to understand the variation between military organizations and differing national approaches to strategy. And it may be that given the peculiar totalizing nature of military organizations that it is; but to achieve this situation, strategic culturalists would have to claim the idea of culture in an essentialist sense as their own (because it is not an appropriate concept for examining whole societies). However, in spite of the undeniable importance of accounting for such differences, the debates over subject matter (how much culture counts in military terms) and over methodology, are, arguably, ultimately limited because the actual idea of culture has not itself been debated, but has simply been assumed to exist *a priori.*

For all strategic culture scholars, the awkward question is not what culture is (because invariably it always turns out to be 'the assumptions, values, norms, beliefs and knowledge' of a collective), rather, the real difficulty resides in conceptualizing how culture works in establishing such things, and in guaranteeing their persistence, only and exclusively for the collective in the first instance. This is a difficulty both for those examining broader national styles and for those focusing solely on military organizations. The idea that culture is simply 'out there' doing what it does, does not assist us; and this is an especially pertinent issue when there are other scholars in the social sciences who would refute the claim.

Yet, these assumptions about culture have served to demonstrate that the idea of culture was now a conventional standard. For these scholars, culture was an acceptable concept and one largely beyond dispute even if its actual relevance to strategic studies could be debated. However, it would have to be noted that the dependency on the anthropological concept of culture has ensured a certain measure of repetition of the difficulties first encountered in anthropology. Criticisms of lack of clarity, homogenization and determinism can all be found in the debate over essentialist conceptions of culture.

Although there has been more debate about the virtues of a cultural approach in strategic culture than any other area of IR, and this has generated larger theoretical questions concerning methodology and epistemology (all of which is to be welcomed), it is clear that many of the problems this area confronts, like those that have dogged International Society theory, derive explicitly from the conception of culture that underpins the research. As work with the anthropological concept in IR expands, so it is inevitable that the inherent conceptual difficulties will expand correspondingly. Neither an increase in the volume of work produced, nor an extension of the subject areas this concept is thought to touch, will diminish the doubts that surround the anthropological concept. So, in spite of the fact that work on strategic culture has produced a growing number of interesting studies and presented significant theoretical challenges to a too narrow-minded application of Realism, it nonetheless remains to be seen what the overall benefits of turning everything cultural are. Indeed, some scholars, Theo Farrell for example, seem to be turning more towards sociology and ideas of institutionalism, and away from anthropologically derived assumptions, in order to bring ideas into the security arena. Until strategic culture theorists tackle the underlying question of how culture works, how it shapes everything and exists everywhere, and are more explicit about the manner in which they conceptualize culture (rather than how they categorize and identify it methodologically), it might be suspected that they are looking at 'something' in ways that are now largely doubted by many anthropologists. Indeed, IR generated considerable concern among anthropologists when an individual scholar (Samuel Huntington) applied the anthropological concept of culture to international relations and attempted to develop a new narrative of international politics.

Culture as a 'clash' of difference

In the summer of 1993, the journal *Foreign Affairs* published Samuel Huntington's article, *The Clash of Civilizations?*, which generated an almost unprecedented level of discussion. The article was subsequently expanded into the volume, *The Clash of Civilizations And The Remaking of World Order*, in 1996. Much criticism and debate followed, most of which was concerned with the implications of his thesis and his failure to define 'civilization' adequately. Some critics took issue with his classification of certain cases, while others objected to his overly generalized view of the world.[10] Yet, even Jeane Kirkpatrick, who found "Huntington's classification of contemporary civilizations ... questionable" (Kirkpatrick in Huntington 1993/1996:50), ended up supporting his basic assumption that the idea of civilization was an "important" one (Kirkpatrick in Huntington 1993/1996:52).

Huntington argued that 'world politics was entering a new phase' and that the future of international relations would be determined by forces generated by cultural difference. He identified seven or eight 'great divisions among humanity,' which he called 'civilizations.'[11] Rather pessimistically, he was convinced that the "most important conflicts of the future will occur along the cultural fault lines separating these civilizations from one another" (Huntington 1993/1996:3). At root then, Huntington's civilizations were inherently incommensurable; while the obvious source of incommensurability was culture.

What was significant about Huntington's work was that in spite of appearing to speak the language of 'civilization,' and gaining notoriety for that language, his thesis actually relied on an essentialist version of the anthropological concept of culture. It was culture that provided the fundamental concept in his theorizing, not civilization and, certainly, not that idea of civilization his predecessors in IR had known. In this respect, Huntington's argument allocated to 'culture' an unprecedentedly prominent and political role in IR. Whereas Hans Morgenthau and Hedley Bull had recognized that cultural differences could be problematic in world politics, Huntington had gone a step further and explicitly identified 'culture' as the source of serious, and potentially violent, confrontation. Borrowing from Roy D'Andrade, 'culture had become a big thing that did big conflicting things in international relations.'

Huntington wrote that:

Civilization and culture both refer to the overall way of life of a people, and a civilization is a culture writ large. They both involve the "values, norms, institutions, and modes of thinking to which successive generations in a given society have attached primary importance."

(Huntington 1996/1998:41)

What Huntington omitted to say was that 'civilization was essentialist culture writ large.' Further, his 'kitchen sink' definition and confusion between civilization and culture were more than a theoretical irritation a century after Edward Tylor.

Following Fernand Braudel and Immanuel Wallerstein among others, Huntington accepted that civilization was a 'cultural area' and one that involved certain cultural processes and/or creativity of a particular group of people (Huntington 1996/1998:41). It would have seemed particularly necessary then to rigorously explicate the meaning of culture and its relationship to civilization, especially in view of the 'fact' that, for Huntington, "civilizations are cultural not political entities" (Huntington 1996/1998:44). Yet, nowhere did Huntington attempt to offer, what might be considered, an adequate account of 'culture,' instead he relied upon generalities.

Despite drawing on the work of Arnold Toynbee and Oswald Spengler, Huntington's interest in civilizations was one oriented towards regionalism and the meta-narrative thereof, and it is important to draw out the distinction between Toynbee's, Spengler's and Huntington's understanding of civilization because it illustrates how marginal the concept of civilization actually was in Huntington's hands. 'Civilization' for Spengler and Toynbee was a matter of progression and organic growth even though they evaluated the development of civilization in contrasting ways.[12] In Huntington, conversely, the old 'organic' idea of civilization was plainly a redundant issue; civilization was reduced to nothing more than a matter of identification based upon an alleged regional similarity. Repeatedly, Huntington made the point that civilization was nothing more than local culture writ large and amounted to little more than a sphere of identification. This stood in sharp contrast to Norman Angell's progressive and accumulative conceptualization of civilization discussed in chapter one, for example.

Whatever the dominant language of the text, it seems clear that 'culture' was Huntington's fundamental concept and that civilizations were only, as he constantly reminded us, "the broadest level of cultural identity" (Huntington 1993/1996:3) and "the broadest cultural entity" (Huntington 1996/1998:43). Echoing Tylor, Huntington argued that civilization "is defined both by common objective elements, such as language, history, religion, customs, institutions, and by the subjective self-identification of people" (Huntington 1996/1998:43). The problem was not one of repetition, of telling us that culture and civilization belonged together, but the lack of a substantial theoretical explanation. The central problem was one of identifying the 'common objective elements' and then being able to situate them together with 'subjective self-identification,' since there was no guarantee that the two should or would coincide.

Huntington was unwilling or unable to distinguish between culture and civilization. Rather oddly, especially for an American scholar, he claimed that past "efforts to distinguish culture and civilization, however, have not caught on, and, outside Germany, there is overwhelming agreement with Braudel that it is 'delusory to wish in the German way to separate *culture* from its foundation *civilization*'" (Huntington 1996/1998:41 – italics in original). The experience of American cultural anthropology clearly tells a very different story from the one Huntington suggested exists here. As the history of the development of the idea of culture shows, the German idea of culture (kultur) is very different from the French understanding of the term, and the impact of the German idea has actually extended well beyond its country of origin.[13] Kultur was not founded on the concept of civilization, but developed in opposition to it. For Fernand Braudel, culture was a 'personal' affair, as he pointed out it was for all French people (Braudel 1963/1995:5–6). Braudel recognized the German concept and acknowledged its distinction from the French idea of culture, but he was more comfortable with the idea of civilization. Indeed, as the above quotation from Huntington indicated, he, Braudel, considered culture was rooted in civilization and could not be 'separated from its foundation.' Huntington clearly reversed this approach, claiming that civilizations were rooted in culture. Braudel and Huntington were working with different understandings of the term 'culture,' which made it all the more important that Huntington elucidated his idea of culture, especially as this was *the* foundational concept in his thought.

That an American social scientist accepted the word of a French historian on matters of culture and civilization was a curiosity. It suggested that Huntington approached this subject via literature on civilization with some 'home-grown' assumptions about 'culture' in tow, rather than from literature on culture theory. Indeed there was a noticeable absence of reference to culture theory and an overt dependence on the civilization theorists.[14] Beyond a couple of general comments, there were only a handful of passing references to anthropologists.[15] Intellectual dependency on civilization theory was not inadequate in itself, but considering that Huntington's idea of civilization derived explicitly from the idea of culture, the lack of recognition of culture theory seemed to be a major omission. In addition, Huntington's refusal to separate culture from civilization required some level of theoretical explanation since it was not possible to rely on both Braudel and Spengler as far as explaining the relationship between culture and civilization was concerned. Braudel and Spengler were at odds with one another on culture and civilization; their differing views deriving from incommensurable ontologies. For Braudel, culture was an inseparable element of civilization, while for Spengler, civilization was the death of culture. Huntington seemed to have missed this important conceptual difference, as well as having managed to lose the progressive and organic nature inherent in the civilization concept.

In Huntington's view:

> Our world is one of overlapping groupings of states brought together in varying degrees by history, culture, religion, language, location and institutions. At the broadest level these groupings are civilizations. To deny their existence is to deny the basic realities of human existence.
>
> (Huntington 1993/1996:63)

Or so he would have us believe. Who would dare to question 'the basic realities of human existence,' or 'deny the existence' of the things that make up civilizations? Whereas most of us would have little difficulty in acknowledging the 'existence' (albeit with some debate) of history, religion, language, locations or institutions, the inclusion of culture in this list of 'basic realities' was highly contentious. Nevertheless, it is a point of major contextual concern that culture had been elevated to the status of an unquestionable 'reality' in the above statement. It confirmed that culture in the essentialist anthropological sense had become a conventional standard – one that could be taken for granted with ease. Huntington further declared that, "the major differences in political and economic development among civilizations are clearly rooted in their different cultures" (Huntington 1996/1998:29). This was a strong assertion to make, and one that seemingly attributed all differences, ultimately, to a cultural cause, and enabled the author to fuel a pessimistic narrative of international relations.

On the surface, Huntington's use of 'culture' appeared to be, at the very least, confused. He conveniently slipped into the realms of hyper-referentialism, which frequently left the reader disorientated and at a loss as to what 'culture' meant beyond vague gestures and grand categories. At times, culture was religion, at others language, in some places it appeared to include values and elsewhere to exclude them in an almost humanist sense.[16] That such an important concept remained overly generalized was problematic, since if one inspected these issues more closely it was hard to see, on the one hand, what benefit was to be gained from aggregating issues under the banner of culture that might have better stood on their own merit, say religion for example. On the other hand, knowing, as we do, that such 'culture' generalizations do not stand up to close interrogation, one had to wonder what benefit the idea of culture could bring to IR, even in Huntington's theory. However, in spite of the obvious confusion in Huntington's thoughts on the matter, it was plain that he conceived of culture as commonality, and beyond this as homogeneity and continuity.

One of the more curious and obvious examples of essentialism, however, concerned the manner in which he conceived of the diffusion of ideas and artifacts. He told us, "China's absorption of Buddhism from India, scholars agree, failed to produce the 'Indianization' of China. The Chinese adapted Buddhism to Chinese purposes and needs. Chinese culture remained Chinese" (Huntington 1996/1998:76). In much the same way that the introduction of the English language into India did not produce an English society (Huntington 1996/1998:62), or that modernization is not creating Westernization, so the absorption of Buddhism from India into China did not undermine the essential 'Chinese-ness' of the Chinese 'culture.' It seemed highly erroneous to assume the 'Indianization' of China, or that China could become a carbon copy of India, even in theory, but the statement itself revealed a number of things. First, it showed that Huntington had a discrete view of 'cultures' as entities – there was a Chinese culture area of Chinese-ness, and an Indian culture area of Indian-ness, and no matter what is/was culturally exchanged, neither could undermine the integrity (or should that be geist?) of the other. Second, it told us that he believed that the 'core' elements or perhaps even characteristic traits of a culture remained undisturbed by 'foreign' imports. This was essentialism at its most radical. 'The tourists' would never be able to undermine 'the natives;' indeed the actual evidence of change only resulted, in Huntington's view, in no cultural change, so much so that the appearance of foreign interlopers seems almost irrelevant. At a later point he says that while politicians "can introduce elements of Western culture, they are unable permanently to suppress or to eliminate the core elements of their indigenous culture" (Huntington 1996/1998:154). These 'core elements' of culture became ahistorical yet deterministic, and, needless to say, there was no substantive evidence of their existence. Indeed, Huntington successfully committed the fundamental error, discussed in chapter three, of citing more and more examples to prove the existence of culture, while the evidence of culture itself did not amount to much.[17] According to Huntington, Asian societies stress "the values of authority, hierarchy, the subordination of individual rights and interests, the importance of consensus, the avoidance of confrontation, 'saving face,' and, in general, the supremacy of the state over society ..." (Huntington 1996/1998:225).[18] Confucianism, on the other hand, emphasized, "thrift, family, work and discipline" (Huntington 1996/1998:108). These were gross generalizations, clichés and unsubstantiated myths that ought to have been critically challenged.

Huntington noted the rise of civilization in the singular sense, but made it clear that he was only interested in civilization in the plural sense and as it first appeared in the nineteenth century.[19] He would have dispensed with the singular notion of civilization altogether but for the fact that it had, he claimed, reappeared; this was the idea of a global culture that had occupied R.J. Vincent's thinking, for example. We can learn a good deal about Huntington's view of culture from the manner in which he dismissed the idea of international culture, since where 'international culture' failed, local and civilizational 'culture' clearly succeeded. According to Huntington, a universal culture implies "the cultural coming together of humanity and the increasing acceptance of common values, beliefs, orientations, practices, and institutions by peoples throughout the world" (Huntington 1996/1998:56). A 'coming together' of this order was not happening at the international level in Huntington's view, as was Hedley Bull's conclusion before him and it was no surprise to find Huntington referring to Bull on this matter. Worse, in Huntington's view, the opposite was taking place – "indigenization."[20] Huntington criticized 'late twentieth century' inhabitants for "the widespread and parochial conceit that the European civilization of the West is now the universal civilization of the world" (Huntington 1996/1998:55). Of course, Huntington committed himself to the same erroneous thinking as Bull. He mistook commonality and a 'coming together' for uniformity, consensus and homogeneity.[21] He even dared to ask whether commonality meant that societies will "necessarily merge into homogeneity?" (Huntington 1996/1998:69).

We were informed, "[o]nly naive arrogance can lead Westerners to assume that non-Westerners will become 'Westernized' by acquiring Western goods" (Huntington 1996/1998:58). One might wonder what kind of naivety leads a theorist to assume that 'Westernization' (and homogenization) can occur so easily, or that this was a meaningful statement in the first instance. That Huntington was waiting for a "significant convergence in attitudes and beliefs" (Huntington 1996/1998:59), betrayed his essentialist conception of culture.[22] He reasoned that as homogeneity and consensus clearly did not exist at the global level, the idea of a universal culture could be easily rejected. The idea of global identification was not worth considering, as there were no 'meaningful' grounds for common identification. It was obvious that globally people did not agree on 'values, beliefs, orientations and practices.'

In both Huntington's and Bull's view the most appropriate level for applying the idea of culture, in a meaningful and homogeneous manner, was local not international. Yet, this argument against homogeneity at the international level was to all intents and purposes, utterly meaningless – Huntington and Bull expected too much from culture at *any* level. Indeed, the 'clash of civilizations' thesis demonstrated, perhaps more obviously than any other theory in IR, how the concept of culture determined, and limited, a narrative about international politics. That the notion of an international culture could be so rudely dismissed by Huntington merely reinforced the point that his theory of clash and indigenization was supported by a nativist conception of culture. In short, his inability to 'see' international culture depended most thoroughly on his definition (or idea) of culture in the first place. Huntington's thesis demanded the language of 'ethnographic trademarks;' of culture 'rooted in community,' fetishism, and radical and *meaningful* otherness.

The most disturbing aspect of Huntington's thesis, however, derived from the lack of politics. As Chris Brown commented:

> whether 'civilizations' clash along particular fault-lines is going to depend on how the inhabitants of those key areas, and their neighbours, near and far, choose to define themselves or allow political entrepreneurs to define them, and this is a political process, not one that follows a cultural recipe book.
>
> (Brown 1999:57)

It was not just the future of international relations that was at stake here, but also the basic political implications of Huntington's theory for day-to-day politics. When culture is invoked as the basis of politics then everything that was once political and read in those terms becomes cultural and approached/accepted on that basis. In his theory, the idea of culture has been elevated to the status of gravity, whose role in life has become unquestionable; which must be grounds for suspicion if not debate. For example, Huntington claimed, "China's Confucian heritage, with its emphasis on authority, order, hierarchy, and the supremacy of the collectivity over the individual, creates obstacles to democratization" (Huntington 1996/1998:238). Similarly, according to Huntington, Islam allegedly accounted for the "failure of democracy" (Huntington 1996/1998:29) in the Muslim world. Both were highly contentious claims and ones deserving of thorough scrutiny.

If 'culture' does create obstacles to democratization then we need to know the precise nature of these obstacles, and in what way they operate. Although Huntington went on to speculate over the future of Chinese politics, the suspicion was that culture, especially in the form of 'core elements', would endure. For which we can read that democracy is a cultural improbability/impossibility as far as China and Islam are concerned.

Whatever the difficulties 'indigenization' may be creating for local and global politics, it was plain that Huntington did not read the evidence of indigenization as evidence of politics but rather as proof of the power of 'culture.' Yet, as Lila Abu-Lughod has pointed out, even those articulating 'culture' in this way (and upon whom Huntington relied) are merely reinforcing the epistemological structure of difference that, ironically, on the surface they appear to challenge and refute. As she pointed out:

> A Gandhian appeal to the greater spirituality of a Hindu Indian, compared with the materialism and violence of the West, and an Islamicist appeal to a greater faith in God, compared with the immorality and corruption of the West, both accept the essentialist terms of Oriental-

ist constructions ['that maps and fixes differences in innate terms'].
While turning them on their heads, they preserve the rigid sense of
difference based on culture.

(Abu-Lughod in Fox 1991:144)

Huntington's theoretical stance, especially where it opposed the notion of
a global culture, was therefore fundamentally flawed. He believed that
through citing evidence of indigenization he could demonstrate a widespread opposition to a dominant mode of thought, and thus refute the
argument for a 'global culture.' Whereas, in actuality, he had merely succeeded in locating examples of people who thought in exactly the same
terms as he did. The argument served only to demonstrate the global
acceptance of 'culture' as a specific form of idea. Far from providing substantive evidence of difference, 'indigenization' actually provided theoretical evidence of international epistemic conformity. It demonstrated
that there was a global commitment to the same idea of culture and the
same values which inform that idea. And during the last decade of the
twentieth century, there was much of this conformity in thought concerning culture to be found in IR.

Vagueness and fundamentalism

The 1990s witnessed a widespread revival of interest in the idea of culture,
although to be sure, paraphrasing Tim Dunne, 'the idea of culture had
never quite gone away for the discipline.' Yet, there was a feeling that
something new was afoot. As Yosef Lapid remarked in 1997, a "swing of
the pendulum toward culture and identity is ... strikingly evident in post-
Cold War IR theorizing" (Lapid and Kratochwil 1997:3). Clearly, Huntington's thesis had given this swing a much needed boost. Even if people did
not agree with Huntington's view of international politics, culture was,
suddenly, everywhere.

Most of this culture, however, was predicated on the underlying
assumptions of the orthodox anthropological idea and plainly exhibited
essentialist tendencies. Culture was thought to be a meaningful some-
thing-or-other for a specific community of people; somehow its underlying
characteristics, or core values, endured, and moreover, it was identified
with difference. What was certain was that cultural difference made problems in international relations, even if these problems came down to a
lack of respect and a less than enthusiastic attitude for embracing culture
in a celebratory manner. The antidote to Huntington's fearful view of the
world of culture was multiculturalism, which exhorted us to celebrate the
diversity of culture.

Multiculturalism owed its development to political theory and had
become a topical subject in the 1990s. Although multicultural theory has
had some influence in IR, it is only mentioned in passing here, primarily

because it also was based on the anthropological concept and can be subjected to criticisms already expressed throughout this book.[23]

In many ways, Huntington had merely stated, perhaps a little too
loudly, what was taken-for-granted elsewhere. In all fairness to Huntington, his theory of 'clash' has served the discipline well; it provided us with
an excellent illustration of where the anthropological concept (especially
as a conventional standard in its essentialist sense) ends up when applied
to international politics. In spite of the debate Huntington generated, no
one, it seemed, felt it necessary to question the actual underlying concept
of culture or the principle idea that cultural differences generate 'clash.'
Culture, as some strategic culturalists pointed out, was seen to shape everything and made us what we were.

Let us examine a statement by Simon Murden, taken from a popular
introductory IR textbook, in which the 'facts' of culture were seemingly
established beyond dispute. Murden says:

> The human experience is one of cultures. Culture and cultural differ-
> ences have been at the heart of human behaviour throughout the
> history of international politics. Indeed, at the end of the twentieth
> century, the significance of culture was being reaffirmed ... The
> 'shrinking' of the globe brought different cultures into closer contact,
> and represented a world-wide challenge to traditional patterns of
> culture ... Peoples across the world were having to face the dilemma
> of what in their cultures could be maintained and what would be lost
> ... Culture is a powerful underlying force, but in the contemporary
> state system it is also one that still struggles to gain a coherent voice.
>   (Murden in Bayliss and Smith 1997:374–5)

There may be much in the statement to solicit a sympathetic response
from the reader, and indeed, many may agree with what has been said,
but the appeal is, fundamentally, to instinctive knowledge and delivers
nothing more than a comprehensive list of unspoken assumptions about
how culture ought to operate. In this respect, Murden's statement is
extremely useful for it was a typical pronouncement on culture, as most
people in 1990s IR understood the idea. It serves as an excellent illustration of essentialist dogma in which individual 'cultures' must "be put in
separate compartments" (Keesing in Borofsky 1994:302) and kept there, if
they are a genuine case. As with Huntington, Murden also provides us
with a useful illustration of the underlying problems that taking the idea
of culture for granted entails.

Chief among these problems is the need to demonstrate that 'cultures'
exist as discrete and coherent entities; and this 'fact' needs to be established before we can begin to accept the argument that cultures are under
threat of extinction from globalization. We would have to know much
more about the nature of culture as a 'powerful underlying force' and be

offered a comprehensive account of 'traditional patterns of culture,' espe-cially, since traditions come and go, are invented and re-invented. The ethnographic trademark of culture would need to be clearly established in order to justify the claim that cultures 'face a dilemma over what to main-tain and lose.' We might also like to know how cultures are going to achieve a solution to this dilemma, or, more importantly, who is going to decide this on their communal behalf. It would need to be explained, fully, why and how 'culture has been at the heart of human experience' before we will allow the author to tell us that this has (categorically) affected international relations. And this would all have to be carried out in theoretical terms rather than what amounts to a, less than obvious, emotive political appeal.

However, Murden was not alone in expressing this view of culture and taking the anthropological concept for granted. Yosef Lapid, who criti-cized Huntington, seemed to believe that the problem with Huntington's view of culture was 'definitional.' Huntington's failure to "move away from categorical, essentialist, and unitary understandings of these concepts" (Lapid and Kratochwil 1997:8) of culture and identity, only resulted, in Lapid's view, in the serious problem of reification. As Lapid pointed out, "[f]ar from being the rare exception, Huntington's failure [to move towards a less or non-essentialist definition] simply confirms that 'reifica-tion is an epistemological problem not easily vanquished, for it pervades the rhetorical and conceptual apparatus of our scientific world-view'" (Lapid and Kratochwil 1997:8). Yet, as the discussion in chapter three indicated, reification and essentialism may not be so serious a charge, especially if the basic, ontological, assumptions underpinning the concept remain. Rather ironically, at the level of ontology Lapid would appear to have more in common with Huntington than he realized. Both scholars would seem to accept that 'culture is a big thing that does things,' even though they may disagree, epistemically, over definitions and the kinds of things 'culture' potentially does.

Stephen Chan also attempted to be "unkind" to Huntington by object-ing to his 'generalized view of the world;' but even Chan accepted that other cultures were worthy of our attention. He suggested that:

> An enlightened (not an Enlightenment) international relations, requires not the business of sketching the Other so generally that it seems abnormal ... but, the business of trying to understand the nature and ingredients of global plurality; of other cultures, and their fears and resistances within the periphery of modernity ...
> (Chan 1997:139)

Taking the idea of culture, and the existence of 'other cultures,' for granted had not only become a widespread presumption it seems, but it was also one with historical saliency.

Beate Jahn (1999) discussed the encounter between the Spanish Conquistadors and the Amerindians, which she described as 'cultural.' Jahn did not define culture nor did she explicate in what way or under which terms this particular encounter could be described as cultural. Yet, in order to secure our understanding as readers and to accept the sense in which this particular encounter could be deemed cultural, we needed, as with Huntington's work, to share in the meaning of the word as a conventional standard. This is especially so, since the word 'culture' did not exist in the terms Jahn employed it at the time the event took place. Indeed a cultural encounter between the Spanish and the Amerindians might have as easily conjured an image of digging up the beach to plant crops, or the exchange of Bibles for beads, as it did a clash of interest. The lack of clarity might have been contagious, but it did confirm that, by the late 1990s, the anthropological concept of culture was being relied upon as a conventional standard across the discipline. Yet, whilst in anthropology the essentialist qualities and nature of the culture concept were being dissected, in IR these developments passed most commentators by.

If cultures were 'struggling to gain a coherent voice,' as Murden (and many a multiculturalist) claimed, then a crucial obstacle might have been that they never had a coherent voice in the first place. Indeed, the experience of the Kayapo Indians affords insight into how a community deliberately constructed a coherent voice for the benefit of a Western audience.[24] However, this general heresy, namely that cultures did not have a coherent voice, was not entertained; instead 'vagueness' became all the rage.

In the Preface to the edited volume *Culture and International Relations*, Jongsuk Chay said that culture is, "perceived as too broad and its boundaries as too vague ..." (Chay 1990:xi), while a few pages later, R.B.J. Walker pointed out that "those who like their concepts to be precisely and operationally defined may find culture to be frustratingly vague and tendentious" (Walker in Chay 1990:7). Yet, the frustrating thing is that A.R. Radcliffe-Brown had dismissed the concept precisely on the grounds Walker described some five decades previously. Radcliffe-Brown's precedent tells us there is no reason to tolerate this situation over half a century later. The anthropological concept of culture might have become popular in IR, but everyone, it seemed, agreed that this was a notoriously difficult subject.[25]

Culture may be a complicated subject as Raymond Williams pointed out, and certainly its history is complex, but it is not a matter beyond our comprehension; after all, people invented the term and the concepts attached to it.[26] No one who has written on this subject has been completely unable to offer an account of what they take culture to mean. For instance, move to the empirical realm and the difficulties instantly disappear. Everyone it seems could produce an example of culture (Joe Public and IR scholar alike); even if defining culture was a tricky business. The examples commentators cited indicated that they must have been operating with a very clear idea of what culture involved. Likely then that the idea of culture was not so vague after all.

In the absence of theoretical clarity, dependence on the idea of culture as a conventional standard left scholars, however well intentioned, vulnerable to the charge of 'cultural fundamentalism.' In 1995, Verena Stolcke argued that, in Europe:

> a perceptible shift in the rhetoric of exclusion can now be detected. From what were once assertions of the differing endowment of human races there has risen since the seventies a rhetoric of inclusion and exclusion that emphasizes the distinctiveness of cultural identity, traditions, and heritage among groups and assumes the closure of culture by territory.
>
> (Stolcke 1995:2)

These 'new boundaries' of culture were creating 'new rhetorics of exclusion' and in the extreme amounted to what Stolcke identified as 'cultural fundamentalism.' Moreover, as she pointed out, "[i]nstead of ordering different cultures hierarchically, cultural fundamentalism segregates them spatially, each culture in its place" (Stolcke 1995:8). Although Huntington had nested cultures hierarchically within his civilizational scheme, the matroushka doll image had, largely, given way to a flatter and overlapping view of cultures; nevertheless, the fundamental ontological principles remained the same. As Stolcke indicated, so long as each culture was believed to occupy its own space and could be separated from its neighbours, the fundamental distinguishing features remained as troubling theoretical concerns. The natives were still conceived by scholars to be essentially different from the tourists.

After Huntington, it was the political consequences of cultural fundamentalism that especially worried anthropologists. Following Stolcke's argument, Christophe Brumann, a reformist who supported the culture concept, was concerned for the political implications of the fundamentalist position.[27] As Brumann explained:

> It [cultural fundamentalism] posits the existence of a finite number of distinct cultural heritages in the world, each tied to a specific place of origin. Since these are taken to be ultimately antagonistic and incommensurable, they and the individuals associated with them are considered best kept separate, ideally in their respective homelands or, if that fails, in ethnically defined quarters . . . Cultural fundamentalism, therefore, will not serve as ideological buttressing for new colonialisms, but for fuelling xenophobic tendencies . . .
>
> (Brumann 1999:10)

The lack of consideration of both the political implications of the culture concept, as well as the kind of politics which maintained that the idea of culture was a useful one, should have been a matter of serious concern. Instead of labouring under the essentialist version of the anthropological concept within IR or exposing ourselves to accusations of cultural fundamentalism, perhaps some reconsideration ought to be entered into.

If we struggle to find culture in the anthropological sense, consider it too vague or too difficult to identify but remain committed to the cause, then perhaps it is time to ask where the problem truly lies. It is possible that the problem lies less in our ability to achieve clarity and more with the nature of the concept (not to mention our assumptions about that concept) itself. As Lila Abu-Lughod, a well-known critic of culture, has pointed out:

> The fact that … [culture] is such a "successful" and popular concept should be cause for suspicion, not self-congratulation. That the concept lends itself to usages so apparently corrupting of the anthropological ones as the pernicious theses of Samuel Huntington's clash of civilizations is, for me, serious. Huntington's glorification of Western superiority and gross simplification and reification of cultures and cultural difference resonate with popular sentiment and racist politics. It seems to me that our role [as anthropologists] is not to use our expertise in "culture" to correct him (by showing that his cultural units are too big or too incommensurate, too homogenized or too crude) but to criticize the very notion of setting up groups of people defined by shared cultures as hostile and opposed.
>
> (Abu-Lughod 1999:14)

Crucially she goes on to say, "[i]f civilizations are extensions of cultures and cultures depend on culture and we do not question the notion of culture, then we are not in a position to mount this critique" (Abu-Lughod 1999:14). Sadly, it had to be said that the kind of critique Abu-Lughod envisaged had not made its mark within IR by the close of the twentieth century.

The interest in differences of 'national style' in strategic culture raises the question as to how different work on culture is compared to that produced on national characteristics that began in the 1940s. This question is pertinent to everyone in IR employing the idea of culture, and is not simply one confined to strategic culturalists or cultural fundamentalists. No matter how sophisticated the study, how elaborate the argument, nor even, how celebratory the tone, if 'culture is a big thing that does things' and that these things are believed only to belong to a specific community of people, then the grounds for distinction are marginal. It may not be necessary to subscribe to the unsubstantiated myths of their time that the Russians have a predilection for 'spying,' or that millions of Chinese 'need to save face' or that Islam prevents the spread of democracy, but if we end up believing that culture represents a permanent source for the distinction between the natives and the tourists, then we must wonder how this concept works and what kind of narratives we are supporting. Beyond this and irrespective of whether the idea of culture is applied to a national grouping as found in Morgenthau's work, or a regional grouping as in Huntington's idea of civilizations, or a sub-group such as a military organization or an indigenous community, the underlying theoretical questions, as raised so far, remain undisturbed.

Ultimately, we must ask ourselves if an essentialist conception of culture, and this kind of causal explanation, is of any value to IR? We may find ourselves agreeing with Lila Abu-Lughod, Joel Kahn and Adam Kuper among others, and wonder why we even continue to work with the idea. It is not only appropriate but also pertinent to ask if the rise of the anthropological concept over the humanist concept has been a useful development in the discipline. Perhaps the time is right for the discipline to consider a cessation of the practice of fetishizing the natives and to elaborate upon conceptual frameworks that welcome the tourists back.

Key points

During the 1990s,

- The synthesis between 'community, culture and difference' became abundant in IR literature.
- Strategic culture focused on the differences between military organizations and national styles.
- Strategic culture encountered methodological and epistemological problems over what to study and how to study it – a debate that continues.
- Samuel Huntington's 'clash of civilizations' depended exclusively on an essentialist conception of culture. Problematically, politics had given way to culture as the source of international difficulty in his thesis.
- Anthropologists expressed concern over the politics of culture and the theoretical implications their concept generated. Huntington's thesis generated much concern in anthropology over the utility and desirability of the idea that culture exists everywhere and affects everything.
- The essentialist nature of the culture concept was being much debated in anthropology, whilst in IR this concept of culture was being taken for granted as a conventional standard.

Conclusion
Fates and futures

What is the future of the concept of culture, where are we today and what does the author think? These are the kinds of questions that readers of a monograph such as this one would like to have the answers to as it comes towards closure, and rightly so. Undoubtedly, since the end of the Cold War, there has been a marked increase in interest in the subject of culture. Literature on multiculturalism, interest in cultural differences and specific regional values, as well as their relationship to international issues, such as human rights, all continue to influence the discipline. Similarly, work on strategic and organizational culture continues to expand. In addition, two developments have seen new avenues for research opening up within IR, much of which is empirically based.

On the one hand, there is the growing interest in popular culture and its international dimension. Jutta Weldes' (1999) study of Star Trek and its reflection of American foreign policy is a good example here.[1] This kind of work leans towards the Cultural Studies approach and is focused on popular activities, and therefore unusual subject matter in IR such as film and television media, music, sport and science fiction, but some of it is also, inevitably, interested in power relationships. The power of global discourses to influence international affairs is perhaps best exemplified by the impact of global mass media, for example, the 'CNN Effect' (Robinson 1999).

On the other hand, there has been a small eruption in work on cultural diplomacy and the cultural policy of specific states and particular periods.[2] Arguably, the recognition that the Cold War had a cultural dimension has contributed to the awakening of interest in this area.

Far from being a neglected subject in the discipline, we seem to have, and have had, more 'culture' than we know what to do with. We have cultural internationalism, cultural diplomacy and cultural policy; the Cultural Studies approach and the interest in the international dimensions of popular culture. Alternatively, there is the culture of specific nations, which makes them characteristically different from one another, and also, interest in multiculturalism, and indigenous culture, and the clash of cultures. There is organizational culture in the form of strategic and diplomatic cultures, and the culture of International Society, world culture and global cultural flows. Yet, each of these developments has its roots, in one way or another, in either the humanist or the anthropological concept of culture.

Whether culture is exemplary or popular is a question generated by the humanist concept. Whether cultural diplomacy furthers mutual understanding or merely promotes a specific way of life, highlights the contrast between the humanist and anthropological concepts. Whether we are looking for ways of accounting for differences between communities, or of respecting cultural diversity (celebrating it even), or need to find mechanisms for living with the prospect of cultural clash, these are all issues that derive explicitly from the anthropological concept.

As important as all of these questions are, the more serious underlying concerns are theoretical. It is the theory behind the thinking that requires discussion, not so much the substance or empirics of the case. And in this respect, working within established theoretical assumptions about the nature of culture does not challenge the fundamental propositions upon which those assumptions are based. In short, there is not much that could be claimed as conceptually new, although much may be novel in IR of course, including many of the questions some scholars have generated. On the whole, scholars in IR are still dependent upon conventional standards drawn from elsewhere, although, as this book has attempted to show, the content of those conventional standards altered substantially from one end of the twentieth century to the other – from the humanist idea of culture to the essentialist's concept.

There is, however, one aspect of international relations that forces us to question our conceptual cultural tools more than any other in IR and that is globalization. Whether we think the idea of culture has a future, and if we wonder what the fate of the natives and the tourists will be, is a matter that depends less on our understanding of globalization and more on our initial understanding of the nature of culture itself. In this sense, globalization requires us to reconsider what we mean by the term 'culture.' It also raises the further consideration of whether either conceptual approach has any future value in the discipline. The processes of globalization present a challenge to both the humanist and anthropological concepts of culture, but in differing ways, while the historical experience of culture within the discipline presents its own challenges as to how we understand the word itself. Ultimately, the twin challenges of globalization and of our disciplinary heritage force us to question how we think about communities and difference and the concepts we employ to inform our narratives about such things.

The fate of the natives

There was a time when I worried that everything would turn out to be the same the world over. I thought that it would be a terrible shame if global diversity came to an abrupt end and we all found ourselves eating the same foods, wearing the same clothes, watching the same films and doing the same things. It bothered me that the only major difference between Birmingham and Beijing might turn out to be in the weather. Nowadays, I worry much less about such mediocre predictions. We need better intellectual equipment than homogeneous and depressing images if we are to think about the consequences of common living, which is beginning to be a hallmark of globalization processes. Besides, on the face of it, what is there to fear if we did all turn out to be doing the same things and living similar lifestyles? I see nothing wrong with the argument that we should all enjoy a similar quality of life and living standard. When life expectancy in Japan averages 81 years and in Sierra Leone only 38.9, the idea of sameness is extremely appealing (under Japanese standards, obviously).[3] Yet, it is precisely this fear of 'sameness' that the processes of globalization are believed to intensify. Regardless of what we think of globalization (whether we are for or against is too simplistic), it is the notion of 'fear' itself that requires interrogation. Fear of what, we may ask?

The underlying fears in arguments involving global similarity are obviously bound up with an essentialist notion of 'culture' and the 'loss of the native.' Globalization is thought to be driving the native into extinction through the establishment or imposition of a single and homogeneous way of life. Local cultural ways of life are believed to be under threat from the international exchange of artifacts, ideas and 'gifts.' The natives are being pushed out or worse still, being destroyed by the tourists, and this fear of globalization (in its cultural aspect) is a frequent complaint.

Hedley Bull worried that local diversity was undermining and inhibiting the prospects of a coherent (or solidarist) international culture. International society would be more effective if it was able to build on the norms of international culture in more meaningful terms; which would mean in Bull's terms, constructing a robust single global culture. Bull grew less hopeful about the prospects for international culture in the face of decolonization and the growing social and political divides. Samuel Huntington, on the other hand, positively trumpeted the re-emergence of local diversity as evidence against the very idea that a single international culture was possible. Instead of an international culture developing, he claimed that the opposite process was taking place with something he called 'indigenization.' Neither theorist got this right in my view; both Bull and Huntington failed to see the diversity and disagreement that exists within local societies when they spoke in cultural terms from an international perspective. In this way, neither had much to offer in terms of how to think about the changes that are taking place at the international level. Both have misunderstood the idea of culture; or to be more precise both have understood culture in its essentialist form and as this form of culture does not exist, neither perspective is going to take us very far when it comes to dealing with the substantive changes taking place under globalization. Denying the possibility of the occurrence of a single global culture by retreating into 'nativism,' or 'indigenization,' is not to say that something is not going on at the international level.

Clearly, we are not building a single international culture whereby we all believe in the same values and live the same lives in the cultural fundamentalist sense. Huntington's observation that the introduction of Buddhism into China did not turn the Chinese into Indians was an accurate one (although, it did not add much to our knowledge of China), but it was based on incorrect theoretical premises. At one level, the kind of homogenization Huntington described did not and will not occur because it is, at the individual human level, a physical and intellectual impossibility.[4] The discourses of life are utterly various and so long as there are different human beings involved in these discourses, the conversations will vary amongst them in multitudinous terms. The arrival of a hamburger outlet in Beijing or Minsk does not make one an American; it simply extends the digestive options of a Chinese or a Belarusian. Even popular and crude complaints about 'McDonald's taking over the world,' do not prevent the locals from taking their families to such establishments in large numbers, even if only out of curiosity. This is not to trivialize the fear that 'McDonald's is taking over the world,' a point discussed in a moment, but it is to say that at the literal and transformative level, the partaking of a hamburger is insufficient to make one an American. In a basic way, swallowing food, wearing clothes, watching films, and so on is not like catching a cold. Ways of life are not contagious, but clearly, the presence of global artifacts in one's community is representative and indicative of some kind of change. Who is to 'blame' for such change is an important question, but an entirely separate issue, to which the answer can be as political as it is economic.

More of us are sharing common living and it is globalization that is creating/enabling this kind of social change. Denying the existence of a single global culture does not help us to approach the questions being generated by the vast array of international connections that globalization brings; neither does it assist us in assessing the impact of these things at the local level. The inadequacy of the approach is especially obvious when the natives appear on television to appeal to the global masses, have access to the Internet, use mobile phones and make full use of other paraphernalia of global living. More importantly, it affords us no way of assessing what is happening on a global scale and from an international (or IR) perspective. Both arguments (popular in international politics), the one that bemoans the lack of global similarity and the one that celebrates it, are two sides of the same coin and they both fail to provide us with adequate frameworks for thinking about global developments.

On the intellectual side, the fears of cultural sameness as well as the arguments against it are selfish ones, especially as it is seemingly not poverty that we fear, but the spread of affluence and an affluent lifestyle. (This is a personal and political complaint on my part.) There is nothing wrong with all of us having effectively the same sanitation system, the same access to clean water, the same quality of medication and education, and so on – even if these things are produced in the local 'dialect' and fit in with the local way of doing things. There is certainly nothing wrong in people being able to buy affordable clothing, or live in decent housing, or being able to provide for their children and offer them a better way of life. There is nothing wrong with all households having a flushing toilet and the same kind of front loading automatic washing machine to take the burden off, largely, women's hands. Or to be more provocative, there is nothing wrong with people wanting to exercise some measure of control over their lives and having a say in how it ought to be organized and by whom, in vaguely similar ways. Not only is there nothing fundamentally wrong or even anything intellectually to object to in this sameness, but it seems that globalization is greatly increasing knowledge of other people's lives, what other people do, the things they possess and so on. All of this is creating, in the process, a greater number of possibilities for people. Far from restricting choices, in many respects globalization is increasing them for large numbers of people around the world – the vast majority of whom happen to live outside the 'wealthy, white and Western' nexus.

Fearing the emergence of sameness is especially problematic when we are ignorant of what local people actually would like for themselves. The essentialist concept of culture is particularly worrying in this respect, especially when detailed substantive research is lacking. But it is not unreasonable to suggest that globalization is not just affecting our knowledge of artifacts (say washing machines) and what might be available to us (HIV/Aids medication), but it is also increasing our knowledge of ideas (equality for example). Many of us now inhabit a world where we know more about other people, the things they do, the way they live, than we did previously – or at least we think we do, inasmuch as we form impressions about other people (an important distinction and one not to be taken lightly as we shall see below). This makes us aware of what is available or possible in ways that we may not have had any knowledge of in the past.

The expansion in the global traffic of information, in this respect, is awe-inspiring and has enabled more people to become aware (for good or ill) of the alternative forms of living that exist in the world, as well as the kinds of things that go on in it. This is a tremendous substantive change, not only in terms of the volume of information moving between people but also for the impact it has and the perceptions it creates. Perhaps, fifty years ago, the idea of democracy was out of many people's grasp and even their imagination. Post-Cold War, this is no longer the case. Some forms of government are beginning to look like dinosaurs from a previous age in these globalized times. The natives are increasingly aware of this and are capable of voicing their own dissent.

When we fear people all doing the same things and ending up with the same culture (in the 'way of life' sense), we are not only being selfish but we are basing that selfishness on two large, yet implicit, assumptions.

The first assumption holds that all things will manifest themselves in precisely the same way in different locations (Huntington's problem). This is not only an intellectual impossibility but also essentialist nonsense. Everything is adapted to the local circumstance and acquires its own native purpose – even debates about global events. There will be, and always have been, local variations as the anti-essentialist criticisms of the suggestion of cultural homogeneity discussed in chapter three indicated.

The second assumption implies that other people should not be expected to want this global lifestyle for themselves (but more detailed ethnographic evidence is required to enable us to debate this assumption). There are problems with global production to be sure, certainly in terms of fair wages and working conditions; however, rejecting the global spread of the flushing toilet and the automatic washing machine in favour of 'saving the natives' from a fate worse than affluence, seems a particularly arrogant stance. If something is good enough for us and other people want the same or similar, then who are we to deny them the opportunity, even in theory? Championing the native against the tide of global change raises the question of whose cause it is that is really being defended. A question that applies both internally, to groups who want to preserve/protect their culture, and externally, to supporters of such claims. The issue of internal preservation, which is seen here as a political matter, will be discussed in the last section of this conclusion.

The generalized idea (and external argument) that natives ought to be preserved in their ancient, and usually life shortening, ways because they are the ones resisting the onset of global culture is a thoroughly privileged one; it is tantamount to saying, 'we, Westerners can change and make our lives easier, but you local, different, native types have to remain the same because it makes us feel better.' And so the line of argument runs, if the natives must shoot seals or harpoon whales, they should do it on foot and by hand; considering labour saving devices like skidoos and .50 calibre rifles goes against our (Western and privileged) conception of (your native) tradition.[5] There is much of this kind of argument about for preservation of the natives, especially when it is deployed as a defence to a perceived notion of, so-called, cultural imperialism.

According to the authors of a recent 'international bestseller,' "[i]ndigenous music has to be torn away from its context and Westernized to be acceptable to those who are supposed to be its inheritors" (Sardar and Davies 2002:125). The message from the authors to young people (who are to be blamed for encouraging this dreadful innovation) seems to be that it is OK to make music so long as you don't go electric. With these kinds of arguments, notions of equality and mutual respect seem to fly out of the window.[6] The 'billiard ball' conceptions of communities and culture, much maligned in anthropology, are still pervasive assumptions, it seems, when it comes to assessing the impact of globalization and providing perspectives on social change. Narratives that fix difference are, arguably, in danger of fixing the privileges of the West and preserving the native in some mythical state.

The fear of global cultural similarity is an entirely imagined one. The fear is unfounded because it assumes we would all turn out to be the same person, which, at a minimum, does not place much faith in the nature of human beings. We are plainly not the *same* people even within the same society. Short of a change in human nature, it is difficult to see how we can even begin to subscribe to the view that we will all end up being the same on a global scale, with or without the concept of culture in tow. The question of homogenization is not a cultural one, but one dependent upon our understanding of human beings and our deployment of other concepts drawn from politics, economics, sociology and other disciplines.

Although the processes of globalization provide a powerful impetus to arguments centred on a fear of the loss of the native, it is clear that we have 'lost' more culture and difference than we can ever remember or a whole university full of historians will ever be able to recapture. It is an epistemological point, but one with political implications. The fact that we may all end up eating pasta and rice and wearing Levi jeans is of no great consequence in comparison to the unknown and unknowable amount of history that has already been lost and beyond our ability to retrieve. This is not intended as a flippant remark, but one that suggests we face certain facts about our existence more squarely. None of us has the 'culture' or way of life we had ten, twenty or a hundred years ago, not even small communities like the Mbuti. The point is, 'cultural' loss is a daily if not hourly occurrence; complaints about 'loss,' which accompany complaints about globalization, are, as discussed in the last section of this conclusion, another species of argument altogether.

The mere fact of loss, however, is nothing unusual. We lose 'culture' and our so-called 'ways of life' and take up with new ones, more frequently than we care to admit. Indeed, since we have lost far more than we can remember or can ever hope to regain, one would presume that we would have got used to the process by now. Maybe, contemporary global living has made us all too nostalgic for our own good. Whatever the case, the epistemological point is clear: the object of loss that we are complaining about, or fear for its disappearance, is only a small aspect of life overall. The value we place on this object of concern is a separate issue – why value this practice or habit or 'way of life' and not the countless others we have lost, and can no longer remember, along the way? The way we answer this question, about the things we value or chose to retain, is more political than we realize.

Why some things become important or have importance attached to them is a matter of choice and power (whose choice and power become pertinent issues), it is not an essentialist cultural given. In this respect, globalization is no more or less a threat to our ways of doing things than we already pose and have posed, to ourselves. Since we did not have a fixed and enduring way of doing things in the past, we will not have one in the future. The natives will come and go, and new natives with different ways of doing things will replace them. We will abandon practices and habits and we will create new ones; whether we abandon theses things in favour of McDonald's or Mitsubishi is another matter and one in which the marketing and the selling of ideas, clearly, plays a considerable role. Should we, however, blame these companies for our careless disregard of habit or is it preferable to see them as symbolic of it? Conversely, we could in theory choose to resurrect any number of practices or habits from our past, but we do not, and perhaps one reason as to why we do not resurrect these past habits is that we do not care about them sufficiently, or, crucially, have not been persuaded to care about them, as much as other practices. If we have changed our practices or habits, then it is the process of change and all that that entails which should intrigue us. The power of politics, religion, economy, marketing ploys and social structure cannot be conveniently papered over. The crucial point is that the loss and/or re-emergence of 'cultural' ways of life (so-called) is a complex political matter and ought to be approached on those terms. It is not simply the case that we had something and now it is gone, the real questions are why did it go, or be replaced, and for what purpose?

In the same way that Michael Carrithers found Ruth Benedict's Digger Indians 'managing to get along somehow' (as discussed in chapter three), in theory and as a result of globalization, we could end up doing the same things in the same way, which would undoubtedly signify considerable social change – but we would get over it and get on. Indeed, we are getting over it and getting on. Traditions, as Eric Hobsbawm (Hobsbawm and Ranger 1983) reminded us, are frequently invented in any case. One minute we might be practising suttee and the next minute not; one moment, wearing Levi jeans and the following one, traditional dress. Our ancestors may have travelled by camel, horse or elephant, and prior to that, they had to walk; but now it is more convenient to use the 4×4. So what. We have the society we have, which is not an argument for the status quo – far from it. Things remain extremely unsatisfactory on a global scale and considering all of the inequalities and injustice, there is plenty of room for improvement. Yet, none of this has anything to do with an essentialist conception of culture. If we are unhappy about our circumstances, then it is a question of politics and economics as to whether we are able to change them and make the situation better, or whether we are limited in the extent of our life choices and chances. It is not a 'cultural' matter because, even if we accepted the basic idea of culture, the substance of culture is not fixed and homogeneous, and never was. 'Culture' will not save us and we will not save 'culture.' The bigger mistake is to replace politics, economics and power with a non-entity called culture. We will all lose 'our culture' in one way or another eventually (we used to call it 'social change'), and while globalization may be speeding this process of change up and rendering it more visible, it can hardly be blamed for initiating the business in the first place. All of which is a call for a more sophisticated approach to what are clearly complex processes currently centred on the impact of globalization.

In the absence of the singular homogeneous international culture, differences *within* a state are as likely to be as great as differences between states. Arguments refuting the idea of a global culture, or even those fearing the emergence of one (the same thing but differently stated), are wide of the mark again in this respect. Arguments that massage fears of homogeneity or applaud so-called local culture in smaller homogeneous terms for resisting global homogeneity, gloss over the complexity and diversity of social life. Differences will persist as long as the differences between individuals exist.

There is an assumption that life is profoundly different between Beijing and Birmingham, and Mumbai and Minsk. Yet, the differences between town and city, between districts and regions can be equally as thought provoking and challenging; an observation easily lost in all the talk of homogenization. At the same time, this range of diversity is also limited in its extent, because all of the differences that we can focus on (or exaggerate) are also underpinned by commonality; commonality that globalization explicitly and successfully appeals to. We tend to like to think that we are all much more various than we really are, especially when we compare one extreme to another. Experience, however, of being a 'tourist' and of actually going elsewhere can teach us that we may not be so profoundly different as individuals and communities after all. If we were that different, we would not be able to live, work and holiday in other locations as much as we do. Indeed this was something the inter-war theorists with their cultural interchange easily recognized. This is not to say that differences do not exist, but it is to say that we can work to understand them, overcome them, learn new habits and practices, and, above all, survive and fit in with or create new discourses, when required. We can exaggerate the differences between communities and have been intellectually excessively prone to do so. A migrant can choose to fit in with his/her surroundings and learn new habits, new discourses and new ways of doing things. The days of pristine isolation and a vast array of difference are long since past – if they ever existed to the extent we like to tell ourselves, in any case.

Anti-essentialist conceptions of culture may have a lot to offer in terms of thinking about the processes of globalization, but they require further research and examination. Plainly, an anti-essentialist version of culture (culture as a verb, or a process of interaction) does away with the relentless 'have we/haven't we' argument, which is fixated on the notion of a single global culture and the demise of the native. Under an anti-essentialist conception of culture, the processes of doing are of greater interest than the (unchallenged and seemingly unchallengeable) *a priori* assumption that culture is the thing that makes us what we are and has to be preserved. In examining the processes that lead to the things we do and attempting to provide reasons for why we do those things in a specific way, there is a greater space for politics, economics and the context in which these things occur. There is much promise in an anti-essentialist approach, but it is suspected that the constructivist wing of IR is most likely to take up that challenge. In the meantime, there are still 'global cultural flows,' to borrow a phrase from David Held and Anthony McGrew (Held and McGrew 1996), and the fate of the tourists to think about.

The fate of the tourists

The things that capture commentators' attention regarding globalization are the speed, extent and intensity of connections, not simply in terms of trade but also in terms of production, finance and communication. One aspect of the globalization process might come under the broad heading of the old humanist version of 'culture.' "[G]lobal flows of culture" (Held and McGrew 1996:327), as artifacts and ideas that flow round the globe overriding state boundaries, have increased markedly in extent and intensity, and will continue to do so into the future as far as most commentators can tell. In popular thinking, globalization is associated with certain global products and international companies – McDonald's, Nike, Hollywood films, Microsoft – much of which is a euphemism for Americanism, or American imperialism.[7]

The actual pattern of the global movement of artifacts, let alone ideas, is not well mapped in the popular mind. However, one thing is certain: it is an increasingly global exchange, however unequal this process of exchange may be in actuality at the present time. Bollywood is more productive at times and has greater global ticket sales than Hollywood. Nokia, Sony, Mitsubishi and L'Oreal, to name a few, are all household names that did not originate in the United States. Food and football are two obvious areas that are not dominated by the Americans. People all round the world eat each other's food these days and while the Americans might be said to be getting better at football (soccer), so are the Japanese and the Koreans.

Yet these are all minor points in comparison to the extent of global cultural flows in information, mass media, production and its techniques, and ideas. Two things are certain though; first, in spite of all the predominately negative speculation, we know very little about the reception and impact of these things on a global scale, while second, although there is a lot of global cultural exchange about, this is not exactly the kind of cultural interchange the inter-war theorists' envisioned.

Let us think back to what constituted the idea of culture in the humanist sense; it was art, literature, the products of human endeavour and the outputs of intellectual achievement. Substantively speaking, much of this made its way around the world historically in any case; think of the movements of books to India, the presence of chinoiserie in European art, or the influence of African music in the United States. Undoubtedly, much of this cultural movement was associated with the age of Empire and the politics of domination and exploitation, but what is perceived as interesting about globalization is not only the dramatic increase in the volume of cultural traffic but also that the variety of products have become more genuinely global. Pueblo pots, dot paintings by indigenous Australians, world music and literature are all global commodities. The film industries of India, Japan and Hong Kong rub shoulders with the American and European ones. This is less true of the film industries in Africa, Central Asia, Russia and Latin America, but no doubt, they too will experience global markets in due course. Fashions for cosmetics and health products like ginseng, tea tree and aloe vera, and for items like pashmina shawls, all have dispersed origins and form part of the global flow. Yet, it is more than a flow of goods and artifacts – this activity influences and affects our lifestyles and ideas about others and ourselves. The question of whether these artifacts ought to be interpreted as more popular than exemplary is left open to debate.

Global cultural flows or cultural interchange is creating a situation whereby the tourists are becoming indistinguishable from the natives. Not only are the tourists leaving a trail for the natives, so to speak, with their food, clothes, music, interests and demands, they are taking some of the same types of things from the natives to take back home again. In some cases, the tourists are rapidly becoming part of the native landscape as images and residents. British pensioners used to retire to Worthing before they went to Spain; now they make the trek to India. Their American equivalent makes similar pilgrimages to Mexico. When Cubans retire to Cumbria and Connecticut, the flow will be more complete. Some Europeans, meantime, are getting their cosmetic surgery done on the cheap in Eastern Europe, while some Indian and Asian women aspire to an idealized version of the 'Western' woman's shape.[8] Immigrants always bring new gifts, and diasporas create new networks and possibilities. There is a considerable amount of this kind of activity going on and it is not all confined to the big names like Nike and McDonald's; it is also in the small everyday things, such as tea and music, and in the way we perceive our bodies, others and ourselves.

There is clearly a considerable global imbalance in the movement of goods, but we should not assume for one moment that this would always be the case. That said, two things are clearly at odds in this process with the humanist concept of culture.

First, lipstick sales do not count as culture under the terms of the old humanist concept, although they would hold appeal to the Cultural Studies end of the market. Much of the substantive content of global cultural flows would fail to pass muster under the inter-war theorists' definition. This suggests that to appreciate the impact of some 'cultural' goods under globalization, we need to disassociate the idea of culture with elitist notions and extend it to more mundane, yet equally influential, matters like lipstick, shampoo and tea. We have to accept that people are more concerned with humbler issues like the hamburger than they are with Hamlet. Although there does not seem to be much interest in the humanist idea, least of all in the terms understood by the inter-war theorists, there is no denying that global culture flows are one of the most important features in contemporary international life. More importantly, this is creating impressions about *others* that are affecting, in turn, international politics. Would the global fear of America be so strong if McDonald's did not exist in most major cities and Microsoft on most computers around the world? It remains to be seen whether a Cultural Studies approach in IR would prove more fruitful than the elitism inherent in the original humanist conception that discounts the hamburger in favour of Hamlet. The project of Cultural Studies, however, does not have the same aims or aspirations as the humanist concept. It merely seeks out the hidden power elements and relationships of human effort and products, and may not serve as a helpful framework when it comes to thinking about the problems cultural interchange seem to be generating in world politics.

This brings us onto the second crucial difference that contemporary globalization has with the humanist concept. The majority of global exchange occurs without any conscious effort; excepting the conscious effort required to make money, or news, of course. There is no obvious attempt involved in the process of trying to get to know other people and to understand them. This is, arguably, one of the most problematic aspects of the cultural interchange associated with globalization.

Global 'gifts' are exchanged, or arrive on the doorstep, but are not sent or received in the deliberative and self-aware manner in which Alfred Zimmern and Gilbert Murray believed they should have been. On the whole, the 'gift' appears and we try to make sense of it after the event. Maybe this was always so, but it is clear that the social consequences of this activity are altering the shape of contemporary life on a vast scale. It is fair to say that much of the detail of this process passes us by, but arguably, cultural interchange of this order is not creating the 'organic relationships' that Zimmern aspired to; nor is it leading to the kind of 'mutual

knowledge' that the inter-war theorists believed would deepen international understanding.

'Tourists,' in the very general sense of global interlopers, do not seem
to travel any more 'intelligently' than they did in Zimmern's day, and
perhaps it is too much to expect them to travel otherwise. Undoubtedly,
though, every aspect of interchange is creating knowledge and does carry
with it impressions and reactions. All of which present us with some
serious challenges both in international relations and in thinking in IR.
This is especially the case when we consider that much contemporary cultural interchange seems to be fuelling negative impressions and forms of
knowledge, rather than the positive ones hoped for by the inter-war theorists. It is not the case that these things make no impression whatsoever, for
plainly they do. One of the most problematic issues might be said to
reside in the area of perceptions and understandings that global interchange generates between differing peoples. This was a problem readily
recognized and easily understood by the inter-war theorists; so much so,
that it provided them with a basis to advocate the promotion of cultural
interchange. Their objective was clear; it was to break down barriers in
international understanding, not to create new ones. There is a need
nowadays, it would seem, for a humanist revival in, at least, this very
important respect.

We have always formed impressions of *others*. For instance, this has been
illustrated by the 'monstrous races' (Friedman 1981) that surround the
edges of medieval Mappae Mundi and by the exotic figures that lurk
around in travel tales. From missionary reports to the diaries of adventur-
ers and from ethnographic monographs to portraits of national characteristics, *the other* has been fictionalized, 'primitive-ized' and 'orientalized'
from a Western perspective. From the non-Western perspective, tales of
strangers permeate oral and written stories, appear in local lore, and grace
the surfaces of caves, pots and paintings around the globe. The foundations of such impressions might be noticeable oddities, gross generalizations, stereotypes, or outright prejudice, but, in the mere art and practice
of impression forming, globalization is not doing anything new when it
adds to this general activity. However, the greater the volume and intensity of cultural interchange, the greater the propensity for bizarre impressions and exotic perceptions. All of which constitute the 'real reality' in
one sense, in so far as this is what people believe about *others* and therefore has to be taken as the thing to be worked with.

Yet, in another sense, in the sense that these impressions are only ever
partial and can be alarmingly negative in their distortions, they present
the possibility for serious difficulties in international politics. In this way, it
is clear that the Realists were wrong in their assessment of the effectiveness of international culture in its humanist form. That they dismissed the
activity for its shortcomings, namely its inability to engender peaceful
international relationships, also meant that they discounted the subtle way

in which culture could and can exert a powerful influence in world affairs. As a result, theoretical questions over the effectiveness of culture (in its humanist sense) have remained in abeyance since the late 1940s.

'Americans' and 'Muslims' (whoever either are, for we know that there are many Islams and many Americans) are probably, and unfortunately, two of the most misunderstood groups of people. Crude perceptions that Americans only care about money and themselves, and that Muslims are to be viewed with suspicion because they are religious fanatics or worse still, potential terrorists, are regular assumptions and a grim contemporary reality. Outside of their own spheres, both communities could use some conscious efforts at fostering mutual understanding; not simply between themselves but with the global public at large. What is easily a recognizable problem for 'Americans' and 'Muslims' is likely to be an issue for everyone touched by the globalization process. Retreating into nativism and shutting the neighbours out is not an option under globalization – this issue touches us all.

Prejudicial and racist assumptions make it very difficult for the victims to move around (as visitors or residents) or even to exist in other communities. Other kinds of perceptions are pernicious on a grand scale; in the social sciences and to some extent among people generally, we have taken on board the criticisms of the prejudice inherent in meta-narratives involving 'primitives' and 'orientalism,' but now it seems, from some people's point of view, that all 'Westerners have no values.' In view of the colossal volume of stereotyping and prejudicial assumptions, there is an obvious and urgent need to reach some measure of understanding. However, a serious interrogation of the origins of such perceptions is required before we can do something to counter the negatives and dispel the myths.

Perceptions of others have become a major part of the globalization process, whether they are warranted or unwarranted, accurate or otherwise. Sadly, it appears that our (new) knowledge of *others* is generating new forms of prejudice and feeding feelings of animosity. All of which is fertile ground for the politician who wants to fan the flames of 'cultural difference:' a problem already recognized by anthropologists with their fear of the politics generated by cultural fundamentalism. Hope for a revival of the old humanist concept might be misplaced, but some variation on the humanist theme must be welcomed. However, any move towards the humanist concept could not simply be a resurrection of the past idea, not least because the original humanist idea was elitist, openly ethnocentric and frequently, racist. Notions of mutual interest and respect, based on presumptions of equality and a genuine curiosity about fellow human beings, not to mention real concerns for *others*, are ideas with which we could begin to navigate our way back to the universalism inherent in the humanist concept.

Undoubtedly, global interchange is the thing that is going to shape the lives of everyone (eventually) living on the planet. Global cultural inter-change is a major and crucial feature of international relations, but what it is doing to our lives and what the consequences are, generates more questions than we are able to answer at the moment.

Chief among the concerns, are the questions as to whether this global interchange will give us cause for fostering mutual understanding or whether it will merely supply a greater number of occasions for creating new forms of prejudice? Will this interchange cleave the world into new kinds of divisions, especially those that divide the 'haves' from the 'have nots'? Will it feed the stereotypes and social incommensurability of the kind that Huntington described? If it does, and there are plenty of examples that might concur with his model of the world these days, it does not mean that Huntington was right. In the first place, it will be politics, as Chris Brown reminded us, not the notion of essential and embedded culture that will determine the form these differences take.

Yet, it is the way we think about differences that will (or will not) allow us to think about political solutions to political problems. Beyond this, and as this book has attempted to illustrate, it is in the concepts we employ that the answers to questions over the way in which we view the world will be determined. There are more possibilities of viewing the world of international relations through the concept of culture than simply those associated with the essentialist notion that culture makes us what we are.

The notion of the distinctive native, suspended in difference across time and space, is plainly untenable. In practical terms, the natives are turning out not to be so very different from the tourists, indeed, separating the two might not be the best thing to do given that they are both intermingling and exchanging 'gifts' at a phenomenal rate. The big question then, is where this leaves our understanding of the term 'culture?'

The future of culture

The history of culture has always been both international and political, and has taken the meaning of culture, paraphrasing Terry Eagleton, from 'pig-farming to Picasso, and from Picasso to the Pitjandjara.' The French took the word from the Italians, and from France it made its way around Europe. The word has travelled extensively in the intervening centuries, but the meaning attached to it has, as Adam Kuper pointed out, always been defined in opposition to something else.

Initially, the idea of culture was defined against bad manners and ill behaviour, and subsequently against the idea of civilization. The Germans defined it against the French idea of civilization, while the British defined it against the vulgar masses and mechanical advance. American anthropologists defined culture against British anthropologists and evolutionary thinking, and fed the idea back to Europe. Where once it was thought that culture was the accumulative intellectual and artistic wealth of humanity, now everyone defines his or her idea of culture as a way of life, in distinction from everyone else. In the light of the changing meaning of culture, it is important to remember that the meaning a current reader attaches to the word may not be the same meaning as that held by other authors at their time of writing. Had we been discussing the subject of culture in 1500, 1800, 1920 or 1990, we would not have been discussing the same thing. Although there may be some doubt over which theorist was working with which concept, and perhaps this is most applicable to International Society theory, the general trend is clear.

It was not possible for a British IR commentator in the 1920s to employ the anthropological concept because the American scholars were still working on the idea. Indeed, scholars of this period did not associate the word culture with communal difference. When they spoke of differences they did so in terms of races and nations, and all within the framework of the civilization concept. What also emerges from this history is the recognition that the relationship between the idea of culture and the civilization concept has been a significant one for IR; although this relationship to the civilization concept has not been examined in depth in this book, it was discussed to ground the history of culture in IR. However, the same word, civilization, was found at both ends of the twentieth century but with different meanings attached to it.

Interest in international relations, in the early twentieth century, centred on the concept of civilization, and, in many ways, that century appeared to close with renewed interest in civilization, although Samuel Huntington's idea of civilization was very different from that informing Norman Angell and his contemporaries. In both cases, the idea of culture found a place in narratives about international relations that were bound up with a notion of civilization. But, as the history contained in chapter one indicated, the meaning of civilization was being debated before IR was officially established. When a number of great issues combined (i.e. the idea of civilization, the place of evolutionary theory in civilization thinking, and the fear for the future of civilization) as they did around the First World War period, they created a space in which the humanist idea of culture could flourish in international politics. All of which brings us back to what culture was defined against.

In IR, the idea of culture that came to prominence during the inter-war period was defined against the uncivilized behaviour in international politics that led to the First World War. In the aftermath of the Second World War, national culture was defined against the humanist ideas that had sought to bring about peace through cultural interchange. Cultural internationalism was undermined, in theory, by cultural nationalism, which signified a major epistemic shift – the anthropological concept was on the rise. International Society theory defined culture against individual states, but increasingly found itself deferring to parochial and native forms of culture. By the end of the twentieth century, the natives were defined against the tourists, either as organizations or as coherent indigenous entities struggling to find their voice or clashing in their expression of it. In each case, the meaning of culture has served a social and political purpose. Culture is an idea that does things.

The critical questions centre on, what is the idea of culture expected to do and for whom? When viewed from within the discipline of international relations, the answer turns out to be more various than perhaps we imagined or have given ourselves credit for.

For inter-war theorists, culture played a part in their cosmopolitan narrative and their internationalist aspirations, and the same holds for International Society theorists, as discussed in chapters two and five respectively. For Hans Morgenthau and the Cold War warriors, culture was about national ways of life and this was examined in chapter four. In the battle between these ways of life, culture was deployed to win hearts and minds for the Americans, and it provided the basis of studies of other states and their national characters. As chapter six illustrated, for strategic culture, the idea of culture was thought to be the means for accounting for the differences between military communities, while Samuel Huntington took this idea much further and declared culture to be the source of difference between regional groupings, or civilizations.

Although some remnants of the old humanist concept remain, for instance in UNESCO and the various national exchange programmes, it was the anthropological concept that came to dominate most people's thinking by the late twentieth century. This historical survey has sought to show that not only has the anthropological concept eclipsed the humanist idea of culture generally, but also that American IR embraced the anthropological concept before British, and British based, scholars. American scholars were familiar with the anthropological concept around the time of the Second World War, while their British counterparts did not fully embrace the concept until the 1970s, or perhaps even later. This situation was perhaps not surprising since American anthropologists had (as demonstrated in chapter three), over the course of several decades, developed the new idea, while the British drew upon a much older heritage in European thought, that was discussed in chapter two. Yet, more than simply providing an intellectual framework within which to situate specific scholars and their work, this review of culture in IR has attempted to demonstrate the interconnections between ideas and the context that spawned them.

We are all victims of our contexts and are compelled to work within the confines of our factory conditions. This is especially relevant with reference to the idea of culture in IR; scholars did not invent the concept of culture they have depended on, nor could they be said to have added too much to the idea, although some did extend this idea to the international realm. In many respects, the ideas of IR theorists not only reflect trends in the social sciences generally, but the way they have applied the idea of culture to international relations tells us much about the conventional standards of their age.

Scholars have tended to employ the term 'culture' as though the meaning was self-evident; assuming that the meaning is, and was, readily understood by the audience and accepted by them. The experience of culture in IR highlights one of the major difficulties of relying upon ideas as a matter of conventional standard, especially when those ideas have been drawn from other disciplines and become taken for granted. Not only does the lack of elucidation make it difficult for future readers to grasp what the author intended, but it also makes it difficult for contemporary and future students to examine and engage with what amounts to an unspoken assumption.

Culture as a conventional standard has presented certain assumptions as though they were the truth; under the humanist concept it was assumed that Shakespeare and intellectuals were the embodiment of culture, whereas under the anthropological concept, it is assumed that all natives have culture and it is this that makes them what they are. With the humanist concept it was believed that cultural interchange would foster mutual understanding and bring international benefits – an assumption that still requires substantiating.

The problems surrounding the acceptance of unspoken assumptions become most troubling when they concern the anthropological concept, which has clearly been invoked in its essentialist form. The debates and difficulties surrounding the essentialist concept in its original discipline of anthropology have been overstepped and the theoretical limitations bypassed, although, undoubtedly, they have been touched on by R.J. Vincent and in the discussions among Strategic Culturalists. Yet, a general lack of awareness of the problems inherent in many conceptualizations of culture means that the difficulties only become replicated in the IR setting, leading not so much to an increase in understanding, but more to a repetition of difficulties already debated in anthropology. This is perhaps most evident in the problems some scholars working with the idea of strategic culture have experienced with relating the idea of culture to social action – a problem that previously presented itself to American cultural anthropologists.

Not many people find 'culture' an easy subject, but few seem keen to doubt the idea's absolute utility these days. Criticizing a concept in the hope of improving on it is one thing, but saying a concept does not exist is problematic. As important a concept as culture has been in IR, it has been a thoroughly 'taken for granted' one – something that can unquestionably be relied upon without too much concern for the content of the idea. Unlike other concepts in IR, sovereignty for example, the idea of culture has not been much dissected or thoroughly debated. The implications of the concept of culture we employ for the kinds of narratives we then produce, and the influence that our construction (or acceptance) has on the stories we tell about international politics, are only beginning to be made transparent. In spite of the current commonplace belief that we all have culture and it makes us what we are, we are not compelled to sub-scribe to the underlying idea; indeed, the criticisms of the essentialist understandings of this concept, made in chapter three, amply demon-strate that there are important reasons for us to resist this notion. This raises the rather serious question as to the place of difference in the discipline and how scholars choose to think about this.

People and their differences, arguably, lie at the heart of the discipline. Differences have always existed and we have always been curious about them. I would say this curiosity about *others* is not only a crucial feature of what it means to be human, but is also an important and central feature of international relations and IR. How we think about differences, which kinds of differences we 'see,' and how we categorize them, are all matters subject to debate. Whether we have thought about these differences in terms of states, classes, races or cultures is a matter of conceptual choice. Inter-war theorists did not see 'cultural' differences; they saw 'racial', national and civilizational differences. But even within the framework of those differences, they did not accept that the differences they saw were the end of the story; rather, they chose to tell a story about international relations that looked beyond difference. They chose the humanist idea of culture to help them in their project. International cultural relations and fostering mutual understanding were an important element in their narrative about international relations. The Cold War context changed thinking about not only fostering mutual understanding but also the very desirability of the project. Perhaps this tells us more about the context of the period than it does about the nature of the differences themselves.

Adda Bozeman worried that "ideas ... [were] not transferable in their authenticity, however adept and dedicated the translators" (Bozeman in Bull and Watson 1984:392). Maybe ideas never do translate in their authenticity, but we still find ways of communicating with one another. The spectre of authenticity was Bozeman's strongest criticism of Inter-national Society theory and the trump card she whipped out onto the table was 'culture.' Bozeman's weakness was that she believed that there was such a thing as an 'authentic culture,' while criticisms of essentialism suggest otherwise.[9] Whatever 'authenticity' amounts to, it would be a mistake to think of it as a timeless matter. We are all capable of learning, not to mention creating, new habitual practice and calling it the (new) 'standard' and the latest in 'authenticity.' Fixing society to an 'authentic' standard that supposedly endures and remains unchanged is not to appre-ciate the dynamic nature of human society. 'If we cannot find two Indians to tell a story alike,' what hope is there of finding the 'real' thing? Worse, the notion of an authentic standard of culture creates obstacles for those designated inauthentic. Although questions of authenticity clearly occupy political leaders and community spokespeople, the problem this presents to academics is most pressing.

R.J. Vincent, it was pointed out in chapter five, recognized that race was a contested category and even a non-existent one in biological terms (Vincent 1982). However, the problem was from his point of view, what we as academics, commentators and otherwise thoughtful people could make of the situation where people made frequent use of the idea of race. By paying close attention to articulations of race, Vincent suggested, we could learn much about the politics behind the idea. And so it is, in my view, with the current conventional standard of essentialist culture that permeates IR. Indeed, in terms of non-existence, Joel Kahn has suggested that in the future the concept of 'culture' might be defined in the following way:

> *Culture.* The common use of the word in English to refer to a group of persons who share common ideational features and form a discrete and separate population unit has no scientific validity, since anthropological theory has long since demonstrated that there are no fixed or discrete cultural groups in human populations ... However, as a folk concept in western and non-western societies the concept of culture is a powerful and important one.
>
> (Kahn 1989:21)

What then, are we, in IR, to make of this folk concept?

Substantively speaking, the idea of culture, like that of race, is one that matters for subjective reasons. It also provides a useful vehicle for strategic social manoeuvring; think of what the idea did for the Kayapo Indians. Like race, it is the idea that serves as the source of difference and distinction between groups of people. When people speak of their 'culture' or of other communities having a different 'culture', we do not learn much about the substantive content of an authentic thing called 'culture' or even of how different people really are. What we glimpse is a vision or statement of how people would like their world to be and of their perceptions of *others*. In short, references to the essentialist concept of culture provide us with a good insight into other people's epistemologies (how they see the world) and better still, their politics. This probably helps to explain why it is always easier to see other people's cultures than our own (we know more about our own societies and are familiar with their internal diversity).

Much of the current debate over 'culture' invokes the notion of authenticity. People often refer to practices, habits, values, that they used to do or did 'before the barbarians came' – either as immigrants or as some manifestation of globalization. When people talk about 'culture' today, they are invariably trying to hang on to some aspect of their contemporary world or are trying to recreate a mythical past. Critical thinking demands to know whose contemporary world and whose mythical past is being invoked, for neither is likely to represent the contemporary world or past of everyone, even for those who share an identifiable geographical space. People believe that they *ought* to be the ones in control of their lives; if they feel that they are not, they are likely to go looking for an explanation. When people complain, as they frequently do, that they are losing their 'culture' or 'those nasty Americans are taking it over,' what we have is a statement about the things that are important to them and an insight into how they view politics in the contemporary world. Simply because the United States is not taking over the world, does not undermine the fear in people's minds that it might (or at least has the acknowledged potential to do so). Yet, the frequency of the fear expressed on behalf of culture tells us that this is, in some way or another, some form of reality for those who express the view. I may disagree vehemently with the notion and even the suggestion that homogenization is a (remote) possibility, but if I am to aspire to thoughtful observation, I must listen carefully to what people have to say on the matter. And what I hear is 'politics;' the politics of fears both imaginary and real.[10] Real in the sense that everyone's society is being lost and maybe at an alarming rate, and imagined in the sense that the image of society that has been lost probably only reflects the speaker's vision (or aspect as in Carrithers' notion of aspectival) of it.

The essentialist conception of culture always conveys, or attempts to convey, an ideal vision of reality. As an audience, we will not learn much about *your* 'culture' if you speak about it, but we might learn a good deal about *your* view of *your* society and *your* politics. In speaking about 'culture' you will reveal much about how you see the world, the things you think are important in it, what you value most and what you worry about. If you speak about *other* people's cultures, we will get some insight into your views of *others* – the fears, the threats, the myths, the condescension, and/or mutual respect. In addition, your attitude towards *others* may reveal as much about your perceptions of security and stability in your own society and as an individual, as it will about your understanding of these things in other societies. I suspect that most of the fears expressed are concerned with fears about power, or feeling powerless in the face of dramatic and visible social change. I suspect also that the fears are about uncertainty – uncertainty about the future in terms of economic well-being and prosperity, about keeping one's job or finding one, about putting food on the table, and about envisioning a better life for the children. I suspect also that these fears are not necessarily held by everyone in society, and that is something I should be intrigued by, in the least, and disturbed by, at most. When one group of people dismisses another on the grounds of culture, or claim the refugees do not belong because they are the wrong cultural type, we should be concerned. Above all, we should be disturbed particularly when the idea of culture is wielded by the powerful, for there is sure to be an abuse of power in there somewhere. When authorities tell us 'we are our culture' and proceed to dictate the terms, we all need to sit up and pay close attention to the sub-text of what is actually being said.

The essentialist concept of culture fuels the politics of segregation, and even if we cannot remove the idea completely, we should at least question it. We can learn much from culture-speak, but it will not be about a 'really existing ontological' thing called culture, because, as the criticisms demonstrate, there is no really existing singular entity that is 'the culture' out there. Like Vincent, I take the view that simply because 'race' does not exist as the nineteenth century theorists imagined, that does not undermine the tremendous part the idea has played and continues to play in social and political life. Similarly, that the cultural fundamentalist's idea of culture does not exist or even happen in the way most people want to speak about it, does not diminish the fact that this idea (or this Western folk concept) of 'culture' plays an incredibly powerful role in society and politics. In short, we would not want to trivialize the things that clearly matter a good deal to some people, but crucially, probably not to all of the people. Human life is not simply distributed, hybridized, an utterance, or, most painfully of all, a performance, it is something to be taken seriously and listened to carefully. For this reason, we need to dissect the ideas behind the words spoken in the name of culture and the fears expressed in its terms.

The essentialist idea of 'culture,' like that of the humanist, serves a purpose. Like the concepts of civilization, race and class that preceded it, culture is an idea that speaks for people. Our task, as students, critics and political beings, is to examine this idea of culture and all it contains, for what it is expected to do and by whom. We need to pay closer attention to the 'politics of difference' and be less easily impressed by differences in politics that attempt to smuggle themselves past us under the guise of 'culture.' Culture is not a truth claim – it is a political statement and as such deserves to be handled with the same measure of intrigue, criticism, suspicion or contempt as any other in the political world of IR. Culture speaks, in my view, with a 'conservative' voice about the nature of human interaction, communities and difference. It is 'conservative' because it attempts to preserve a discourse and to conserve society. All too frequently, it looks backwards, maybe too nostalgically, and it views change negatively instead of trying to identify what good might be forged out of the new. Ultimately, we require alternative theories for thinking about culture other than ones based (however vaguely) on totalizing and essentializing conceptions of people and their differences.

The essentialist concept of culture fuels narratives that fetishize our differences and elevates them to stand as a barrier between us. The British used to think about themselves in terms of class and race, but somewhere between the 1970s and the 1980s, Britain stopped being a 'class ridden' society and became a 'multicultural' one instead. This may not be wrong, but we need to be clear about what it is we are taking on here. It is too easy, sometimes, to assume that differences are a matter of culture and not the outcome of religious belief, politics, economic disparities, a local discourse or simply a clash of interest. We especially need to be critical of ideas that we take for granted, for those ideas might not be quite as innocuous as they appear.

IR disciplinary history demonstrates that there are alternative ways of thinking about culture, even if we have not always continued to be aware of them. In this sense, this historiography serves its own critical purpose. We do not have to accept that culture is the source of differences between us; it can be the language of commonality. The humanist concept is capable of informing cosmopolitan narratives, while the anthropological concept necessarily invites particularist ones. In many cases, it is quite clear that the term 'culture' can easily be replaced by the term 'society;' similarly, the idea of 'cultural differences' would be better served if it were substituted by other ideas, say those of political differences, economic, religious or ideological ones. Certainly, greater clarity and conceptual precision could be obtained, for often it is not transparent what kind of work the term 'culture' is expected to perform. More importantly, the normative weight we selectively assign to differences is an equally critical intellectual matter. As commentators, we have an intellectual duty not to create or fuel prejudice but to visualize conceptual solutions to problems. We need to ask ourselves, as some anthropologists have before us, whether or not we are comfortable with the synthesis between notions of difference, whole communities and something called 'culture.' And we need to remind ourselves that we did not always see the world in this way.

Criticisms of the essentialist conception of culture tell us that there are always people who dissent from the government line, and people who inhabit different worlds from the ones we know and are familiar with. Medieval peasants did not inhabit the same world as the aristocrats whose histories are, perhaps, better known. Nineteenth century factory workers did not live in the same world as the industrializing middle classes. The rural Chinese do not live in the same world as the globalizing city dwellers. Subsistence farmers the world over do not inhabit the same sphere as the international business travellers. Frequently, women and men operate in different dimensions, have different concerns and alternative priorities. The question then, is whose culture is this? Whose fear is it that this 'culture' will be eroded away or is being threatened by globalization? Ultimately, it becomes a question of who speaks for whom and why? Experience tells us that for every Dr Mohammed in Malaysia there is an Anwar Ibrahim; for every Samuel Huntington, a Lila Abu-Lughod; and for every conservative looking to conserve, there is a radical looking for a different answer to the question. This is the value of Vincent's attitude towards race, I believe; it has the capacity to steer us, at once, towards a sceptical and discriminating view of 'culture.' Sceptical because the idea of 'culture' in its anthropological guise is not a fact to be swallowed completely, but is something to be scrutinized. Discriminating because we should take it seriously where it is espoused and subject it to critical examination for its politics, its economics, and, above all, its underlying epistemology.

This book began by doubting Margaret Mead's claim that 'we are our culture.' It ends with refuting the suggestion entirely. Not only is this idea ridiculous, but it is dangerous. It may be convenient and useful to totalize communities and to abstract stereotypes and generalities, but it is dangerous to absent politics, economics and other issues involving power from the scene. Moreover, we need to be sensitive to the damage caused to those people and issues that do not fit the image or are unable to conform to the assumed standard of culture. It is easy to find theoretical fault with the essentialist assumption that we are our culture; it is empirically problematic, intellectually suspect, and too close to race theory for comfort. We need to reject the assumption that someone can speak for everyone through the medium of culture; moreover, we must challenge the faith that this is the only way to view the differences that exist. Through charting the history of the ideas attached to the word culture, and by mapping the relationship between these ideas and IR, I hoped to demonstrate that alternative ways of thinking about culture have existed and continue to exist in the discipline. By demonstrating that two concepts of culture have fed narratives about international relations and have affected political practice, I hoped to make a deeper critical point. The way we see the world and the stories we tell about it are enhanced and inhibited by the concepts we possess. We do not have to be our culture, indeed, given our disciplinary heritage, there is considerable ground for thinking that other cultural futures are not only possible, but increasingly desirable.

Key points

- The narrative possibilities involving an idea of culture within IR are numerous – but they all have their conceptual roots in either the humanist or the anthropological ideas of culture.
- Processes of globalization challenge both the humanist and anthropological concepts of culture and require us to think carefully about the nature of our concepts.
- Globalization reveals the paucity of the essentialist version of the anthropological concept – fears of and resistance to global homogeneity are not cultural issues.
- Globalization can be seen as a form of global cultural interchange – but this is not fostering mutual understanding, rather it seems to be creating negative impressions between people.

- Ultimately, our use of the concept of culture depends on what kind of story we want to tell about international relations. Do we want to tell a cosmopolitan story that includes both the natives and the tourists, or do we want to continue to fetishize the natives? It is our conceptual choice.
- We need to draw a distinction between the politics of culture and cultural politics – to be more sensitive to articulations of culture for what they reveal to us in political terms.

Notes

Introduction

1 In 1830 Coleridge wrote, "[b]ut civilisation is itself but a mixed good, if not far more corrupting influence, the hectic of disease, not the bloom of health, and a nation so distinguished more fitly to be called a varnished than a polished people, where this civilisation is not grounded in cultivation, in the harmonious development of those qualities and faculties that characterise our humanity." Samuel Taylor Coleridge's 'On The Constitution Of Church And State According To The Idea Of Each' (cited in Williams 1958/1993:61).

2 The problem that bothered Quentin Skinner was whether it was possible to accuse Plato of 'totalitarianism' when totalitarianism was a twentieth century concept and unknown by Plato. Skinner argues that there are no 'tenseless propositions' as he calls it – meaning there are no concepts that endure, unchangingly so, through the past, present and into the future, that we can apply to authors past and present. I accept that Skinner has a point here, but do not agree entirely with him in respect of the futility of employing ideas in a tenseless sense. There is some merit in applying new ideas to old work, and not least because Skinner does this himself. One of the weaknesses in Skinner's contextualism is that he appears to accept the idea of 'culture' as a kind of tenseless proposition. Clearly, this is not the case as this book attempts to demonstrate; the idea of culture has a history – it has a past, a present and presumably some kind of future.

3 Michaels employs the example of the New York Jew to demonstrate some of the problems with James Clifford's (1988/1994) idea of Mashpee Indian culture (see Michaels 1995:176–8 note 224).

1 The civilizing mission of culture

1 See Norbert Elias (1939/1978) Adam Kuper (1999) and Raymond Williams (1958/1993).

2 The word 'cultura' originally derived from another Latin word, *colere* that had a variety of meanings including "inhabit, cultivate, protect, honour with worship" (Williams 1976/1988:87).

3 The Pitjandjara live in central Australia, in the region surrounding Uluru.

4 The term civilization, like that of culture owes much to a Latin root term – *civilis*, meaning 'to make civil' in the legal sense of pertaining to citizens. Under Roman jurisdiction, an act of judgement in law turned a criminal process 'civil'. Although the civil aspect of law is still very much an important aspect of contemporary jurisprudence, it is the notion of 'making civil' in the normative sense that concerns us most here. It is from civil acts, or the

French term, *civilité*, for these acts, that the word 'civilization' owes its biggest debt.

5 According to Elias (1939/1978:38), the first evidence of the term civilization is found in Mirabeau's work in the 1760s. The term 'civilization' is, from its early use, contrasted with "simpler and socially inferior people" (Elias 1939/1978:39).

6 The essayist/diarist James Boswell gives us an insight into the changes taking place. In 1772, he tells us; "[o]n Monday, March 23, I found him [Dr. Johnson] busy, preparing a fourth edition of his folio Dictionary ... He would not admit *civilization*, but only *civility*. With great deference to him, I thought *civilization* from *to civilize*, better in the sense opposed to *barbarity*, than *civility*" (Oxford English Dictionary 1994:256).

7 As Raymond Williams points out, "[t]he contrast between 'grows' and 'made' was to become the contrast between 'organic' and 'mechanical' which lies at the very centre of a tradition which has continued to our own day" (Williams 1958/1993:37).

8 Kultur is not simply a nationalist idea or expression in its early form; as Adam Kuper has shown, there is more to the early idea of culture than simple nationalism (Kuper 1999: see chapter one). It is also a mistake to link Herder to nationalism, as Robert Clark points out: "Herder's idea of 'humanity' was incompatible with a 'nationally awakened point of view'" (Clark 1955:336–7). Herder condemned all forms of imperialism and had disagreed with Kant over race, so it is not easy to link him to nationalism, especially in its more virulent form. See also Clark (1955) chapter ten generally and F.M. Barnard (1969).

9 All cultures were linked together in Herder's view; they continued in a 'great chain' and were the local expression of universal traits. More importantly, cultures were not conceived of as fixed entities, but were prone to change. See A. Gillies (1945) especially chapters six and seven.

10 Arnold was an Inspector of Schools and wrote several pieces on education. It is also worth noting that Wilhelm Von Humboldt, whom Arnold refers to in *Culture and Anarchy*, was the Minister of Education in Prussia.

11 Leavis (1930) was writing for the people who had read, or were aware of, the Lynds' famous study of Middletown and had been disturbed by its findings. Robert S. Lynd and Helen Merrell Lynd, *Middletown: A Study in American Culture* (London: Constable and Co. Ltd. 1929). See Adam Kuper (1999:44) for comments on Leavis and the Lynds.

12 Raymond Williams indicates that Eliot's miscellany merely "translates the older specialised sense of 'culture' (arts, philosophy) into 'popular culture' (sport, food and the Gothic churches)" (Williams 1958/1993:234). It is also important to note that in Eliot's terms 'culture' was not synonymous with a whole way of life – although he recognized the anthropological meaning of the term, he considered it relevant for the study of primitive societies (Eliot 1948:22). European society was too complex and "highly developed" (Eliot 1948:22), in his view, for the anthropological meaning to be applied.

13 John Bright is an obvious example in this respect. Arnold quotes John Bright's contemptuous comment: "[p]eople who talk about what they call *culture*! ... by which they mean a smattering of the two dead languages of Greek and Latin" (Arnold 1869/1994:28).

14 Before 1860, Raymond Williams found no hostility to the word culture, but after that point he detects a change of voice, which leads to "the common English hostility" (Williams 1958/1993:126) and derision, in some circles, to the term.

15 *Humanitat* was the means by way of which individuals could bring together and share their common humanity. In *humanitat* the "local and the universal in humanity are fused together" (Gillies 1945:106 see also chapter eight).

16 See Gillies (1945) especially chapter five and Clarke (1955) chapter five.

17 Elias says Goethe is an exception here (Elias 1939/1978:20).

18 The reader needs to be aware that kultur had acquired greater nationalist 'precision' by the time of the Second World War, but the role that the state played in determining this is significant. This is especially noticeable when comparing the meaning attached to the idea of kultur at the time of the First World War to that of the Second World War.

19 Alfred G. Meyer, 'Appendix A: Historical notes on ideological aspects of the concept of culture in Germany and Russia' in Kroeber and Kluckhohn (1952:405).

20 George Stocking suggests that Jean-Baptiste de Lamarck's conception of the processes of biological evolution were well suited to the behavioural sciences. Lamarckian thinking influenced Herbert Spencer in Britain and John Wesley Powell, Lester Frank Ward, John Dewey and Woodrow Wilson in the United States. George Stocking (1968/1982) chapter ten.

21 The term Social Darwinism is misleading, primarily because many social scientists turn out to be more influenced by Lamarck than Darwin. Strictly speaking, Darwinian theory is a matter of biological selection, while many theorists also factored the environment into their thesis. Herbert Spencer who coined the phrase 'survival of the fittest' was "a crude Lamarckian" (Kuper 1988:2), as is Norman Angell who was influenced by Spencer. See Kuper (1988) chapter one.

22 As Stocking points out, this "change from 'civilization' to 'race' can be seen as a development of the idea of civilization itself" (Stocking 1968/1982:37).

23 Ivan Hannaford (1996), see chapter ten especially.

24 Consider the Civil Rights Movement in the United States and ongoing debates about equality in Europe, for example. Also see Elazar Barkan (1992) for a discussion of the inter-war period.

25 Elazar Barkan points out that "[b]ecause racism nowadays is perceived as irrational and unscientific, its elimination from culture and science is deemed, at least implicitly, to have been inevitable: once Nazi atrocities had been revealed, racism was rejected. An extension of this view is the historical misconception that Nazi racism was renounced as early as the 1930s. In fact, the response in both the United States and Britain was neither immediate nor of sufficient strength to discredit theories of racial superiority. By 1938 only a small segment of the educated public had reformulated its attitude on the question of race in response to the Nazi menace" (Barkan 1992:1).

26 See also Roxann Wheeler (2000) for an analysis of eighteenth century attitudes towards race.

27 Barkan indicates that scientific race theory caused British anthropologists difficulty much later than it did for some of their American counterparts, notably the Boasians (discussed in chapter three this book). Indeed, it appears that the fear of Nazism, rather than problems with the concept of race, placed the race issue on the British agenda. Unlike the United States, where the question of race had been central to the development of cultural anthropology, "in Britain the question of race did not become prominent until after 1933, before that date the primary debate had been over class relations" (Barkan 1992:285). This places the criticisms of biological determinism made in international politics in a slightly different perspective; although no-one explicitly challenged the scientific 'fact' of race, the challenge to biological determinism is being voiced. In some ways, the early British international relations theorists are performing a similarly critical role to that of the Boasians in the United States – they are questioning the conventional standards of determinism and assumptions surrounding the nature of civilization.

28 Although I only raise this issue here, it does appear that the question of the relationship between IR and racial thinking requires deeper examination. If we want to know how early thinkers approached the subject of world politics around the time of the discipline's formation, we would do well to look at the subject of race as a defining feature of international relations, especially since all commentators refer to different races in a taken for granted sense.

29 *The Journal of Race Development* was founded at Clark University, USA, in 1910. *The Journal of International Relations* was eventually superseded, in 1922, by the journal *Foreign Affairs*. I am grateful to Mott Linn of Clark University for confirming these points for me.

30 As Iriye points out, Nazi Germany could not recognize Japan in terms of racial equality, but they could accept Japan on the grounds of culture (Iriye 1997 chapter three).

31 The 20th January 1920 was the official birth date of the organization, but the idea had been circulating for several years. C. Howard-Ellis said that there was very little that was new in the League, although the League itself was new (Howard-Ellis 1928:67–8).

32 The following small sample of NGOs illustrate the variety of organizations: The International Committee of the Red Cross emerged out of a committee set up in 1863, the International Telegraphic Union founded in 1865, the Universal Postal Service was established in 1874, the International Friends of Nature was founded in 1895, the International Transport Workers' Federation in 1896, and the Nobel Prizes were first awarded in 1901. Other conferences and congresses include: the First International Sanitary Conference in 1851, the International Congress of Women in 1888, the First International Working Men's Association founded in 1864 and the second in 1889, The Hague Disarmament Conferences of 1899 and 1907, and the World Congress of Esperanto 1905.

33 Angell (1911/1972). See chapter two, part two in particular for evidence of progress.

34 For a list of mechanical changes (Angell 1911/1972:229) and for values of the Middle Ages (Angell 1911/1972:235).

35 On duels (Angell 1911/1972:160 and 175); reference to Herbert Spencer and Lord Roberts (Angell 1911/1972:159).

36 These theorists had a range of ideas on the matter from the establishment of an international organization (which they all subscribed to), to Philip Noel Baker's ideas about strengthening international law, from David Davies' argument for an international police force to Norman Angell's thesis of the inevitable growth in economic interdependency. See Long and Wilson (1995).

37 Angell refers to contemporary figures and examples, which sheds light on who the opposition are and which ideas Angell found problematic. He frequently draws upon articles and letters published in *The Times*, the *Spectator* and the *Daily Mail*. He opposes, among others, Theodore Roosevelt, General Homer Lea and Admiral Mahan (Angell 1911/1972:137–8).

38 See Norman Angell (1911/1972), chapter four, part two.

39 Angell is clearly disgruntled with General Lea and Admiral Mahan – for references to Lea (Angell 1911/1972:168–70); and for Mahan (Angell 1911/1972:35). Force is not the 'foundation of civilized life' for Angell as it was for Professor Spenser Wilkinson with whom he also takes issue (Angell 1911/1972:247–50).

40 The influence of evolutionary theory within IR has been considerable. Some three decades after Angell, E.H. Carr can be found also arguing against biological determinism (Carr 1939/1995:46–9 and 150).

41 Murray records that in 1919 Robert Cecil was heckled as a traitor at a public meeting (Murray 1948:2).

42 C. Howard-Ellis (1928) counted the thousands of visitors who flocked to Geneva, its summer schools and numerous international institutions as well as the work of smaller states, among the League's successes.

43 Hughes was a "champion of the cause of White Supremacy" (Zimmern 1936:258) according to Alfred Zimmern.

2 Cultural internationalism

1 Peter Wilson says, "Carr distinguished between the first inter-war decade and the second. He claimed that '[t]he characteristic feature of the present crisis ... has been the abrupt descent from the visionary hopes of the first post-war decade to the grim despair of the second.' These comments suggest that Carr himself felt the monopoly of the utopians had come to an end well before 1939" (Long and Wilson 1995:7). See also Gilbert Murray (1948); Alfred Zimmern (1936) and E.H. Carr (1939/1995).

2 The West had unified the world in technological terms, and had the most extensive global reach of all known civilizations. More importantly in Toynbee's view, "the West is today still an unfinished story" (Toynbee 1961:518).

3 Iriye goes on to say that: "[a]t the end of the twentieth century, however, the limits of power, whether it be nuclear weapons or localized police force, are quite evident. If power alone cannot maintain order, culture must assume an increasing measure of responsibility" (Iriye 1997:12).

4 http://www.cloudband.com/frames.mhtml/magazine/articles1q01/feat_day_cradle3_0201.html (10th December 2003).

5 http://www.royal.gov.uk/output/Page1634.asp (11th August 2003).

6 Gift exchange tells you a lot about the state of relations, of whom it is worth ingratiating oneself or simply keeping on good terms with – you also learn a lot about the order of importance and priority regarding the states that do and do not receive gifts. Mapping the gift of pandas, for example, sent by the People's Republic of China from 1953 to 1982, when the practice ceased, reflects state priorities.

7 http://www.jimmycarterlibrary.org/documents/stgifts.phtml (10th December 2003).

8 Ruth McMurry and Muna Lee (1947) describe it as 'another way,' Philip Coombs (1964) as the 'fourth dimension,' while J.M. Mitchell (1986) calls it the 'third dimension.'

9 Esperanto was developed by Ludwik Zamenhof whose textbook *International Language* had been published in 1887. A number of conferences were held in the 1920s and 1930s and attracted a large number of participants, i.e. Oxford 1930 had 1,000 delegates from 30 countries (see Iriye 1997 especially p. 77). There is a more detailed discussion of this subject by Young S. Kim in John Boli and George M. Thomas (1999).

10 It might be said that the question of how diverse peoples can live more peacefully and respectfully together has been a persistent theme within the discipline.

11 Zimmern acknowledged differences without reference to the term 'culture.' "Do not let the Englishman," he said, "try to gesticulate like a Frenchman, or encourage the Frenchman to imitate our English reserve. Our starch is real starch and is acceptable because it is real. French starch would be unreal and therefore only ridiculous" (Zimmern 1929:71).

12 I find it particularly interesting that Zimmern should equate intellectual exchanges with the giving of 'gifts' in this statement, especially since he plainly wants to avoid all notions of imposition and dominance. Where 'gifts'

(however they are defined) are given freely, in mutual recognition and on the basis of human equality, the idea of exchanging 'gifts' strikes me as an inspiring way to look at international relations.

13　http://www2.britishcouncil.org/history/history-why/history-why-selling-uk.htm (3rd August 2003).

14　The Committee itself and its Secretariat, which were based at Geneva, is sometimes referred to under the acronym CIC (see Murray 1948), while the Institute at Paris is referred to as the IICI following its French title of the Institut International de Cooperation Intellectuelle. The Institute opened in 1925 and was provided by the French government.

15　On the ICIC, see also Zimmern (1936:316–17).

16　F.P. Walters (1952:192) says that the League Assembly granted the Committee a budget of less than five thousand pounds.

17　Preamble – http://www.unesco.org/shs/human_rights/hrpreamble.htm (9th December 2003). The American poet Archibald McLeish, who had worked for the United States Office of War Information, wrote the preamble.

18　The problems centred on the 'New World Information and Communication Order' that UNESCO sought to implement.

19　The British Council began by promoting British culture and supporting teacher training in developing countries. In 1949, its remit was limited to English language teaching. The 1954 Drogheda report recommended withdrawal from Europe and the Council worked with the Overseas Development Agency focusing on developing countries. The 1969 Duncan Report recommended an expansion of work in the arts, science and technology – lifting the focus off English language. The 1980s saw major cutbacks in the work of the Council, but the late 1980s saw a reversal of this. With the changing international environment, the British Council began working in Eastern Europe, Russia and parts of the former Soviet Union – this saw the beginnings of an expansion in activity (1989) and funding (1988). Today the British Council is moving away from English language support and back towards the idea of 'culture' in the broader, humanist, sense. It sponsored an exhibition of Art Houses of Britain in Washington, 1985, sent rap DJs to counter racism in Eastern Europe, and in 2001 launched a Football Culture website in conjunction with the BBC.

20　http://education.vsnl.com.iccr/ (11th August 2003).

21　The Japan Foundation Law, Article 1, http://www.jpf.go.jp/e/about/bground.html (11th August 2003).

22　Anthony Parsons (1985) admonishes the British for failing to employ cultural diplomacy with the same measure of pride as the French. Mitchell (1986) has a chapter on France.

23　http://exchanges.state.gov/education/ivp/history.htm (3rd August 2003).

24　Nelson Rockefeller became the co-ordinator of a government exchange programme between the United States and Latin America in 1940.

25　For an overview of American attitudes, see John Brown, 'The anti-propaganda tradition in the United States,' http://www.publicdiplomacy.org/19.htm (10th November 2003).

26　http://exchanges.state.gov/education/ (3rd August 2003).

27　I am grateful to William P. Kiehl for bringing to my attention the distinction between attitudes of those within the ECA based in America and its operatives in the field.

28　The question of motives and integrity becomes especially apparent when assessing the cultural programmes of the Cold War period. Early on, the "infant USIA was badly mauled in the last stages of McCarthyism: the effects of this notorious campaign in USIA and the Voice of America ... were severe"

(Mitchell 1986:57). Recently, it has been revealed (see Saunders 1999 for example) that some USIA activities were funded by the CIA, although what we make of this is discussed in chapter four. However, it should be noted that CIA funding was extensive during the Cold War and therefore, the source of funding may not be the most significant feature of these cultural activities. I am grateful to Thomas R. Seitz for drawing the range of CIA funding to my attention.

29 http://exchanges.state.gov/education/ivp/history.htm (3rd August 2003).
30 Mitchell (1986) discusses the problem of propaganda and national projection.
31 See http://www2.britishcouncil.org/ (3rd August 2003) for example.
32 For example, see Walter D. Mignolo, 'Globalization, Civilization Processes, and the Relocation of Languages and Cultures,' in Jameson and Miyoshi (1998).
33 http://www2.britishcouncil.org/history/history-why/history-why-selling-uk.htm (3rd August 2003).
34 Sarah Womack, 'Japanese fans flock to worship Beckham,' *Daily Telegraph*, 31/07/02, http://www.telegraph.co.uk/news/ (13th December 2003).
35 The British Council, for example, has independent and charitable status but still is accused of 'propaganda.' See http://www2.britishcouncil.org/history/history-why/history-why-selling-uk.htm (3rd August 2003).
36 The *Stavros S. Niarchos* sailed into Portsmouth on the 31st July 2003, as part of a joint project between the Sail Training Association and ENCOMPASS, 'The Daniel Braden Reconciliation Trust'. The trust was established in the memory of Daniel Braden who died as a result of one of the Bali bomb attacks in October 2002.

3 The ever disappearing native

1 Edward B. Tylor took the first, British, academic chair in anthropology at Oxford in 1896.
2 A point that T.S. Eliot also drew upon in his work. Eliot referred to Tylor and the anthropological concept in his *Notes* (Eliot 1948:22), but decided the concept was only applicable to primitive society.
3 Kroeber and Kluckhohn's book of definitions also requires understanding in context: it sought to establish/confirm the credibility of the anthropological concept of culture in American social science. See Adam Kuper (1999).
4 Culture is still in Tylor's view a matter of higher pursuit (art, literature and intellectual achievement), but something that he wanted to demonstrate was the outcome of progressive (evolutionary) development. See Stocking (1968/1982), chapter four.
5 Founding Cultural Anthropology should not to be confused with Anthropology as such, since clearly Anthropology existed before Boas, as the work of John Wesley Powell demonstrates.
6 Boas originally studied mathematics and physics before moving to geography and ethnography.
7 Boas was drawn to the work of both Alexander and Wilhelm von Humboldt early in his career. He was 'influenced by Bastian the ethnologist and the anatomist Virchow while he was in Berlin,' and studied geography under Fischer at Kiel. For a more detailed survey, see Stocking (1996) and Kuper (1988) chapter seven.
8 Boas had made field trips to Baffinland in 1883 and British Columbia in 1886 before emigrating. Franz Boas, 'The Occurrence of Similar Inventions in Areas Widely Apart,' *Science*, Vol. 9, 485–6, 1887, and 'Museums of Ethnology and Their Classification,' *Science*, Vol. 9, 587–9, 1887. See Stocking (1974:57–8 and 61–7). Adam Kuper also discusses this dispute (Kuper 1988:130–2).

9 Boas did continue to employ Larmarckian ideas and aspects of race theory, which seems to cause some critics difficulty. See, for example, Kamala Visweswaran (1998).

10 Judith Berman has pointed out that much of the criticism levelled at Boas has misunderstood his anthropological work and its subtle theorizing. Judith Berman in Stocking ed. (1996).

11 Boas argued against racism throughout his life – right until the moment of his death, "when in a discussion on how to combat racism at the age of 85, at a Columbia Faculty Club luncheon, 'Boas, with a comment on the need to press its exposure ... and without further sound, fell over backwards in his chair, dead'" (cited in Barkan 1992:77).

12 For an overview see Freeman (1983/1996), especially chapters one to four.

13 See Franz Boas, 'Eugenics,' *Scientific Monthly*, Vol. 3, 1916; A.L. Kroeber, 'The Superorganic,' *American Anthropologist*, Vol. 19, 1917; R.H. Lowie, 'Alfred Russel Wallace,' *New Republic*, Vol. 9, 1916.

14 Williams (1947) also demonstrated that Ruth Benedict did not adhere to her egalitarian principles; she clearly worked her own normative distinction between 'acceptable and asocial traits' into her theory.

15 The 1921 and 1924 Immigration Acts placed major restrictions on the numbers and types of immigrants to the United States. See Walter Benn Michaels (1995) for a detailed discussion of the literature of America during the pre- and post-First World War period. Akira Iriye (1997:62) also refers to Madison Grant.

16 Michaels argues "that nativism in the period just after World War 1 involved not only a reassertion of the distinction between American and un-American but a crucial redefinition of the terms in which it might be made. America would mean something different in 1925 from what it had meant at, say, the turn of the century; indeed, the very idea of national identity would be altered" (Michaels 1995:2). This new national identity depended on both nativism (establishing who the natives are) and a modernist expression of it, one that included culture theory.

17 It is also interesting to note that ethical concerns, race thinking and the idea of culture had a different effect on A.R Radcliffe-Brown. During the 1920s, Radcliffe-Brown was teaching in South Africa when anthropologists there (i.e. W.W.M. Eiselen) began to argue for the separate development of cultures, which would, eventually, provide the intellectual basis of the apartheid system. Radcliffe-Brown argued against the idea of cultural segregation on the grounds that South Africa was a single society – there was a shared social structure and economy for example.

18 See Stocking (1968/1982), chapter four. Kroeber and Kluckhohn also found the number of definitions of culture rapidly increased during the 1920s and 1930s, indicating the concept's growth.

19 In 1947 the American Anthropological Association numbered 408 members (cited in Kuper 1999:54). The significant developmental shift was from studying indigenous American Indians to the Third World and I am grateful to Adam Kuper for bringing this point to my attention.

20 Kahn (1989) suggests that common issues are: treating cultures in their 'otherness,' an interest in tradition, an acceptance that culture is something that is shared, especially shared meaning.

21 Whether a culture can be studied scientifically and reduced to an ideal type, or whether it is something that is distributed, to be interpreted or mapped out, are all different methodologies that depend upon the assumption that there is 'something' out there called culture to be studied in the first place.

22 Criticisms similar to those levelled against the idea of culture can also be made of totalizing religious categories, i.e. Christian, Muslim, etc.

23 P.G. Wilson, 'The Problem with Simple Folk,' *Natural History*, December 1977, cited by Andrew Vayda in Robert Borofsky ed. (1994:321).

24 This still holds for people who accept internal diversity. Speaking of a particular culture makes no sense, or none that can be qualified in cultural terms, if some level of homogeneity is not entered into by the people under discussion (i.e. the Balinese, etc.). Unless, of course, we accept that the idea of culture is fiction.

25 Clifford Geertz (1973/1993) famously suggested that ethnographers read a culture like a book and then write about it. Geertz says, "[t]he ethnographer 'inscribes' social discourse; *he writes it down*" (Geertz 1973/1993:19). Yet, as Joel Kahn has pointed out, this would seem to imply that the only 'culture' ethnographers uncovered was that which they had published. "If culture is, as Geertz is honest enough to say, an anthropological construction, then the text is, in fact, the culture itself. Culture is, then, according to anthropological tradition, something extrinsic to the peoples under study not because it is a superorganic phenomenon with an ontological reality in North Africa or Indonesia, but because it occupies a space, albeit a small one, in the culture from which the anthropologist comes" (Kahn 1989:12).

26 See James Clifford (1988/1994); James Clifford and George Marcus ed. (1986); George Marcus and Michael Fischer (1986); and Renato Rosaldo (1989/1993).

27 Robert Brightman (1995) demonstrates that, for most part, these critical scholars have set up 'straw-men' in their arguments and has usefully discussed the key problems that critics associate with the culture concept.

28 "The ideal authority for any statement in this book," Benedict says, "would be the proverbial man in the street" (Benedict 1946:16).

29 Clifford, for example, revels in his criticisms of Malinowski, which would more than suggest that a major piece of Malinowski's life's work was little more than a waste of time.

30 The notion of hybridity is a particularly malevolent form of essentialism in my view. The 'hybrid' (person or group) is neither one thing nor the other but the 'freakish' amalgam of two 'pure' cultures, usually the home and host cultures. The 'hybrid' is not an original nor is it permitted to be itself – it belongs in its own special category.

31 See Joel Kahn (1989) and Walter Benn Michaels (1995) for criticisms of the implicit retention of essentialist assumptions.

32 The same principles of argument also apply to the present. If we learn everything there is to know about a culture and are still seen as outsiders, then it must be something prior to learning that prevents us from being accepted or recognized as part of the culture. What we actually know would seem to matter less than who we are and to whom we are born.

33 This question, what prevents the New York Jew becoming a Mashpee Indian, is borrowed from Walter Benn Michaels, who in turn is referring to James Clifford (Michaels 1995:176–7 note 224).

34 We can see this process (of race turning into culture and maintaining racial divides) more clearly in South Africa, where the idea of culture provided the intellectual basis for the apartheid system.

35 The idea that people 'form a' culture suggests that Eagleton conceives of culture as noun in the singular.

36 Ideas involving 'processes of meaning making,' 'intelligible connections,' and 'intersubjectivity,' present an interesting challenge in terms of delineating the subject matter and how we, as scholars, decide to close enquiry. It seems to be one of the implications of anti-essentialism that scholars need to be more self-aware about the kinds of closure they impose on their subject matter.

37 Brian Barry (2001) has discussed the problems that the idea of culture generates in politics. Barry particularly objects to the concept's apparent ability to undermine universal aspirations and a cosmopolitan discourse.

4 The nationalization of culture

1 The comment was made by Uda Hisashi, a Japanese official (cited in Iriye 1997:124).
2 A more obvious and extreme example of the communist state's manipulation of culture to that of the Soviet Union occurred in the People's Republic of China with the Proletarian Cultural Revolution under Mao Tse-tung. But ruthless state controlled cultural programmes have been conducted by numerous authoritarian states, notably Cambodia under Pol Pot and Afghanistan under the Taliban.
3 'Notes of Freedom,' BBC Radio 4, 17th June 2003.
4 The CIA funded and supported a wide range of cultural activities during the Cold War. See Frances Stonor Saunders (1999).
5 This raises an important theoretical question: how appropriate is it to attribute to people ideas that they did not possess? The contextual method opposes this line of questioning and rejects the idea of writing history backwards. Moreover, the question itself demands a more complex explanation of the events of the period than those offered by the conspiratorial approach, of, say, that found in Saunders' (1999) book for example. The more difficult questions are to what extent state funding (or in this case CIA funding) of cultural activities matters, under what terms and in what way does it matter? This is an area where cultural diplomacy theorizing is at its weakest.
6 Key advocates of the nationalist approach included, George Kennan, William Benton and W.R. Tyler of the State department.
7 Although the Soviets and the Americans appear to be doing the same thing (scoring points off each other via culture), the supporting ideologies were very different. This raises some important theoretical questions: how do we distinguish between not only, the 'normal' everyday cultural diplomacy that most, if not all, states engage in, and propaganda in general (even if we accept that propaganda is a distortion of policy in some way), and beyond this, between these two issues and the Cold War in general. Also, on what grounds do we distinguish between Russian and American activity during this period from their behaviour during non-Cold War periods? Nuanced explanations and distinctions are inhibited here by the theoretical limitations.
8 The secretive element is also reflected in the popular language of the time; 'cultural attachés' based in embassies became something of a by-word for espionage.
9 For a critical review of Saunders' book see Walter Laqueur, 'You Had To Be There,' *The National Interest*, No. 58. Winter 1999/2000 cited in Brown http://www.unc.edu/depts/diplomat/archives_roll/2002_07-09/brown_pubdipl/brown_pubdipl.html (12th December 2003).
10 Early evidence of the scientific interest in national characteristics can be found in Morris Ginsberg (1956). In a paper written in 1935 on 'National character and national sentiments,' Ginsberg drew heavily on the work of Franz Boas. Gabriel Almond (1950) also devoted a chapter on the 'American character and foreign policy.'
11 http://www.cnn.com/SPECIALS/cold.war/episodes/02/documents/kennan/ (16th December 2003).
12 Kenneth Waltz (1979) is a foremost critic of Morgenthau, contending that Morgenthau did not develop a theory of international relations. Also see Peter Gellman (1988).

13 Zimmern complained that; "[t]o preach education, then, according to the prescription set forth by Matthew Arnold and other students of Continental culture and organization, is to attack our island defences at the point where we are most impregnable" (Zimmern 1929:22). 'To preach education' in the manner of Arnold is to miss the point in Zimmern's view – this is not to teach proper education at all, but some spurious and lesser Continental (Germanic) version of it. Zimmern is drawing a direct link here between Arnold's interest in German romantic philosophy and the German idea of kultur. But the context in which these words were written needs to be taken into consideration, before we assume that Zimmern was rejecting Arnold completely. Zimmern clearly shares a sympathy with Arnold for humanism (and this is more obvious in his work from 1922 than seven years later when the above piece was written), in this quotation, however, Zimmern is reacting to the parochial expression of culture and the German state's appropriation of it, which was increasingly visible on the eve of the 1930s. Rightly, Zimmern is concerned about the influence of kultur and suspicious of anyone who thinks they can 'preach' about it rather than put in the sustained effort, as he saw it, required to restore civilization to its former glory at this point in time.

14 Morgenthau does use the term civilization but employs it, largely, in relation to Western civilization. It is clear that culture is the concept that he relies upon more than civilization. He defines civilization thus: "[w]hat we call civilization is in a sense nothing but the automatic reactions of the members of a society to the rules of conduct by which that society endeavors to make its members conform to certain objective standards, to restrain their aspirations for power, and to domesticate and pacify them in all socially important respects" (Morgenthau 1948/1962:231). There is an air of artifice about this definition of civilization (civilization is something that happens to people); there is no mention of achievement or progression, which should not surprise us in view of Morgenthau's German heritage. Culture is the organic and more natural element in his thought.

15 Morgenthau (1948/1962); on 'moral' issues see chapters fifteen and twenty; on 'propaganda' see chapter twenty, and on 'world public opinion' see chapter seventeen.

16 We are certainly made aware by Morgenthau that 'news' information can appear very differently in 'the *New York Times*, *Pravda*, and *Hindustan Times*,' because it means something different in each community (Morgenthau 1948/1962:265).

17 Frances Stonor Saunders cites the appearance of Herbert von Karajan in New York in 1955 and Wilhelm Furtwängler in 1953–4 (Saunders 1999:226).

18 It is one of the ethical and moral dilemmas in art, and indeed politics, as to whether one should judge a painting, piece of music or literature, or policy even, by the personal failings of the person behind it all.

19 Frances Stonor Saunders has difficulty with the distinction between art and politics during this period, for example. But she has 'written history backwards' and has passed a normative judgment on it. Not only were the CIA's activities conspiratorial, but they appear morally questionable in her account of the Cold War.

20 Leni Riefenstahl's work fell into this category; her films, *The Triumph of the Will* (1935) and *Olympia* (1938) were seen to glorify the Nazi regime. Her career never recovered from the stigma.

21 In a letter to Nicolas Nabokov, Kennan wrote: "I can think of no group of people who have done more to hold our world together in these last years than you and your associates in the Congress [for Cultural Freedom]. In this

country [the United States] in particular, few will ever understand the dimensions and significance of your accomplishment" (cited in Kramer 1999:305).

22 Charles Frankel raises similar concerns about contact and fostering mutual understanding, but did not address the issue directly. Charles Frankel (1966) chapter six, especially pp. 82–5.

23 Morgenthau (1948/1962) see chapters seven, sixteen and twenty.

24 Cultural identities are the most popular source of interest these days, rather than national culture, as was Morgenthau's concern.

25 I am grateful to Professor John Simpson for drawing this aspect of disciplinary history to my attention. See for example, Herbert C. Kelman ed. (1965).

26 Morgenthau (1948/1962) see for example p. 50, pp. 262–3, and p. 344, and on 'propaganda as psychological warfare,' pp. 338–9. On the 'psycho-sociological' element in Morgenthau see Chris Brown (1997/2001:31).

27 Morgenthau (1948/1962). See especially chapter seventeen on 'World Public Opinion,' in which Morgenthau discusses the 'Psychological Unity of the World' while also acknowledging cultural variation and differences in understanding and values. See also, chapter seven 'The Ideological Element in International Policies,' which invokes the language of psychological rather than cultural forces.

5   International cultural society

1 Sujata Chakrabarti Pasic (in Lapid and Kratochwil ed. 1997) is one exception here; although she criticizes Bull for essentialism, she retains the anthropological conception of culture.

2 This is a good example of the distinction that James Tully has drawn our attention to (as discussed in the Introduction) that 'the points of a text relative to available conventions and an author's own ideological points in writing,' are not the same thing. What is available in the context does not mean an author has to accept or work with those ideas – the author's own understanding and intentions are central to understanding a text.

3 See Martin Wight (1946/1978:105) and also Tim Dunne's discussion (1998:53).

4 Rather revealingly, Daniel says, "the old dictionary definition [of culture as], 'the intellectual side of civilisation' is no longer useful. We are not sure what is a civilization, or what is intellectual; but we realise that the most characteristic art of any society is the way it lives, its 'manners and customs.' I cannot use 'culture' just to mean 'artistic and literary,' but equally, of course, that is included in the total definition" (Daniel 1975:3). This is a good illustration of a point of intellectual transition in Britain. The civilization concept is no longer conceptually tenable – Daniel is not even certain as to what that term pertains to any more. Similarly, the old humanist definition of culture is too limited in his view, whereas, the holistic anthropological definition of culture, as he quite rightly acknowledges, simply subsumes the old definition under its whole way of life approach.

5 Tim Dunne informs us however, "members of the British Committee were divided on the question of whether a common culture was a necessary condition for the existence of a states-system" (Dunne 1998:124–5).

6 Wight also says, "I have wondered if it would be accurate to exemplify the greater richness and complexity of modern international thought by saying that, in the modern states-system, the notion of international public opinion comes close to meaning the spirit and purpose of mankind. Its connotation is multilateral; its objects are general and universal" (Wight 1977:71–2).

7 In 'Triangles and Duels,' written in 1972, Wight says, "[a] states-system pre-

supposes both regularity of diplomatic intercourse and homogeneity of culture: it is the political articulation of a macro-culture" (Wight 1977:175). Wight seemed to be refining his ideas in the light of a changing context of culture thinking.

8 Under the section 'Cultural Questions,' Wight asks, "[a]re we going to concern ourselves with what might be called the sociology of states-systems?" (Wight 1977:33).

9 Similarly, in *Power Politics*, the question arises in the editors' Introduction, as to "whether or not the global states-system of today is founded upon any common culture, and if not whether it has any prospect of survival" (Wight 1946/1978:13).

10 See also Nicholas Wheeler and Timothy Dunne (1996).

11 Wheeler and Dunne tell us that Bull "first used the terms 'pluralism' and 'solidarism' in his early British Committee papers, later published in *Diplomatic investigations*" (Wheeler and Dunne 1996:94). I am less concerned with the nature of these terms here, than the fact that they are a persistent element in his work and one that seems to supplant his interest in international culture.

12 Bull tells us, "international society is a primitive or embryonic society . . ." (Bull 1983:18).

13 Specifically, the liberal-democratic, the communist and the underdeveloped worlds.

14 The problem with the notion of a resurgence or rediscovery of culture is the presumption of the existence of something meaningful to 'rediscover' in the first place. If this is rediscovered as a matter of politics then there are no inherent theoretical difficulties, it is when this is assumed to be 'culture' (as an *a priori* set of distinctive meanings) that the ontological problems surface.

15 Ruth Benedict and Clifford Geertz are both referred to in *Human Rights* (1986/1995), *The Factor of Culture* (1980) and *Race* (1982). Margaret Mead appears in *The Factor of Culture* (1980).

16 See Vincent (1986/1995) especially pages 39, 48 and 54.

17 For a critical review of Geertz, see Adam Kuper (1999) chapter three.

18 The text in question is M. Fortes and E.E. Evans-Pritchard's *African Political Systems* (Oxford: Oxford University Press, 1940) and is referred to in *The Factor of Culture* (Vincent 1980:260).

19 This is, perhaps, best illustrated by his analysis of different cultural perspectives and possible research projects in *The Factor of Culture* (1980).

20 Frank Ninkovich has similarly expressed difficulties of working with the anthropological idea in international relations. In view of the problems, it might lead us to suspect that this concept is not appropriate for IR scholars.

6 Strategies, civilizations and difference

1 Strategic studies began in the 1950s. Previously strategy had been the province of experts in military organizations and was based on the planning and winning of wars. The advent of nuclear weapons changed this situation – nuclear weapons, obviously, problematized war planning and the prospects of winning it. This opened the way for academic thinking on the matter.

2 Allison's three models were the rational, organizational and governmental, each of which yielded different answers to the same questions.

3 Clifford Geertz has proven to be one of the most influential scholars, of his generation of anthropologists, across the social sciences. However, a note of caution ought to be injected into IR; Geertz's idea of culture has not been without criticism in anthropology, and relying on Geertz, as the key authority

on culture, would be a bit like the equivalent of depending on Kenneth Waltz as the main voice in IR.

4 See for example: Desmond Ball, 'Strategic Culture in the Asia-Pacific Region,' *Security Studies*, Vol. 3, No. 1, Autumn 1993; Colin Gray, 'National Styles in Strategy: The American Example,' *International Security*, Vol. 6, No. 2, Fall 1981; Carl G. Jacobsen ed. *Strategic Power: USA/USSR* (London: Macmillan, 1990); Bradley Klein, 'Hegemony and Strategic Culture: American Power Projection and Alliance Defence Politics,' *Review of International Studies*, Vol. 14, No. 2, 1988.

5 The debate between Colin Gray (1999) and Alastair Iain Johnston (1995 and 1999) is based on the distinction between three generations.

6 It has been recognized that the initial advantage of a cultural approach was in accounting for the anomalies Realism failed to explain, but the research agenda is expanding in its own right.

7 Booth and Macmillan offered a detailed list of directives for the contributors to the Booth and Trood volume to work with (Booth and Trood 1999:Appendix).

8 In some ways, the discussions over subject matter (what to study) anticipate some of the difficulties that an anti-essentialist conception, if it were applied in IR, would involve. If culture is what people do, or as Brian Street has suggested is an active process of meaning making, then it is not obvious that the subject matter is self-delineating – meaning it cannot be taken as self-evident that the culture of the Mashpee Indians, or the Jains, is the logical object of study. Indeed, given the fluidity of an anti-essentialist concept of culture, it would seem necessary for the scholar to justify why they are looking at any bounded entity to begin with rather than to proceed as though this were an established axiomatic fact from the outset. Indeed, the orthodox understanding of boundary in the anthropological sense (i.e. this is the culture of the Mashpee) would seem to be challenged by anti-essentialism. It would appear that the scholar needs to be more aware of the kinds of boundaries s/he draws around the subject matter when employing this approach.

9 Colin Gray, for example, appears to want to say that culture is what we do but at the same time tell us that culture makes us what we are. It appears that Gray would like to approach the subject of culture in anti-essentialist terms but with an essentialist concept in tow.

10 See for example: *Foreign Affairs*, September/October 1993; *Issues and Studies*, Vol. 34, October 1998; Stephen Chan (1997); B.M. Russett, J.R. Oneal and M. Cox, 'Clash of Civilizations, or Realism and Liberalism Déjà Vu? Some Evidence,' *Journal of Peace Research*, Vol. 37, 2000.

11 According to Huntington, "[t]hese include Western, Confucian, Japanese, Islamic, Hindu, Slavic-Orthodox, Latin American and possibly African civilization" (Huntington 1993/1996:3). Huntington's lack of precision is reminiscent of problems that R.J. Vincent noted (1986/1995 see p. 48) in that Huntington relies upon four religions (Confucian, Islamic, Hindu and Slavic-Orthodox), one country (Japan), two large geographic areas (Latin America and possibly Africa), and one abstract idea (the West).

12 Oswald Spengler thought civilization was the death or last phase of culture, whereas Arnold Toynbee considered that Western civilization, at least, had the potential to continue growing and improving since it was the most universal of all known civilizations.

13 Norbert Elias (1939/1978) and Adam Kuper (1999) are particularly good at explaining the distinction. Braudel himself recognizes the differences between the German and French ideas of culture but underplays the significance of the German concept. He notes the anthropological development but, like T.S.

Eliot, assigns their idea of 'culture' to 'primitive society.' Fernand Braudel (1963/1995) chapter one.

14 Principally, Huntington appears to rely on Toynbee, Braudel and Spengler.

15 Huntington (1996/1998) makes a few general references to anthropologists, see pages 41 and 57. In addition, Ernest Gellner is mentioned on p. 113, A.L. Kroeber on p. 40, Marcel Mauss on p. 41 and Sidney Mintz on p. 136. Clifford Geertz is not mentioned at all. Fernand Braudel, Oswald Spengler and Arnold Toynbee all receive greater attention than the anthropologists.

16 See (Huntington 1996/1998); for example on page 68 he writes of "[t]he attitudes, values, knowledge, and culture of people ..."; that culture is added on at the end implies that it is something other than 'attitudes, values, and knowledge.' On page 91, culture is linked to power, which reminds the reader of a Cultural Studies approach. Huntington says, "[t]he distribution of cultures in the world reflects the distribution of power. Trade may or may not follow the flag, but culture almost always follows power." Expanding powers experience a flowering of culture that they impose on others. This almost suggests that culture is a matter of artifice, art, literature, intellectual and scientific and other achievements that Cultural Studies people might be interested in. Elsewhere, on page 253, he tells us that religion "is the principal defining characteristic of civilizations."

17 A good example here is the list of events that took place over a six month period in 1993. Since this list appeared in both the book and the article in which he replied to his critics, it can be seen as having considerable importance for the author. Huntington (1996/1998:38–9) and (1993/1996:58–9).

18 Asians need to save face apparently; of course, Huntington does not explain how and in what manner 'the Asians' (whoever they are) 'save-face' in a way that Westerners do not or never feel the need to.

19 See Huntington (1996/1998) chapters two and three, part one.

20 Huntington (1996/1998), see part two, 'The Shifting Balance of Civilizations.'

21 The homogeneity argument was pursued along several lines as universal culture, modernization and Westernization. See Huntington (1996/1998), especially chapter three, part one.

22 Huntington was critical elsewhere of what he called the "common world culture" (Huntington 1996/1998:67).

23 The problems that are associated with the anthropological concept are as pertinent to multiculturalism as they are elsewhere in the social sciences, but for reasons of space cannot be entered into here. Key multicultural theorists include: Will Kymlicka (1995), Charles Taylor (1992) and James Tully (1995). A major critic of multiculturalism is Brian Barry (2001).

24 Terence Turner introduced the term 'culture' to the Kayapo of Brazil (see Wright 1998). The concept was unknown to the Kayapo prior to Turner's intervention; they then employed the idea for political purposes. They abandoned Western-style dress for a more 'traditional' mode of clothing and solicited Western support as a culture under threat in their disputes with the Brazilian government. However, as Susan Wright points out, the homogeneous appearance obscured internal debate behind the scenes as to what should be presented as Kayapo culture. The Kayapo "defined 'culture' for themselves and used it to set the terms of their relations with the 'outside world'" (Wright 1998:14). Commenting later on some of the changes Kayapo society had experienced, Turner said of the Kayapo: "They are not losing culture, they are changing it in a way that affords them a viable expression of what's worth living for in their society. It's a cultural change, but it's still a viable, independent culture." Terence Turner, 'Neoliberal Ecopolitics and Indigenous Peoples:

The Kayapo, The "Rainforest Harvest," and The Body Shop' http://www.yale.edu/environment/publications/bulletin/098pdfs/98turner.pdf page 15 (13th December 2003). As it could be said that all cultures (for want of a better term) are dependent in some way or another, the important question ought to be, what does an unviable culture look like?

25 Murden, for example, says, "[c]ulture is a social construction that is so multi-faceted that it may be difficult to define precisely" (Murden in Bayliss and Smith ed. 1997:376).

26 Raymond Williams described culture as "one of the two or three most complicated words in the English language" (Williams 1976/1988:87).

27 In this paper, Brumann (1999) widens Stolcke's thesis beyond the European context, to the concept of culture more generally.

Conclusion: fates and futures

1 *Millennium* (Vol. 30, No. 3, 2001) had a special subsection devoted to Science Fiction.

2 See for example: the work of John Brown and Frank Ninkovich, plus the debate surrounding Frances Stonor Saunders' book, especially on the Internet.

3 United Nations Human Development Report 2002, data from 2000. Japan enjoys the greatest life expectancy from birth, whereas Sierra Leone experiences the least, http://hdr.undp.org/reports/global/2002/en/indicator/indicator.cfm?File (13th August 2003).

4 The individual societies that have come closest to attaining an homogenized state have all been societies on the verge of, for want of a better term, 'mass insanity.' Think of Stalin's Soviet Union, Mao's China, or Pol Pot's Cambodia – no one would describe these instances as anything approaching the normal state of affairs in human relationships.

5 Arguments based on the traditional methods of hunting seals and whales have been used as a source of criticism against the modern techniques employed by the Inuit and Makah Indians. Organizations such as The Cetacean Society and Sea Shepherd Conservation Society obviously object to any harvesting of seals and whales, but their anti-traditionalist arguments powerfully suggest that this activity is contrary to native culture (or at least their conception of it). Sea Shepherd Conservation Society, 'Makah tribe to use high-caliber military assault weapons against migrating Gray whales,' 30th July 1997 – http://www.seashepherd.org/ author's own collection. For an insight into the Makah whaling debate see, http://www.highnorth.no/Library/Culture/ne-fr-in.htm (13th December 2003).

6 Brian Barry (2001) confronts this matter in his book.

7 This fear is not new. We find F.R. Leavis complaining, "[i]t is a commonplace that we are being Americanised ..." (Leavis 1930:7).

8 Beatrix Campbell, 'Nations on a knife-edge' *The Independent on Sunday*, 15th August 1999. See also Sander L. Gilman, *Making the Body Beautiful: A Cultural History of Aesthetic Surgery* (Princeton: Princeton University Press, 2001) and *Creating Beauty to Cure the Soul: Race, Psychology in the Shaping of Aesthetic Surgery* (Durham and London: Duke University Press, 1998).

9 The more serious question, and one that occupied Bozeman's work, is to what extent we should allow the past (history) to determine, or dictate, the terms of the present?

10 Anthropologists have developed an interest in the politics of culture, especially since Robert Thornton reminded them not to confuse the politics of 'what culture is' with 'what culture does' (cited in Street 1993:32/3). See also Susan Wright (1998).

Bibliography

Aberystwyth, The University of Wales. (13th December 1918) Council Minute item nine.

Aberystwyth, The University of Wales. (1950) *Report on the Wilson Chair of International Politics – submitted by the Special Committee Appointed by Council on 9th December 1949*, Aberystwyth: The Cambrian News Ltd.

Abu-Lughod, Lila. (1999) 'Comments,' *Current Anthropology*, Vol. 40, February, pp. 13–15.

Alexander, Jeffrey C. (1991) *Culture and Society: Contemporary Debates*, Cambridge: Cambridge University Press.

Allison, Graham T. (1971) *The Essence of Decision: Explaining the Cuban Missile Crisis*, Boston: Little, Brown and Company.

Almond, Gabriel A. (1950) *The American People and Foreign Policy*, New York: Harcourt, Brace and Company.

Almond, Gabriel A. and Verba, Sidney. (1963/1989) *The Civic Culture: Political Attitudes and Democracy in Five Nations*, Newbury Park, California: Sage Publications Inc.

Angell, Norman. (1911/1972) *The Great Illusion: A Study of the Relation of Military Power in Nations to Their Economic and Social Advantage*, New York and London: Garland Publishing Inc.

Angell, Norman. (1914) *The Foundations of International Polity*, London: William Heinemann.

Arnold, Matthew. (1869/1994) *Culture and Anarchy*, Samuel Lipman (ed.), New Haven and London: Yale University Press.

Asad, Talal. (1979) 'Anthropology and the Analysis of Ideology,' *Man*, Vol. 14.

Bailey, Thomas A. (1944/1963) *Woodrow Wilson and the Lost Peace*, Chicago: Quadrangle Books.

Barkan, Elazar. (1992) *The Retreat of Scientific Racism: Changing Concepts of Race in Britain and the United States Between the World Wars*, Cambridge: Cambridge University Press.

Barnard, F.M. (ed.). (1969) *J.G. Herder on Social and Political Culture*, Cambridge: Cambridge University Press.

Barry, Brian. (1998) 'The Limits of Cultural Politics,' *Review of International Studies*, Vol. 24, No. 3, July.

Barry, Brian. (2001) *Culture and Equality*, Cambridge: Polity Press.

Bayliss, John and Smith, Steve (eds). (1997) *The Globalization of World Politics: An Introduction to International Relations*, Oxford: Oxford University Press.

Beattie, John. (1964/1993) *Other Cultures: Aims, Methods and Achievements in Social Anthropology*, London: Routledge.

Bell, Clive. (1928/1932) *Civilisation: an Essay*, London: Chatto & Windus.

Benedict, Ruth. (1935/1952) *Patterns of Culture*, London: Routledge & Kegan Paul Ltd.

Benedict, Ruth. (1946) *The Chrysanthemum and the Sword: Patterns of Japanese Culture*, Boston: Houghton Mifflin Company.

Bernard, Russell H. (1984) 'Editorial: On the Tenacity of Culture among Anthropologists,' *American Anthropologist*, Vol. 86, No. 2.

Bidney, David. (1944) 'On the Concept of Culture and Some Cultural Fallacies,' *American Anthropologist*, Vol. 46.

Bidney, David. (1947) 'Human Nature and the Cultural Process,' *American Anthropologist*, Vol. 49.

Boli, John and Thomas, George M. (eds). (1999) *Constructing World Culture: International Nongovernmental Organizations Since 1875*, Stanford, California: Stanford University Press.

Booth, Ken. (1979) *Strategy and Ethnocentrism*, London: Croom Helm.

Booth, Ken. (1991) 'Security in Anarchy: Utopian Realism in Theory and Practice,' *International Affairs*, Vol. 67, No. 3.

Booth, Ken and Trood, Russell (eds). (1999) *Strategic Cultures in the Asia-Pacific Region*, London: Macmillan Press Ltd.

Borofsky, Robert (ed.). (1994) *Assessing Cultural Anthropology*, New York: McGraw-Hill Inc.

Bozeman, Adda. (1960) *Politics and Culture in International History*, Princeton: Princeton University Press.

Braudel, Fernand. (1963/1995) *A History of Civilizations*, New York: Penguin Books. Translated by Richard Mayne. First published in France 1963.

Brewin, Christopher. (1992) 'Research in a Global Context: a Discussion of Toynbee's Legacy,' *Review of International Studies*, Vol. 18, No. 2.

Brightman, Robert. (1995) 'Forget Culture: Replacement, Transcendence, Reflexification,' *Cultural Anthropology*, Vol. 10, No. 4.

http://www2.britishcouncil.org/ (3rd August 2003). The British Council.

http://www2.britishcouncil.org/history/history-why/history-why-selling-uk.htm (3rd August 2003). Essays on the role of the British Council.

Brown, Chris. (1997: 2nd edn 2001) *Understanding International Relations*, Basingstoke: Palgrave Press.

Brown, Chris. (1999) 'History Ends, Worlds Collide,' *Review of International Studies – Special Issue*, Vol. 25.

Brown, Chris. (2000) 'Cultural Diversity and International Political Theory: from the *Requirement* to "Mutual Respect"?', *Review of International Studies*, Vol. 26, No. 2.

Brown, Donald E. (1991) *Human Universals*, US: McGraw-Hill Inc.

Brown, John. 'The Anti-propaganda Tradition in the United States,' http://www.publicdiplomacy.org/19.htm (10th November 2003).

Brown, John. 'The Purposes and Cross-purposes of American Public Diplomacy,' http://www.unc.edu/depts/diplomat/archives_roll/2002_07-09/brown_pubdipl/brown_pubdipl.html (12th December 2003).

Brumann, Christophe. (1999) 'Writing Culture: Why a Successful Concept Should

Not Be Discarded,' *Current Anthropology – Special Issue*, Vol. 40, Supplement, February.

Bull, Hedley. (1977: 2nd edn 1995) *The Anarchical Society: A Study of Order in World Politics*, Basingstoke and London: Macmillan Press Ltd.

Bull, Hedley. (1983) 'Justice in International Relations,' paper presented at *The Hagey Lectures*, Ontario: University of Waterloo.

Bull, Hedley and Watson, Adam (eds). (1984) *The Expansion of International Society*, Oxford: Clarendon Press.

Butterfield, Herbert and Wight, Martin (eds). (1966) *Diplomatic Investigations: Essays in the Theory of International Politics*, London: George Allen & Unwin Ltd.

Buzan, Barry. (1993) 'From International System to International Society: Structural Realism and Regime Theory Meet the English School,' *International Organization*, Vol. 47, No. 3, Summer.

Carr, E.H. (1939: 2nd edn 1946/1995) *The Twenty Years Crisis 1919–1939: An Introduction to the Study of International Relations*, London: Papermac.

Carr, E.H. (1945) *Nationalism and After*, London: Macmillan & Co. Ltd.

Carrithers, Michael. (1992) *Why Humans Have Cultures: Explaining Anthropology and Diversity*, Oxford: Oxford University Press.

Cecil, Viscount, *et al.* (1934) *Challenge to Death*, London: Constable & Co. Ltd.

Chan, Stephen. (1997) 'Too Neat and Under-Thought A World Order: Huntington and Civilisations,' *Millennium*, Vol. 26, No. 1.

Chay, Jongsuk (ed.). (1990) *Culture and International Relations*, New York: Praeger.

Clark, Jon; Heinemann, Margot; Margolies, David and Snee, Carole (eds). (1979) *Culture and Crisis in Britain in the Thirties*, London: Lawrence and Wishart.

Clark Jr., Robert T. (1955) *Herder: His Life and Thought*, Berkeley and Los Angeles: University of California Press.

Clark, Romy J. (1993) 'Developing Practices of Resistance: Critical Reading for Students of Politics' in *Language and Culture*, Graddol, David; Thompson, Linda and Byram, Mike. (eds) Clevedon, Avon: British Association of Applied Linguistics in association with Multilingual Matters Ltd.

Clausewitz, Carl von. (1976) *On War*, Princeton: Princeton University Press. Translated and edited by Michael Howard and Peter Paret.

Clifford, James. (1988/1994) *The Predicament of Culture: Twentieth-Century Ethnography, Literature and Art*, Cambridge, Mass: Harvard University Press.

Clifford, James and Marcus, George E. (eds). (1986) *Writing Culture*, Berkeley: University of California Press.

http://www.cloudband.com/frames.mhtml/magazine/articles1q01/feat_day_cradle3_0201.html (10th December 2003). Carpets and textiles website.

http://www.cnn.com/SPECIALS/cold.war/episodes/02/documents/kennan/ (16th December 2003). Excerpts froom George Kennan's 'Long Telegram.'

Cohen, Raymond. (1991: revised edn 1997) *Negotiating Across Cultures: International Communication in an Interdependent World*, Washington DC: United States Institute of Peace Press.

Coleridge, Samuel Taylor. (1978) *Essays on His Own Times in* The Morning Post *and* The Courier, Vol. II, London: Routledge & Kegan Paul Ltd.

Coombs, Philip H. (1964) *The Fourth Dimension of Foreign Policy: Educational and Cultural Affairs*, New York and Evanston: Harper & Row.

D'Andrade, Roy. (1999) In *Current Anthropology – Special Issue*, Vol. 40, Supplement, February.

Daniel, Norman. (1975) *The Cultural Barrier: Problems in the Exchange of Ideas*, Edinburgh: Edinburgh University Press.

Desch, Michael C. (1998) 'Culture Clash: Assessing the Importance of Ideas in Security Studies,' *International Security*, Vol. 23, No. 1, Summer.

Doyle, William. (1978: 2nd edn 1992) *The Old European Order: 1600–1800*, Oxford: Oxford University Press.

Duff, Andrew; Pinder, John and Pryce, Roy for the Federal Trust (eds). (1994) *Maastricht and Beyond: Building the European Union*, London: Routledge.

Duffield, John. (1999) 'Political culture and state behavior: why Germany confounds neorealism,' *International Organization*, Vol. 53, No. 4.

Dunne, Timothy. (1997) 'Colonial Encounters in International Relations: Reading Wight, Writing Australia,' *Australian Journal of International Affairs*, Vol. 51, No. 3.

Dunne, Tim. (1998) *Inventing International Society: A History of the English School*, Basingstoke and London: Macmillan Press in association with St. Antony's College, Oxford.

Eagleton, Terry. (2000) *The Idea of Culture*, Oxford: Blackwell Publishers Ltd.

http://education.vsnl.com.iccr/ (11th August 2003). The Indian Council for Cultural Relations.

Elias, Norbert. (1939/1978) *The Civilizing Process: The History of Manners*, Vol. 1. Oxford: Basil Blackwell. First published in Switzerland 1939.

Eliot, T.S. (1948/1949) *Notes Towards the Definition of Culture*, London: Faber and Faber Limited.

Eller, Jack David. (1997) 'Anti-Anti-Multiculturalism,' *American Anthropologist*, Vol. 99, No. 2, June.

http://exchanges.state.gov/education/ (3rd August 2003). Bureau of Educational and Cultural Affairs (USA).

http://exchanges.state.gov/education/ivp/history.htm (3rd August 2003). ECA history.

Farrell, Theo. (1998) 'Culture and Military Power,' *Review of International Studies*, Vol. 24, No. 3, July.

Forster, Michael N. (ed. and translated). (2002) *Johann Gottfried Von Herder: Philosophical Writings*, Cambridge: Cambridge University Press.

Fox, Richard (ed.). (1991) *Recapturing Anthropology*, Santa Fe, New Mexico: School of American Research Press.

Fox, Richard. (1995) 'Editorial: The Breakdown of Culture,' *Current Anthropology*, Vol. 36, No. 1, February.

Frankel, Charles. (1966) *The Neglected Aspect of Foreign Affairs*, Washington, DC: The Brookings Institute.

Freeman, Derek. (1983/1996) *Margaret Mead and the Heretic: The Making and Unmaking of an Anthropological Myth*, Ringwood, Australia: Penguin Books.

Friedman, John Block. (1981) *The Monstrous Races in Medieval Art and Thought*, Cambridge, Mass: Harvard University Press.

Friedman, Jonathan. (1994) *Cultural Identity and Global Process*, London: Sage.

Gamble, Ray. (1993) 'International Management of Whales and Whaling: An Historical Review of the Regulation of Commercial and Aboriginal Subsistence Whaling,' *Arctic*, Vol. 46, No. 2, June.

Gargan, Edward T. (ed.). (1961) *The Intent of Toynbee's History*, Chicago: Loyola University Press.

Geertz, Clifford. (1973/1993) *The Interpretation of Cultures*, London: Fontana Press.

Geertz, Clifford. (1984) 'Distinguished Lecture: Anti Anti-Relativism,' *American Anthropologist*, Vol. 86, No. 2, June.

Gellman, Peter. (1988) 'Hans J. Morgenthau and the legacy of political realism,' *Review of International Studies*, Vol. 14.

Gillies, A. (1945) *Herder*, Oxford: Basil Blackwell.

Ginsberg, Morris. (1956) *Essays in Sociology and Social Philosophy: Volume One: On the Diversity of Morals*, London: William Heinemann Ltd.

Gong, Gerrit. W. (1984) *The Standard of 'Civilization' in International Society*, Oxford: Clarendon Press.

Goodrich, Leland M.; Hambro, Edvard and Simons, Anne Patricia. (1969) *Charter of the United Nations: Commentary and Documents*, New York and London: Columbia University Press.

Goody, Jack. (1996) *The East in the West*, Cambridge: Cambridge University Press.

Grant, Madison. (1916) *The Passing of the Great Race or the Racial Basis of European History*, New York: C. Scribner's Sons.

Gray, Colin S. (1999) 'Strategic Culture as Context: The First Generation of Theory Strikes Back,' *Review of International Studies*, Vol. 25, No. 1.

Gray, Colin S. (2003) 'In Praise of Strategy,' *Review of International Studies*, Vol. 29, No. 2.

Gray, John. (1998) 'Global Utopias and Clashing Civilizations: Misunderstanding the Present,' *International Affairs*, Vol. 74, No. 1, January.

Groom, A.J.R. and Light, Margot. (1994) *Contemporary International Relations: A Guide to Theory*, London: Pinter Publishers Ltd.

Haigh, Anthony. (1974) *Cultural Diplomacy in Europe*, Strasbourg: Council of Europe.

Hall, Stuart and du Gay, Paul (eds). (1996) *Questions of Cultural Identity*, London: Sage.

Halliday, Fred. (1992) 'International Society as Homogeneity: Burke, Marx, Fukuyama,' *Millennium*, Vol. 21, No. 3.

Hannaford, Ivan. (1996) *Race: The History of an Idea in the West*, Washington DC: The Woodrow Wilson Center Press and Baltimore: The Johns Hopkins University Press.

Harrison, Faye V. (1995) 'The Persistent Power of "Race" in the Culture and Political Economy of Racism,' *Annual Review of Anthropology*, Vol. 24.

Hatch, Elvin. (1973) *Theories of Man and Culture*, New York: Columbia University Press.

http://hdr.undp.org/reports/global/2002/en/indicator/indicator.cfm?File (13th August 2003). UN Human Development Report 2002.

Heider, Karl G. (1998) 'The Rashomon Effect: When Ethnographers Disagree,' *American Anthropologist*, Vol. 90, No. 1, March.

Held, David and McGrew, Anthony; Goldblatt, David and Perraton, Jonathan. (1996) *Global Transformations: Politics, Economics and Culture*, Cambridge: Polity Press.

http://www.highnorth.no/Library/Culture/ne-fr-in.htm (13th December 2003). High North News.

Hill, Christopher. (1989) '1939: the Origins of Liberal Realism,' *Review of International Studies*, Vol. 15, No. 4.

Hobsbawm, Eric and Ranger, Terence (eds). (1983) *The Invention of Tradition*, Cambridge: Cambridge University Press.

Hoffman, Stanley. (1986) 'Hedley Bull and his Contribution to International Relations,' *International Affairs*, Vol. 62, No. 2, Spring.

Holsti, K.J. (1967/1972) *International Politics: A Framework for Analysis*, Englewood Cliffs, New Jersey: Prentice-Hall Inc.

Hopf, Ted. (1998) 'The Promise of Constructivism in International Relations Theory,' *International Security*, Vol. 23, No. 1, Summer.

Howard-Ellis, C. (1928) *The Origin, Structure and Working of the League of Nations*, London: George Allen and Unwin.

Huntington, Samuel P. (1996/1998) *The Clash of Civilizations and the Remaking of World Order*, London: Touchstone Books.

Huntington, Samuel P. (1997) ' "The Clash of Civilizations" – A Response,' *Millennium*, Vol. 26.

Huntington, Samuel P. *et al.* (1993/1996) *Samuel P. Huntington's 'The Clash of Civilizations?' The Debate*, New York: Foreign Affairs.

Huxley, Julian S. and Haddon, A.C. (1935) *We Europeans: a Survey of 'Racial' Problems*, London: Jonathan Cape.

Iriye, Akira. (1977) *From Nationalism to Internationalism: US Foreign Policy to 1914*, London: Routledge & Kegan Paul.

Iriye, Akira. (1997) *Cultural Internationalism and World Order*, Baltimore and London: The Johns Hopkins University Press.

Jacobsen, Carl G. (ed.). (1990) *Strategic Power: USA/USSR*, London: Macmillan.

Jahn, Beate. (1999) 'IR and the State of Nature: the Cultural Origins of a Ruling Ideology,' *Review of International Studies*, Vol. 25, No. 3.

Jameson, Fredric and Miyoshi, Masao. (1998) *The Cultures of Globalization*, Durham and London: Duke University Press.

http://www.jimmycarterlibrary.org/documents/stgifts.phtml (10th December 2003). Head of State Gifts.

Johnson, Lesley. (1979) *The Cultural Critics: From Matthew Arnold to Raymond Williams*, London: Routledge & Kegan Paul.

Johnston, Alastair Iain. (1995) 'Thinking about Strategic Culture,' *International Security*, Vol. 19, No. 4.

Johnston, Alastair Iain. (1999) 'A Reply to Colin Gray,' *Review of International Studies*, Vol. 25, No. 3, July.

Joll, James. (1973; 4th edn 1990) *Europe Since 1870: An International History*, London: Penguin Books Ltd.

Joll, James. (1982) 'The Ideal and the Real: Changing Concepts of the International System, 1815–1982,' *International Affairs*, Vol. 58, No. 2, Spring.

Joll, James. (1985) 'Two Prophets of the Twentieth Century: Spengler and Toynbee,' *Review of International Studies*, Vol. 11, No. 2.

Jones, W.R. (1971) 'The Image of the Barbarian in Medieval Europe,' *Comparative Studies in Society and History*, Vol. 13.

http://www.jpf.go.jp/e/about/bground.html (11th August 2003). The Japan Foundation.

Kahn, Joel. (1989) 'Culture: Demise or Resurrection?' *Critique of Anthropology*, Vol. 9, No. 2.

Katzenstein, Peter J. (1996a) *Cultural Norms and National Security: Police and Military in Postwar Japan*, New York: Cornell University Press.

Katzenstein, Peter J. (ed.). (1996b) *The Culture of National Security: Norms and Identity in World Politics*, New York: Columbia University Press.

Keesing, Roger M. (1974) 'Theories of Culture,' *Annual Review of Anthropology*, Vol. 3.

Kelman, Herbert C. (ed.). (1965) *International Behavior: A Social-Psychological Analysis*, New York: Holt, Rinehart and Winston Inc.

Kennan, George F. (1952) *American Diplomacy: 1900–1950*, London: Secker & Warburg.

Kennan, George F. (1954) *Realities of American Foreign Policy*, London: Oxford University Press.

Kennan, George F. (1977) *The Cloud of Danger: Current Realities of American Foreign Policy*, Boston: Little, Brown and Company.

Kier, Elizabeth. (1997) *Imagining War: French and British Military Doctrine Between the Wars*, Princeton, New Jersey: Princeton University Press.

Klein, Yitzhak. (1991) 'A Theory of Strategic Culture,' *Journal of Comparative Strategy*, Vol. 5, No. 3.

Kramer, Hilton. (1999) *The Twilight of the Intellectuals: Culture and Politics in the Era of the Cold War*, Chicago: Ivan R. Dee Publishers.

Kroeber, Alfred and Kluckhohn, Clyde. (1952) *Culture: A Critical Review of Concepts and Definitions*, New York: Vintage Books.

Kuper, Adam. (1988) *The Invention of Primitive Society: Transformations of an Illusion*, London: Routledge.

Kuper, Adam. (1994) 'Culture, Identity and the Project of a Cosmopolitan Anthropology,' *Man*, Vol. 29, September.

Kuper, Adam. (1996) *Anthropology and Anthropologists: The Modern British School*, London: Routledge.

Kuper, Adam. (1999) *Culture: The Anthropologists' Account*, Cambridge, Massachusetts: Harvard University Press.

Kymlicka, Will (ed.). (1995) *The Rights of Minority Cultures*, Oxford: Oxford University Press.

Lapid, Yosef and Kratochwil, Friedrich (eds). (1997) *The Return of Culture and Identity in IR Theory*, London: Lynne Reinner Publishers Inc.

Lawson, Stephanie. (1998) 'Dogmas of Difference: Culture and Nationalism in Theories of International Politics,' *Critical Review of International Social and Political Philosophy*, Vol. 1, No. 4.

Leavis, F.R. (1930) *Mass Civilisation and Minority Culture*, Cambridge: The Minority Press.

Lee, J.M. (1998) 'British Cultural Diplomacy and the Cold War: 1946–61,' *Diplomacy and Statecraft*, Vol. 19, No. 1, March.

Levin Jr., Gordon N. (1968) *Woodrow Wilson and World Politics: America's Response to War and Revolution*, New York: Oxford University Press.

Link, Arthur S. (1954) *Woodrow Wilson and the Progressive Era, 1910–1917*, London: Hamish Hamilton.

Little, Richard and Smith, Michael (eds). (1991: 2nd edn 1994) *Perspectives on World Politics*, London and New York: Routledge.

Long, David and Wilson, Peter (eds). (1995) *Thinkers of the Twenty Years' Crisis: Inter-War Idealism Reassessed*, Oxford: Clarendon Press.

Lyons, F.S.L. (1963) *Internationalism in Europe 1815–1914*, Leyden: A.W. Sythoff.

McMurry, Ruth Emily and Lee, Muna. (1947) *The Cultural Approach: Another Way in International Relations*, Chapel Hill: The University of North Carolina Press.

Mair, L.P. (1928) *The Protection of Minorities: The Working and Scope of the Minorities' Treaties under the League of Nations*, London: Christophers.

Mair, Lucy. (1965: 2nd edn 1983) *An Introduction to Social Anthropology*, Oxford: Oxford University Press.

Malinowski, Bronislaw. (1922) *Argonauts of the Western Pacific: An Account of Native Enterprise and Adventure in the Archipelagoes of Melanesian New Guinea*, London: Routledge & Kegan Paul.

Malinowski, Bronislaw. (1967) *A Diary in the Strict Sense*, London: Routledge & Kegan Paul.

Marcus, George E. and Fischer, Michael M.J. (1986) *Anthropology as Cultural Critique*, Chicago: University of Chicago Press.

Markwell, D.J. (1986) 'Sir Alfred Zimmern Revisited: Fifty Years On,' *Review of International Studies*, Vol. 12, No. 4.

Mauss, Marcel. (1950/1997) *The Gift: The Form and Reason for Exchange in Archaic Societies*, London: Routledge. Translated by W.D. Halls. First published in France.

Mazrui, Ali A. (1980–1) 'Changing the Guards from Hindus to Muslims: Collective Third World Security in a Cultural Perspective,' *International Affairs*, Vol. 57, No. 1.

Mead, Margaret. (1928) *Coming of Age in Samoa*, New York: William Morrow.

Mead, Margaret. (1942/1943) *And Keep Your Powder Dry: An Anthropologist Looks at America*, New York: William Morrow & Company.

Michaels, Walter Benn. (1992) 'Race into Culture: A Critical Genealogy of Cultural Identity,' *Critical Inquiry*, Vol. 18, Summer.

Michaels, Walter Benn. (1995) *Our America: Nativism, Modernism and Pluralism*, Durham and London: Duke University Press.

Midgley, E.B.F. (1979) 'Natural Law and the "Anglo-Saxons" – Some Reflections in response to Hedley Bull,' *British Journal of International Studies*, Vol. 5, No. 3, October.

Millennium Special Issue on Culture, Winter 1993, Vol. 22, No. 3.

Mintz, Sidney W. (1971) 'Groups, Group Boundary and the Perception of "Race,"' *Comparative Studies in Society and History*, Vol. 13.

Mitchell, J.M. (1986) *International Cultural Relations*, London: Allen and Unwin in association with The British Council.

Morgenthau, Hans J. (1946/1962) *Scientific Man vs. Power Politics*, Chicago: The University of Chicago Press.

Morgenthau, Hans J. (1948: 3rd edn 1962) *Politics Among Nations: The Struggle for Power and Peace*, New York: Alfred A. Knopf.

Murdock, G.P. (1951) 'British Social Anthropology,' *American Anthropologist*, Vol. 53, No. 4, Part 1, October–December.

Murray, A.J.H. (1996) 'The Moral Politics of Hans Morgenthau,' *The Review of Politics*, Vol. 58, No. 1, Winter.

Murray, Gilbert. (1948) *From the League to the U.N.*, London: Oxford University Press.

Navari, Cornelia. (1989) 'The Great Illusion Revisited: the International Theory of Norman Angell,' *Review of International Studies*, Vol. 15, No. 4.

Navari, Cornelia. (2000) 'Arnold Toynbee (1889–1975): Prophecy and Civilization,' *Review of International Studies*, Vol. 26, No. 2.

Niebuhr, Reinhold. (1932) *Moral Man and Immoral Society*, New York: Charles Scribner's Sons.

Niebuhr, Reinhold. (1944) *The Children of Light and The Children of Darkness: A Vindication of Democracy and a Critique of its Traditional Defense*, New York: Charles Scribner's Sons.

Ninkovich, Frank A. (1981) *The Diplomacy of Ideas: U.S. Foreign Policy and Cultural Relations, 1938–1950*, Cambridge: Cambridge University Press.

Noel-Baker, Philip. (1925) *The Geneva Protocol for the Pacific Settlement of International Disputes*, London: P.S. King & Son Ltd.

Northrop, F.S.C. and Livingston, Helen H. (eds). (1964) *Cross-cultural Understanding: Epistemology in Anthropology*, New York: Harper & Row Publishers.

Olson, William C. and Groom, A.J.R. (1991) *International Relations Then & Now: Origins and Trends in Interpretation*, London: HarperCollins Academic.

Ortner, Sherry B. (1984) 'Theory in Anthropology Since the Sixties,' *Comparative Studies in Society and History*, Vol. 26.

Oxford English Dictionary. (1994) Oxford: Oxford University Press.

Parsons, Anthony. (1985) '"Vultures and Philistines": British Attitudes to Culture and Cultural Diplomacy,' *International Affairs*, Vol. 16, No. 1, Winter.

Perry, W.J. (1924) *The Growth of Civilisation*, London: Methuen and Co. Ltd.

Pilcher, Hans-Karl. (1998) 'The Godfathers of "Truth": Max Weber and Carl Schmitt in Morgenthau's Theory of Power Politics,' *Review of International Studies*, Vol. 24, No. 2.

Poore, Stuart E. (2000) *Strategic Culture and Non-Nuclear Weapon Outcomes: The Cases of Australia, South Africa and Sweden*, unpublished thesis, University of Southampton, UK.

Poore, Stuart. (2003) 'What is Strategic Culture?' *Review of International Studies*, Vol. 29, No. 2, April.

Porter, Brian. (1989) 'David Davies: a Hunter After Peace,' *Review of International Studies*, Vol. 15, No. 1.

Robinson, Piers. (1999) 'The CNN Effect,' *Review of International Studies*, Vol. 25, No. 2.

Rodseth, Lars. (1998) 'Distributive Models of Culture: A Sapirian Alternative to Essentialism,' *American Anthropology*, Vol. 100, No. 1, March.

Rosaldo, Renato. (1989/1993) *Culture and Truth: The Remaking of Social Analysis*, London: Routledge.

Rosaldo, Renato. (1994) 'Whose Cultural Studies?' *American Anthropologist*, Vol. 96, No. 3, September.

http://www.royal.gov.uk/output/Page1634.asp (11th August 2003). Royal Website (UK).

Said, Edward W. (1994) *Culture and Imperialism*, London: Vintage.

Sardar, Ziauddin and Davies, Merryl Wyn. (2002) *Why Do People Hate America?*, Cambridge: Icon Books.

Saunders, Frances Stonor. (1999) *Who Paid the Piper? The CIA and the Cultural Cold War*, London: Granta Books.

Schmidt, Brian C. (1998) *The Political Discourse of Anarchy: A Disciplinary History of International Relations*, Albany: State University of New York Press.

Sewell, James P. (1975) *UNESCO and World Politics*, Princeton: Princeton University Press.

Sils, David L. (ed.). (1968) *International Encyclopaedia of the Social Sciences*, London: The Macmillan Company and The Free Press.

Smith, Philip (ed.). (1998) *The New American Cultural Sociology*, Cambridge: Cambridge University Press.

Snyder, Jack. (1977) *The Soviet Strategic Culture: Implications for Nuclear Options*, Santa Monica, California: Rand -2154-AF.

Snyder, Jack. (2002) 'Anarchy and Culture: Insights from the Anthropology of War,' *International Organization*, Vol. 56, No. 1, Winter.

Spengler, Oswald. (1926/1939) *The Decline of the West*, translated by Charles Francis Atkinson, New York: Alfred A. Knopf Inc. Volume One, *Form and Actuality*, first published 1926, originally published in 1918 in München. Volume Two, *Perspectives on World History*, first published 1928, originally published in München.

Stocking Jr., George W. (1968/1982) *Race, Culture, and Evolution: Essays in the History of Anthropology*, Chicago and London: The University of Chicago Press.

Stocking Jr., George W. (ed.). (1974) *The Shaping of American Anthropology 1883–1911: A Franz Boas Reader*, New York: Basic Books Inc.

Stocking Jr., George W. (ed.). (1995) *After Tylor: British Social Anthropology 1888–1951*, Madison, Wisconsin: University of Wisconsin Press.

Stocking Jr., George W. (ed.). (1996) *Volksgeist as Method and Ethic. Essays on Boasian Ethnography and the German Anthropological Tradition*, Madison, Wisconsin: University of Wisconsin Press.

Stoddard, Lothrop. (1920) *The Rising Tide of Color Against White World Supremacy*, New York: Blue Ribbon Books.

Stolcke, Verena. (1995) 'Talking Culture: New Boundaries, New Rhetorics of Exclusion in Europe,' *Current Anthropology*, Vol. 36, No. 1.

Storey, John (ed.). (1996) *What is Cultural Studies? A Reader*, London: Arnold.

Street, Brian V. (1993) 'Culture is a Verb: Anthropological Aspects of Language and Cultural Process,' in *Language and Culture*, Graddol, David; Thompson, Linda and Byram, Mike. (eds), Clevedon, Avon: British Association of Applied Linguistics in association with Multilingual Matters Ltd.

Taylor, Charles. (1992) *Multiculturalism and "The Politics of Recognition,"* Princeton, New Jersey: Princeton University Press.

http://www.telegraph.co.uk/news/ (13th December 2003). The Telegraph Newspaper.

Thomas, Nicholas. (1996) 'Cold Fusion,' *American Anthropologist*, Vol. 98, No. 1, March.

Thompson, Kenneth and Myers, Robert J. (eds). (1984) *Truth and Tragedy: A Tribute to Hans J. Morgenthau*, New Brunswick and London: Transaction Books.

Toynbee, Arnold J. (1934) *A Study of History – Volume 1*, London: Oxford University Press.

Toynbee, Arnold J. (1947/1949) *Civilization on Trial*, London: Oxford University Press.

Toynbee, Arnold J. (1954a) *A Study of History – Volume 8*, London: Oxford University Press.

Toynbee, Arnold J. (1954b) *A Study of History – Volume 9*, London: Oxford University Press.

Toynbee, Arnold J. (1961) *A Study of History – Volume 12, Reconsiderations*, London: Oxford University Press.

Trouillot, Michel-Rolph. (2001) 'The Anthropology of the State in the Age of Globalization: Close Encounters of the Deceptive Kind,' *Current Anthropology*, Vol. 42, No. 1, February.

Tully, James (ed.). (1988) *Meaning and Context: Quentin Skinner and his Critics*, Cambridge and Oxford: Polity Press in association with Basil Blackwell.

Tully, James. (1995) *Strange Multiplicity: Constitutionalism in an Age of Diversity*, Cambridge: Cambridge University Press.

Turner, Terence, 'Neoliberal Ecopolitics and Indigenous Peoples: The Kayapo, The "Rainforest Harvest," and The Body Shop,' http://www.yale.edu/environment/publications/bulletin/098pdfs/98turner.pdf page 15, (13th December 2003).

Tylor, Edward B. (1871/1903) *Primitive Culture: Researches into the Development of Mythology, Philosophy, Religion, Language, Art and Custom*, Vol. 1, London: John Murray.

Tylor, Edward B. (1881) *Anthropology: An Introduction to the Study of Man and Civilization*, London: Macmillan and Co.

http://www.unc.edu/depts/diplomat/archives_roll/2002_07-09/brown_pubdipl/brown_pubdipl.html (12th December 2003). John Brown article.

http://www.unesco.org/shs/human_rights/hrpreamble.htm (9th December 2003). UNESCO – Preamble.

Vincent, R.J. (1978) 'Western Conceptions of a Universal Moral Order,' *British Journal of International Studies*, Vol. 4, No. 1, April.

Vincent, R.J. (1980) 'The Factor of Culture in the Global International Order,' *Yearbook of World Affairs*, Vol. 34.

Vincent, R.J. (1982) 'Race in International Relations,' *International Affairs*, Vol. 58, No. 4, Autumn.

Vincent, R.J. (1986/1995) *Human Rights and International Relations*, Cambridge: Cambridge University Press in association with The Royal Institute of International Affairs.

Visweswaran, Kamala. (1998) 'Race and the Culture of Anthropology,' *American Anthropologist*, Vol. 100, No. 1, March.

Waever, Ole. (1992) 'International Society – Theoretical Promises Unfulfilled?' *Cooperation and Conflict*, Vol. 27, No. 1.

Walker, R.B.J. (1993) *Inside/Outside: International Relations as Political Theory*, Cambridge: Cambridge University Press.

Walters, F.P. (1952) *A History of the League of Nations*, Vol. 1, London: Oxford University Press.

Waltz, Kenneth. (1979) *Theory of International Relations*, Reading, Mass: Addison-Wesley.

Webster, C.K. and Herbert, Sidney. (1933) *The League of Nations in Theory and Practice*, London: George Allen & Unwin Ltd.

Weldes, Jutta. (1999) 'Going Cultural: Star Trek, State Action and Popular Culture,' *Millennium*, Vol. 28, No. 1.

Wheeler, Nicholas J. (1992) 'Pluralist or Solidarist Conceptions of International Society: Bull and Vincent on Humanitarian Intervention,' *Millennium*, Vol. 21, No. 3.

Wheeler, Nicholas J. and Dunne, Timothy. (1996) 'Hedley Bull's Pluralism of the Intellect and Solidarism of the Will,' *International Affairs*, Vol. 72, No. 1, January.

Wheeler, Roxann. (2000) *The Complexion of Race: Categories of Difference in Eighteenth-Century British Culture*, Philadelphia: University of Pennsylvania Press.

White, Haydn. (1987) *The Content of the Form: Narrative Discourse and Historical Representation*, Baltimore: Johns Hopkins University Press.

Wierzbicka, Anna. (1986) 'Human Emotions: Universal or Culture Specific?' *American Anthropologist*, Vol. 88, No. 3, September.

Wight, Gabriele and Porter, Brian (eds). (1991/1994) *International Theory: The Three Traditions – Martin Wight*, London: Leicester University Press.

Wight, Martin. (1946/1978) *Power Politics*, Bull, Hedley and Holbraad, Carsten (eds), Leicester: Leicester University Press.

Wight, Martin. (1977) *System of States*, Bull, Hedley (ed.), Leicester: Leicester University Press in association with The London School of Economic and Political Science.

Williams, Elgin. (1947) 'Anthropology for the Common Man,' *American Anthropologist*, Vol. 49.

Williams, Raymond. (1958/1993) *Culture and Society*, London: The Hogarth Press.

Williams, Raymond. (1976/1988) *Keywords: A Vocabulary of Culture and Society*, London: Fontana Press.

Williams, Raymond. (1977/1986) *Marxism and Literature*, Oxford: Oxford University Press.

Williams, Raymond. (1981/1989) *Culture*, London: Fontana Press.

Wolf, Eric R. (1982/1997) *Europe and The People Without History*, Berkeley: University of California Press.

Wolf, Eric R. (1994) 'Perilous Ideas: Race, Culture, People,' *Current Anthropology*, Vol. 35, No. 1.

Woolf, L.S. (1916) *International Government*, London: The Fabian Society and George Allen & Unwin Ltd.

Woollacott, Martin. (1997) 'Coke and Big Macs aren't the Real Thing,' the *Guardian*, 4th January.

Wright, Susan. (1998) 'The Politicization of "Culture",' *Anthropology Today*, Vol. 14, No. 1, February.

Yengoyan, Aram A. (1986) 'Theory in Anthropology: On the Demise of the Concept of Culture,' *Comparative Studies in Society and History*, Vol. 28.

Zimmern, Alfred E. (1922) *Europe in Convalescence*, London: Mills & Boon Ltd.

Zimmern, Alfred E. (1929) *The Prospects of Democracy and Other Essays*, London: Chatto & Windus.

Zimmern, Alfred E. (1936) *The League of Nations and the Rule of Law 1918–1935*, London: Macmillan & Co. Ltd.

Zimmern, Alfred E. (ed.). (1939) *Modern Political Doctrines*, London: Oxford University Press.

Index

Made in the USA
Middletown, DE
22 August 2017